LONE PURSUIT

LONE PURSUIT

Distrust and Defensive Individualism
Among the Black Poor

Sandra Susan Smith

Russell Sage Foundation • New York

The Russell Sage Foundation

The Russell Sage Foundation, one of the oldest of America's general purpose foundations, was established in 1907 by Mrs. Margaret Olivia Sage for "the improvement of social and living conditions in the United States." The Foundation seeks to fulfill this mandate by fostering the development and dissemination of knowledge about the country's political, social, and economic problems. While the Foundation endeavors to assure the accuracy and objectivity of each book it publishes, the conclusions and interpretations in Russell Sage Foundation publications are those of the authors and not of the Foundation, its Trustees, or its staff. Publication by Russell Sage, therefore, does not imply Foundation endorsement.

Library of Congress Cataloging-in-Publication Data

Smith, Sandra Susan.
  Lone pursuit : distrust and defensive individualism among the black poor / Sandra Susan Smith.
    p. cm.
  Includes bibliographical references and index.
  ISBN 978-0-87154-773-6 (alk. paper)
  1. African Americans—Employment—Michigan. 2. Unemployed—Psychology—Michigan. 3. Unemployed—Services for—Michigan. 4. Discrimination in employment—Michigan. I. Title.
  HD8081.A65S65 2007
  331.6'396073—dc22

                                                                2007008380

Text design by Suzanne Nichols.

RUSSELL SAGE FOUNDATION
112 East 64th Street, New York, New York 10021
10 9 8 7 6 5 4 3 2 1

Contents

About the Author

Sandra Susan Smith is an assistant professor in the Department of Sociology at the University of California, Berkeley.

To Mummy, Daddy, and Junior

Acknowledgments

Without question, I could have written a book about job finding, distrust, and individualism among the black poor without any input from those in my social and professional network of relations. It would be insincere to say otherwise. Had I done so, however, *Lone Pursuit* would have been a very different book—less interesting, less insightful, less coherent, less engaged with relevant literatures—and its contribution to our current understanding of the problem of chronic joblessness among the black poor would have been diminished. Indeed, *Lone Pursuit* would probably not have been the book's title. Furthermore, without input from others, my own fate would have been much the same as the book's. I would have emerged from the process of writing it less interesting, less insightful, less coherent, less engaged, and so on. Happily, luckily, gratefully, I was the beneficiary of a great deal of emotional, financial, and intellectual support from a host of incredibly generous and insightful individuals, groups, and institutions, most of whom I spotlight here.

The seeds for this project were planted during a conversation with my mother, June Smith, who, before she retired, was a group leader at a factory producing high-technology products. My mother was no-nonsense on the job (and at home for that matter!). With little effort, she commanded a great deal of respect from her charges, her supervisors and managers, and the owner of the corporation for which she worked for almost twenty years, and she did so by insisting on excellence from herself and from everyone around her. Given her role as group leader and her impressive reputation on the job, my mother could easily and successfully have assisted in the hire of anyone in her network of relations, and she had many opportunities to do so. Nevertheless, she often chose not to.

Her decisions to assist were based on her assessments of others' trustworthiness, and these assessments were based largely on her observations of their behavior. As I learned in one of our regular long-distance telephone conversations, my mother refused to assist one relation who was struggling to make ends meet because she did not approve of the way this relation parented and cleaned house. She also had concerns about the relation's dating habits. Each of these assessments made my mother question her relation's judgment and distrust her ability to act appropriately and productively on the job. Just as important, my mother did not want her relation's behavior to soil her own stellar reputation on the job. Within weeks, however, my mother was helping this relation's daughter, who, from my mother's perspective, seemed to make up for a number of her mother's moral shortcomings. Unlike her mother, the daughter had proven herself morally worthy of assistance. Pondering this conversation with my mother, I tried to make sense of her decisionmaking process and its implications for job finding among the black poor, given the state of the literature at the time. It became clear to me then that an important aspect of the job-finding process had been neglected.

I was fortunate enough to come to this realization when I was a Ford Foundation postdoctoral fellow at the University of Michigan's Poverty Research and Training Center (PRTC), now the National Poverty Center. The PRTC was run by Sheldon Danziger, whose reputation for excellent mentorship of graduate students and postdocs is unrivaled. Before arriving on campus, I had learned of Sheldon's reputation, which was embodied in the red pens he used to provide critical feedback on students' and colleagues' work. Soon after arriving, I had my own run-ins with his red pens, and I loved it. When I shared my realization with him, he used a red pen to approve a supplemental research grant from the Ford Foundation to the Program on Poverty, the Underclass, and Public Policy, which got the project off the ground. He also wisely suggested that I either collaborate or consult with a number of other scholars and researchers on campus on various aspects of the project I wanted to undertake; Nathaniel Anderson, Mary Corcoran, Sandy Danziger, and Kristin Seefeldt would each help shape the project early on and in important ways.

Sheldon's suggestion that I team up with Alford Young Jr., then an assistant professor of sociology at the University of Michigan, probably had the most profound effect on the development of this project. Although Al and I had known each other since our days as graduate students at the University of Chicago, I'd never worked with him before. We had in common a desire to understand how the black poor make sense of their lives, but we were interested in addressing very different research questions, and so, until Sheldon's suggestion, we had not considered working together. With this project, we collaborated on the study design and survey instruments. Once the data were collected, our collaboration ended, but Al remains an incredible resource to me, intellectually, socially, and emotionally. After leaving Michigan for my first faculty position, I would return periodically to conduct interviews, and when I did, Al and his wife, Carla O'Connor, then an assistant professor in the School of Education at the University of Michigan, opened their home to me, providing me with a place to stay, meals to eat, and opportunities to debrief after hours of what were often very difficult interviews. They also provided a space within which I could discuss the arguments I would later articulate in this book, a space that was both safe and challenging, a space that forced me to consider my unquestioned assumptions, and a space that encouraged me to grow. In so many ways theirs is my home away from home and they are my family, my big brother and big sister. Jennifer Barber and Bill Axinn also provided a home away from home for me, and to them too I am eternally grateful.

In addition to the financial support I received while at the PRTC, I also received a small grant from the Center for Advanced Social Science Research and a grant from the University Research Challenge Fund at New York University, where I held my first faculty position in the Department of Sociology. Both grants were extremely helpful and came at critical times in the process, allowing me to hire graduate students as research assistants, buy materials needed to further the research, and attend conferences to present my work.

My efforts to write this book were also generously supported by the Russell Sage Foundation, where I was a visiting scholar in 2002–2003 and where I began writing *Lone Pursuit*. The foundation's scholars program provides excellent opportunities to develop one's work because it buffers scholars from all the obligations associated with their faculty positions and provides office space, excellent research assistance, and scrumptious lunches expertly prepared by Jackie Cholmondeley. The program also provides daily opportunities to share work and interact with other scholars who have overlapping interests but often divergent perspectives.

My year at Russell Sage marked a turning point in my intellectual life for another reason. It was there that I met Michael Burawoy, who has become my mentor, my colleague, and my very dear friend. From the start, not only did Michael convince me that I had a worthy contribution to make, but he insisted that I communicate my insights in book form; then he guided me through *every single step* of the book-writing process with patience, compassion, wisdom, critical insight, and generosity of time and spirit. I could not imagine undertaking and completing this process without him. Few others have garnered my respect and complete adoration the way Michael has, and, impressively, I know that I am just one of the masses of people who feel this way.

Soon after my year at Russell Sage ended, I left New York University and joined the Department of Sociology at the University of California at Berkeley, where I have received an amazing amount of feedback from some of the most intellectually engaged people I've ever met. Upon my arrival, the junior faculty members formed a reading group that met every two weeks to discuss each other's work. It was in this context that I came to know, respect, and connect with my same-rank colleagues. It was also within this context that I received a great deal of very helpful, incredibly insightful feedback. This group included the analytically astute and ever-efficient Irene Bloemraad; the ultimate intellectual, Marion Fourcade-Gourinchas; the profound and provocative Dawne Moon; and the intensely engaged Dylan Riley. Dawne deserves special thanks for reading all but one draft chapter of the manuscript and providing excellent feedback, both substantive and editorial. Collectively, their feedback has been invaluable to the development of the book and to my development as a scholar.

The same can be said of the social and intellectual support I have received from my senior colleagues, many of whom have read at least one chapter and shared great insights. They include Vicki Bonnell, Claude Fischer, Arlie Hochschild, Mike Hout, Kristin Luker, Raka Ray, Martin Sanchez-Jankowski, Ann Swidler, and Barrie Thorne. During her yearlong visit to the Berkeley campus, Leslie Salzinger also provided very helpful suggestions that, along with comments from Barrie Thorne and Raka Ray, helped me a great deal in thinking about the role of gender in my analyses.

Among my senior colleagues, one other person deserves special note. Although she deftly avoided reading any of my chapters, Laura Enriquez, another mentor and very dear friend, helped keep me sane throughout this process. Our regular walks and talks through the hills of North Berkeley and the marina provided me with opportunities to share my fears, reasonable or not, to kvetch, to release whatever thoughts were burdening me at the time. Laura always listened intently, suggested alternative (i.e., sane) ways of thinking about things, and advised me on ways of structuring my life so that I could complete the manuscript. Furthermore, she threatened to "box" me if I did not abide! Not surprisingly, I listened to just about every word. Just as importantly, however, Laura constantly reminded me that I *could* complete the book, and that I *would*. Laura has truly been the most wonderful gift to me.

Throughout the process of writing this book, I have also received tremendously helpful comments on drafts of chapters and presentations of my work from a number of people and groups, and these reactions have helped me rethink my interpretation of the data and thus strengthen my arguments. I am especially grateful to Katherine Newman and Bill Wilson, both of whom have been constant sources of tremendous opportunities and support for me over the years. I cannot thank either enough. For many years now I have also received incredibly insightful comments and words of encouragement from Xavier de Sousa Briggs and Mario Small. And I've found conversations and correspondence with Nancy DiTomaso, Bonnie Erickson, Herb Gans, Rosamond King, Nan Lin, Deirdre Royster, and Stacey Sutton quite illuminating. Participants in a number of workshops and colloquia have also provided thoughtful comments and suggestions, including those at the Summer Workshop of the Institute for Research on Poverty at the University of Wisconsin at Madison; UC Berkeley's Department of Sociology; UC Berkeley's Institute for Industrial Relations; UC Davis's Department of Sociology; UC Davis's Consortium for Women and Research, Labor, and Labor Organizing; Northwestern University's Department of Sociology and Inequality Workshop; and the National Poverty Center at the University of Michigan.

And of course, a task of this nature cannot be completed without the assistance of those willing and able to share in the grunt work. I have been lucky to have assistants who have done so with adeptness and grace. Shawn Christian, Alfred Defreece, Trevor Gardner, Kareem Johnson, and Robyn Kent conducted interviews during the early stages of the project. While at New York University, I benefited from the assistance of graduate students Meghan Falvey and Giselle Hendrie, who created datasets for me in Atlas.ti and SPSS, did some initial data analysis, and also provided thoughtful feedback on early drafts. Christine Hooker, an undergraduate at NYU at the time, tracked down and summarized relevant literature for me. While at Russell Sage, Hannah Pierce became invaluable to me, and at Berkeley, assistance from Tamera Lee Stover and Molly Ward was crucial to making steady progress on the book manuscript. Finally, I cannot thank enough some of the staff members from my own department at UC Berkeley. Sue Thur, Judy Haier, Bill Gentry, Belinda White, and John Dailly have often guided me through the slow-grinding bureaucratic behemoth that is the UC system, and, given their overwhelming responsibilities, they've done so with amazing patience and grace. I cannot articulate my level of appreciation for what they do daily to keep the department running smoothly and for giving me reasons to smile.

Although most of the empirical analysis of the book is new, parts of chapter 3 were published as " 'Don't Put Your Name On It': Social Capital Activation and Job Finding Assistance Among the Black Urban Poor," *American Journal of Sociology* 111:1–57. As I did with the publication of this article, I would like to express my greatest appreciation to the *AJS* reviewers, who provided amazing feedback that pushed me beyond what I perceived my limits to be.

Finally, I would like to thank members of my family, including my partner, Amy Graf, who has shown me unconditional love and affection, supported my efforts to get the book done, and reminded me to take time for myself. Being with Amy lessens much of the guilt associated with trying to live a balanced life and replaces that guilt with pure contentment and joy. And to my mother, father, and brother, your love, support, and belief in me has meant more to me than you will ever know. My first book is dedicated to you.

Chapter 1

Explaining Persistent Black Joblessness

Forty-two weeks after losing the only steady job he had ever held, Anthony Redmond, a thirty-six-year-old high school dropout and convicted felon, remained jobless and became increasingly frustrated. He had gone to great lengths to find work, submitting numerous applications daily in the hopes of securing at least one interview in which he would tell the employer, "I'm a hard worker. I do whatever you want me to do the way you want me to do it. I can start now if you want me to." These pronouncements, he thought, would allay employers' concerns about his competence, pliability, and work ethic and increase the likelihood that he would be offered a job. However, his efforts were to no avail. No matter how many applications he submitted, no matter the form or content of his entreaties, he could not convince employers to hire him.

Sadly, Anthony's circumstances are hardly exceptional. Instead, they mirror the experiences of young, less-educated black men and women across the country whose relatively weak labor force attachment has been the source of much scholarly debate for at least five decades. One of the first to sound the alarm about the extent of joblessness in the black community was Daniel Patrick Moynihan. After the passage of the Civil Rights Act of 1964, Moynihan, then assistant secretary in the Office of Policy Planning and Research at the U.S. Department of Labor, released the report *The Negro Family: The Case for National Action* (1967), now commonly referred to as *The Moynihan Report*. In it he warned of the impending "new crisis in race relations," explaining that contrary to the great expectations of some and the fervent hopes of others, equality between blacks and whites would probably not come to pass for several generations. Indeed, he argued, the crisis was already in evidence, as indicated by at least three decades of data on joblessness. Moynihan (1967, 66) wrote, "The fundamental, overwhelming fact is that *Negro unemployment*, with the exception of a few years during World War II and the Korean War, *has continued at disaster levels for 35 years*," such that by 1940, "the 2 to 1 white-Negro un-

1

employment rate that persists to this day had clearly emerged" (emphasis in original).

Twenty years later, in *The Truly Disadvantaged* (1987), William Julius Wilson provided another stark reminder. Characterizing rates of inner-city joblessness as a tragedy, Wilson showed that while employment among young white men had hardly changed at all, employment among their black counterparts had fallen "sharply and steadily." By 1984 just 58 percent of all young black men were employed; among those age eighteen to nineteen and those age sixteen to seventeen, figures were as low as 34 and 16 percent, respectively.

While some have argued that the 1990s brought signs of hope, for others the outlook was bleaker than ever. The economists Richard Freeman and William Rodgers (2000) show that employment among less-educated, young black men responded positively to the economic expansion of the 1990s. However, the economists Harry Holzer, Paul Offner, and Elaine Sorensen (2004, 2) contend that the improvements highlighted by Freeman and Rodgers were only *cyclical* in nature, reflecting the business cycle, and not great enough to "offset the negative *secular* trend that has been reducing employment and labor force activity among these young men for the past several decades" (emphasis added; see also Holzer and Offner 2002; Holzer, Offner, and Sorensen 2005). Instead, their analysis reveals, young black men's employment not only declined significantly during the 1980s but fell even more sharply through the 1990s (Holzer and Offner 2002).

In the new millennium, it appears that the crisis is only worsening. In 2004 the Community Service Society, an independent, nonprofit organization in New York City, released its annual report, *A Crisis of Black Male Employment* (Levitan, 2004). The report indicated that in 2003, 52 percent of New York City's working-age black men were jobless, the employment-population ratio having fallen some twelve percentage points since 2000. By far, this decline represented the sharpest experienced by any other subgroup of workers they studied.[1] At 57 percent, even black women in the area had higher levels of employment.

Despite the male-centered focus of the joblessness literature, black women's rates of employment have been troubling as well. Until the late 1960s, employment among black women was quite high. According to Mary Corcoran, almost 73 percent of young black women were employed in 1969, a rate roughly equivalent to that of white women. Between 1969 and 1991, however, employment among young black women deteriorated substantially, and the gap in employment between black and white women grew. Correspondingly, during this period unemployment rates among black women were very high and surpassed those of white women by a margin of no less than two-to-one. As Corcoran (1999, 54) explained, "At every education level and every year (with the single exception of college graduates in 1970), African American women's unemployment rates were much higher than white women." Owing to a combination of factors, including welfare reforms, the economic expansion, and the expansion of the Earned Income Tax Credit (EITC) (Ellwood 2000; Meyer and Rosenbaum 2001; Noonan, Smith, and Corcoran 2007; O'Neill and Hill 2001; Schoeni and Blank 2000), black women made noteworthy employment gains throughout the 1990s, but persistent joblessness among them remains a very troubling concern.

How do we explain the crisis of joblessness that Anthony Redmond suffered for at least forty-two weeks and that each year is regularly endured by growing numbers of similar young black men and, to a lesser extent, black women? Four theoretical perspectives dominate current debates. Chronic black joblessness is most often explained in terms of pervasive employer discrimination, the changing structure of urban economies, cultural deficiencies, poor access to social capital, or some combination of the above. Each of these theoretical frames of persistent joblessness is compelling and each has wide appeal, but whether considered singly or taken together, they provide an incomplete understanding of the causes of joblessness because, to varying degrees, they do not examine closely or systematically the process of finding work that the black poor undertake (exceptions include Newman 1999). By failing to do so, they overlook—or, as in the case of the cultural deficiency perspective, critically misstate—the meanings that the black poor attach to their labor market experiences. They fail as well to see that the meanings that inform behaviors are produced within the context of interpersonal relations. These relations matter because it is through social interactions and engagements that the poor diagnose problems of joblessness, theorizing about its primary causes and possible solutions. It is through social interactions as well that the joblessness discourses they produce have their ultimate consequences, shaping how poor blacks engage with each other as actors, specifically as job-seekers and job-holders, in ways that affect their labor market outcomes above and beyond the initiating factors deemed to cause joblessness.

By examining the process of finding work closely and systematically, I learned that interpersonal relations between job-seekers and job-holders were characterized by a pervasive distrust that deterred cooperation between these two sets of actors. The majority of job-holders were disinclined to assist their job-seeking relations, citing job-seekers' lack of motivation, neediness, and irresponsible behavior as reasons for their unwillingness. In response, and in an effort to save face, a significant minority of job-seekers were reluctant to seek assistance or to accept it when offered. These interpersonal dynamics played out in a low-wage labor market where employers relied heavily on job referral networks for recruitment and screening. Thus, in addition to and in the context of declining employment opportunities, employer discrimination, presumed cultural deficiencies, and a lack of access to social resources, interpersonal dynamics between black poor job-seekers and their labor market intermediaries also have a profound effect, I contend, on the employment chances of the black poor. Furthermore, I propose that the centrality of interpersonal dynamics highlights the role that micro-level processes play in the reproduction of inequality, essentially cementing the disadvantage initiated by larger macro- and meso-level forces.

In what follows, I briefly describe and then critique the major theoretical frameworks that social scientists deploy to explain chronic joblessness.

Anthony's Insights

To explain his chronic joblessness, Anthony provided a laundry list of structural barriers and individual constraints, a list implicating employer discrimination, deindustrialization and related spatial and skills mismatches, and cultural preferences. In so doing, he provided proponents of three of the major theoretical frameworks on black joblessness evidence to support their theories about its root causes.

Employer Discrimination

According to Anthony, as a black man with a felony conviction, he began every job search with no less than three strikes against him. From his experience, employers were generally unwilling to extend a second chance to men of his ilk. Instead, "white folks" received all of the opportunities. They were given "a better shot." "I can't speak of the whole United States, but for black men here in Michigan, it's hard. Black males here from the age of, say, sixteen on up to forty, and they been convicted or something, all white society look at us like we are no good, you know. You're just going to come back out there and do more wrong. And you're not given more options to do right. [They] just shut [the] door." Indeed, he felt as if the only jobs that black men like him *were allowed* to hold were the lowest-level service-sector jobs at car washes and fast-food restaurants, poorly paid jobs that he felt were best left for teenagers, not for grown men trying to raise families (even though Anthony himself had yet to establish one). Thus, Anthony cited employer discrimination against black men, especially felons, as his greatest obstacle to employment and the primary reason for his chronic joblessness.

Proponents of the employer discrimination perspective would point to mountains of evidence supporting Anthony's claims. First, they would cite studies of employers' perceptions of and preferences for applicants by race and ethnicity. Not surprisingly, the accumulated findings in this area indicate that applicants' race matters—employers perceive black workers to be less competent, productive, and dependable than labor market competitors from other racial and ethnic groups. For instance, Kathryn Neckerman and Joleen Kirschenman (1991) investigated the hiring strategies of Chicago-area employers for entry-level jobs and found that they held such negative stereotypes about inner-city blacks, perceiving them to be deficient in hard and soft skills, work ethic, dependability, and positive attitude, that they employed recruitment strategies that effectively excluded these applicants from their pool of potential applicants.

Employers also perceive black workers, particularly black women, to be more distracted by familial obligations. Drawing from in-depth interviews with employers in the Atlanta metropolitan area, Irene Browne and Ivy Kennelly (1999) investigated how applicants' race and gender affected employers' perceptions and hiring preferences. They discovered that employers viewed black women as poor, single mothers who either struggled to balance work and family obligations, and so were prone to absenteeism and tardiness, or were so desperate in their efforts to support their children that they would take any position available.[2] Neither image led employers to feel inclined to hire black women. Employers either considered such applicants too great a risk or chose not to hire them because they contemptuously viewed black women's desire to work as based in a search for a means of survival, not a belief in work as a moral good. Although highly problematic, these images were far superior to those they held of black men, whom employers viewed only in the most negative light. Not surprisingly, then, black men were the least favored of all job applicants.

Finally, employers characterize black workers as less pliable and obedient than other racial and ethnic groups of workers. Johanna Shih's (2002) examination of Los Angeles employers revealed that they were less concerned with workers' competence than with workers' pliability, obedience, and manageability. Because employers perceived low-skilled black workers to be far less submissive and deferential than their Latino immigrant counterparts, they were reluctant to hire black applicants. Overall, these findings indicate a clear pattern of disfavor toward black workers that makes their hire less likely, especially in smaller firms, firms located in the suburbs, and firms that cater primarily to white customers (Holzer 1997; Holzer and Ihlanfeldt 1998).

Proponents of the employer discrimination perspective would also highlight the compelling evidence based on hiring audit studies (Bertrand and Mullainathan 2004; Turner, Fix, and Struyk 1991). In an audit study, pairs of white and black or Latino testers are matched on a variety of attributes, save race or ethnicity, in an effort to control for most of the factors that employers take into consideration when making hiring decisions. These pairs, whether as real or fictitious applicants, are sent out to apply for vacant positions randomly selected from help-wanted ads in newspapers. Discrimination is determined to have occurred when testers of one race or ethnicity systematically make it further in the hiring process than their equally qualified other-race counterparts.

These studies have revealed that differential treatment does occur, most often to the detriment of black job candidates. Black testers are two to three times less likely to receive callbacks or formal interviews (Bertrand and Mullainathan 2004; Turner et al. 1991). Among those who receive interviews, black testers wait longer to be interviewed, receive shorter interviews, are interviewed by fewer members of personnel, and receive fewer positive comments than their white counterparts. They are also half as likely to receive offers (Turner et al. 1991).

The stigma of a prior conviction only makes matters worse. Incarceration represents a major factor in joblessness because employers are averse to hiring ex-offenders. According to the economists Harry Holzer, Steven Raphael, and Michael Stoll (2002a), fewer than 13 percent of employers would definitely hire ex-offenders, and almost two-thirds indicated that they probably would not or definitely would not.[3] From a supply-side standpoint, this resistance could at least in part be attributed to the time offenders spend in prison, since incarceration takes away from time that could otherwise have been spent accumulating valuable education, work experience, or training. Employers may also be disinclined toward hiring ex-offenders because ex-offenders are far more likely to be high school dropouts and illiterates (Holzer et al. 2005).

Even if human capital deficiencies were not an issue, however, ex-offenders would still have difficulty securing work.[4] In an audit study designed to examine the effect of having a criminal record on hiring, Devah Pager (2002) showed that employers were twice as likely to call back non-offenders than equally qualified ex-offenders, and the effect of race only magnified this gap. While white non-offenders were two times more likely to receive callbacks than equally qualified white ex-offenders, the ratio among blacks was three-to-one.[5] Furthermore, a higher percentage of white ex-offenders received callbacks than equally qualified *non*-offending black applicants—17 versus 14 percent (Pager 2002). Thus, by association, black *non*-offenders are also at a significant disadvantage. Because such a high percentage of young black men have been incarcerated, employers often associate black males with criminality (Holzer, Raphael, and Stoll 2002b). Many who have not been convicted of a crime are disregarded for positions because they are identified with a group among whom rates of incarceration are staggeringly high.[6] Consistent with Anthony's own analysis of his situation, then, proponents of the discrimination thesis would locate his chronic joblessness foremost in employers' distaste for hiring blacks and their particular aversion to black ex-offenders.

Deindustrialization

As if being a black felon were not enough to destroy his chances of getting a job, Anthony highlighted other constraints as well. First, without a driver's license and a car, he had great difficulty getting to the suburbs where he believed good-paying jobs could be found, and he found public transportation, which provided neither frequent nor reliable service, of little practical value. This lack of reliable transportation essentially left him only able to seek positions relatively close to home. However, he was disinclined to accept these positions because they offered such low wages and few, if any, opportunities for advancement; that he would continue struggling to sustain himself would be all but assured if he took such a job.

Second, Anthony felt thwarted by his limited human capital. Again, he had little desire to work at poorly paid jobs such as those at fast-food joints and car washes. However, as a high school dropout who had been incarcerated for most of his adult life, he lacked the education, training, and work experience to compete for jobs that were both physically proximate and relatively well paid. Expressing his frustration, Anthony exclaimed, "There's more jobs out there, but you got to have more education. They want associate's degrees, bachelor's degrees, for everything. I was shocked when they told me that you have somebody with a bachelor degree to be a janitor." Thus, not only did he link his joblessness to the spatial mismatch he faced, but he felt limited by a profound skills mismatch as well.

Proponents of the deindustrialization perspective would find much in Anthony's narrative to support their theory. Foremost among the proponents of this thesis is William Julius Wilson (1987, 1996), who argues convincingly that black joblessness is largely, though not entirely, the result of the changes in the structure of urban economies, particularly in the northeastern and midwestern regions of the country. Specifically, during the latter half of the 1960s, the deindustrialization of urban economies set a transformation in motion: jobs shifted from centers of production and distribution of material goods (which had offered well-paid jobs to those with limited educational credentials) to centers of administration, information exchange, and higher-order service provision (which offered well-paid jobs to those with extensive education, training, and skills). As manufacturing jobs left the central cities of the North, relocating to the suburbs, exurbs, and commercial centers of the Third World, they were replaced by jobs better suited for those with higher levels of education. Drawing from the work of John Kasarda, Wilson has shown that between 1970 and 1984 every major central city in the Northeast and Midwest experienced sharp declines in the number of jobs for which educational requirements were low while showing noteworthy increases in the number of jobs for which the average level of education was higher. New York, for instance, posted losses of almost 500,000 jobs requiring less than a high school diploma, but gained over 250,000 jobs requiring more education. Although Philadelphia lost 172,000 low-skilled jobs, it gained 39,000 that were high-skilled. St. Louis lost ground on both counts—89,000 low-skilled jobs coupled with 2,000 high-skilled positions. As a result, during the 1980s alone, "the central counties of the Frostbelt's 28 largest metropolitan areas lost nearly one million manufacturing jobs and over $28 billion in manufacturing worker earnings" (Kasarda 1995, 215).

Although blue-collar workers of all racial and ethnic stripes were negatively affected by these declines, black men were by far the hardest hit. Not only were they most heavily concentrated in the industries that lost the most jobs and that had jobs that required the least in terms of education, training, and skills, but their representation was far lower in the industries that experienced job gains and those with jobs that required higher levels of education and skills.[7] In areas of the country that had not undergone industrial restructuring of this type (the South and West), employment among black men suffered much less.[8] Thus, according to this approach, at least through the 1980s black joblessness was largely a function of diminishing opportunities due to deindustrialization and related spatial and skills mismatches.[9]

From the diminishing opportunities perspective, then, Anthony's prolonged joblessness is not surprising. Anthony, like many low-skilled black men of his generation, has confronted a labor market that has few decent jobs to offer that are relatively close to his residence and for which he is qualified. Indeed, between 1967 and 1987 (in 1987 Anthony was convicted of breaking and entering and grand theft auto), southeastern Michigan had lost over 100,000 manufacturing jobs—half of its total—while gaining two and a half times that number in trade and high-level service jobs between 1977 and 1987 alone. Unfortunately, Anthony Redmond had fallen victim to the changing structure of the urban economic landscape.

Cultural Deficiency

By and large, proponents of the cultural deficiency perspective would argue that Anthony's "crisis" is of his own making—or, more accurately, that it is a product of the precepts of his culture, whose norms, if not values, are incompatible with those of the mainstream. As evidence, they would point out that Anthony, rather than taking personal responsibility for his plight of joblessness, rationalized his prolonged unemployment by highlighting a number of factors seemingly outside his control: employers discriminated against him, showed little compassion toward him, and were easily intimidated by him; the public transportation system was inadequate; and jobs for which he was qualified were too demeaning. His many excuses for nonwork revealed the extent to which Anthony did not view work as an obligation of citizenship and as a productive enterprise unto itself. Instead, his excuses were evidence that, at best, he viewed work as something to aspire to only when all necessary preconditions had been met (Mead 1992).

Although there are a number of variants on this approach, including those that problematize the supposedly matriarchal structure of the black family (Moynihan 1967; Patterson 1998), Lawrence Mead, political scientist and author of *The New Politics of Poverty* (1992), arguably provides the most sophisticated, if a somewhat contradictory, treatment of the cultural deficiency perspective, employing what appears to be a fair and balanced approach that belies his blame-the-victim viewpoint of the joblessness crisis.[10] Mead asserts that blacks' difficulties are rooted in subcultures of defeatism and resistance. Defeatism expresses itself whenever blacks are faced with the logistical difficulties of finding and keeping work. When tasks such as finding a job, arranging safe and dependable child care, and obtaining reliable transportation become too difficult, Mead argues, blacks surrender, blaming everything and everybody for their inability to secure work while waiting for others (read: whites) to initiate change that will better their circumstances. Their refusal to take personal responsibility, Mead contends (1992, 149), masks a deeply ingrained learned helplessness, the seeds of which were planted in slavery when blacks developed a "paradoxical reliance on the oppressor to undo oppression." Thus, when opportunities do arise, blacks, convinced that they cannot succeed, do not make the effort.[11]

Mead argues for the existence of another subculture as well—that of resistance. In this case, however, blacks are not overwhelmed by the logistics involved in securing jobs. Instead, they find morally repulsive the opportunities to which they have access, characterizing the positions for which they are qualified as too demeaning, too dirty, too difficult, and too poorly paid. Consequently, they resist, forsaking these positions even though they generally lack the credentials necessary to compete for jobs that do not offend their sense of themselves as workers and their sense of what jobs should offer. Unlike the subculture of defeatism, in which blacks have *too little* pride to succeed, in the subculture of resistance they have *too much* pride. Thus, Mead asserts, high rates of joblessness should be attributed to the black poor's refusal to lower their expectations and accept positions that they consider menial.

Summary and Critique

In Anthony's narrative, proponents of each of these three theoretical frameworks for explaining chronic black joblessness would find evidence to support their theory about its root causes. Scholars such as William Julius Wilson (1987, 1996) and John Kasarda (1995) would highlight the difficulty that Anthony had in finding decent-paying jobs within reasonable proximity to his home as evidence of the disproportionately negative impact that deindustrialization and resulting spatial and skills mismatches have had on the employment of lesser-educated black men and women in the inner city. Proponents of the employer discrimination perspective would focus on Anthony's contention that employers are disinclined to hire young black men, especially ex-felons, and point to mountains of evidence from research on employers' perceptions (Browne and Kennelly 1991; Neckerman and Kirschenman 1991; Shih 2002) and audit studies (Bertrand and Mullainathan 2004; Pager 2002; Turner et al. 1991) to support their argument. Cultural deficiency scholars such as Lawrence Mead (1992) would point to Anthony himself and his subculture as the primary source of his chronic joblessness.

None of these perspectives, however, facilitates a full understanding of the problem of black joblessness. This is true of both the structural and cultural perspectives. Structural accounts of black joblessness, although profoundly insightful, often fail to consider the meanings that the black poor attribute to objective factors. While several theories of joblessness compete for dominance as discourses in the minds of poor people, and while any theory can be deployed within a particular context to explain persistent joblessness, it seems that the black poor largely understand persistent joblessness as a failure on the part of individuals to uplift themselves. In fact, prior survey research suggests that among the black poor, structural factors such as discrimination do not register as major impediments to achieving their goals. Paradoxically, even as employers are loath to hire them except under the tightest of labor market conditions (Kasinitz and Rosenberg 1996; Kirschenman and Neckerman 1991; Neckerman and Kirschenman 1991; Wilson 1996), even as they intuit widespread prejudice and discrimination from employers specifically (Harris and Associates 1989; Kasschau 1977) and from white society generally (Sigelman and Tuch 1997; Sigelman and Welch 1991), and even as they confess how little control they feel they have over their own lives (Hochschild 1995), they are far more likely than expected—and more likely than the black middle class and, in some cases, than even poor whites—to explain their relatively low socioeconomic attainment in terms of deficient motivation and individual effort (Hochschild 1995; MacLeod 1995; Parent 1985; Schlozman and Verba 1979).

In *Facing Up to the American Dream* (1995), Jennifer Hochschild explains this apparent paradox by arguing that although most poor blacks acknowledge the importance of discrimination in the daily lives of blacks generally, they are less likely to feel personally affected by it and, more importantly, *they do not perceive it as the most important force shaping their life chances.* Often, it is the least mentioned factor of those volunteered (Harris and Associates 1989). And in *The Minds of Marginalized Black Men* (2004), Alford Young's elaborate cultural analysis of how young, inner-city black men make sense of mobility and opportunity in the United States, he finds that although some men linked theirs and others' mobility to the structure of economic opportunities, highlighting such obstacles as race- and class-based discrimination, the common understanding linking all of his respondents was that the individual is largely responsible for creating or taking advantage of opportunities that lead to his or her own mobility. Young (2004, 138) explains: "Echoing once again the moralism of the language of individualism and the American Dream, all the men underscored individual effort and initiative as the principle driving force behind mobility." Consequently, even while acknowledging the prevalence of discrimination and other structural constraints, poor blacks nonetheless largely concluded that hard work and individual resolve were most essential for blacks' achievement. The assumption is that if blacks do not achieve—for instance, if they are struggling with chronic joblessness—they have only themselves to blame.

My own interviews bear this out. To ascertain how respondents made sense of joblessness, I asked, "How hard is it to find a job, any job?" Given that slightly over half of my sample were unemployed at the time of the interview and that many more had experienced extended periods of joblessness in the past, not only did I expect that the majority of respondents would report that finding a job, any job, was difficult, but I largely expected respondents to situate their difficulty in structural constraints. Indeed, theorists of both structural and cultural deficiency accounts would probably have hazarded such a guess. Both sets of theorists, however, would have been incorrect. The majority of my respondents, six in ten, indicated that finding a job was not difficult at all. Just three in ten thought it was.

Furthermore, what distinguished respondents in the first category from those in the second were their base assumptions about how the U.S. stratification system works. Those in the majority had little doubt about the system's openness. After all, they argued, jobs are readily available, and to the extent that they are not, *those with perseverance will nevertheless succeed, because any job-seeker with motivation and drive can find one.* Others reasoned that the abundance of formal intermediaries, programs, and services available to aid the transition to employment deprives the jobless of any credible defense for their joblessness. Those favoring this view generally argued that anyone who claims an inability to find work simply cannot be looking and that joblessness indicates a weakness of character, a failure of the individual, who either lacks the desire to work or the internal fortitude to gain employment.

These understandings of the roots of joblessness not only have consequences for the behaviors of the black poor in the labor market, as both job-seekers and job-holders, but they also affect how they engage with others who are trying to find work. However, because the dominant structural perspectives generally neglect the interactional nature of the job search process, they ignore the significance of patterned social relations and the meanings that emerge from these and shape how job-seekers understand joblessness and engage the job search process. By failing to consider how the black poor make sense of these objective factors—which they see as diminishing their chances for employment, and rightfully so—proponents of this perspective also overlook how these understandings inform the behaviors of the job-seeking black poor in ways that affect the outcome of joblessness above and beyond the objective factors deemed to bring joblessness about.

Unlike the structural approaches, the cultural deficiency perspective ignores or disputes the significance of structural constraints while locating the crisis of black joblessness solely in the meanings that the poor attach to work, meanings that proponents of this perspective would argue are disconnected from objective reality (Mead 1992; Patterson 1998; Thernstrom and Thernstrom 1998). For instance, Mead argues that poor blacks' chronic joblessness is rooted in their subcultures of defeatism and resistance to low-wage work, such that even when job opportunities are plentiful, they are unwilling to take advantage of them to better their circumstances. However, because Mead does not examine closely and systematically the process of finding work that the black poor undertake, he critically misstates the meanings that the black poor attach to work, job finding, and joblessness.

Indeed, the weight of the evidence indicates that the black poor are not resistant to low-wage work. While Harry Holzer's (1986) analysis of racial differences in reservation wages indicates that as much as 40 percent of the employment gap between young black and white men can be explained by black men's higher reservation wages, in his replication of Holzer's study, which focused on a longer period of time, Stephen Petterson (1997) found no evidence indicating that young black men's joblessness was linked to higher reservation wages. In addition, in their study of Harlem's working poor, Katherine Newman and Chauncy Lennon (1995) found that at the fast-food restaurants they studied, for every one vacant position there were fourteen applicants. Furthermore, after tracking ninety-three job-seekers who had not been hired and who remained unemployed one year later, Newman and Lennon found that their reservation wage was just $4.59 per hour on average. Although this was slightly higher than the minimum wage at the time, given the substantially higher cost of living in New York City, this desired wage was meager at best. Such evidence does not support a description of a subculture of resistance.

Nor is there much evidence that they are defeatists. Newman (1999) argues that the urban poor do adhere to mainstream values, do want to work, and do go out of their way to find and keep jobs. Newman criticizes urban poverty scholars for focusing so much attention on the minority of low-income blacks and Latinos who do not work to the exclusion of the majority who do. By studying in ethnographic detail the working poor's labor market experiences, Newman found that even within the context of shrinking opportunities and low-wage, low-skilled jobs, many of them dead-end, most urban residents continue to "soldier on." "One of their greatest assets," Newman (1999, xv) notes,

> is the commitment they share with more affluent Americans to the importance of the work ethic. These are not people whose values need reengineering. They work hard at jobs the rest of us would not want because they believe in the dignity of work. In many instances they are not only not better off, they are actually worse off from a financial perspective for having eschewed welfare and stayed on the job.

Others have made similar arguments and presented similar evidence (Iversen and Farber 1996; Jones and Luo 1999; Wilson 1996).

By failing to examine closely the process of finding work, a process whose nature is interactional, and basing their determinations of defeatism and resistance almost solely on the outcomes of persistent joblessness alone, cultural deficiency theorists also critically misstate the meanings that the black poor find in work, job finding, and joblessness, and they fail to see the central role that interpersonal relations and social interactions play in producing these meanings. Thus, they are ill equipped to explain behaviors that deviate from their assumptions about the defeatism and resistance of the black poor. In what follows, I elaborate on how we might gain further leverage on the problem of chronic joblessness by examining in much greater detail the interactional nature of the process of finding work.

Social Capital and Its (Im)Mobilization

The social capital perspective assumes what the other perspectives have neglected—that personal networks play a major role in the job-finding process. For instance, in his classic 1974 study, *Getting a Job*, Mark Granovetter examined how 282 professional, technical, and managerial workers from Newton, Massachusetts, found their jobs. He discovered that for the overwhelming majority of workers, personal contacts with whom they had interacted during ordinary social activities had made the match. Furthermore, Granovetter found that those who used personal contacts had better employment outcomes overall. An instant classic, *Getting a Job* revealed what remains to this day an incredible insight—that while we may assume that economic activities and outcomes have nothing to do with social relationships, they are in fact products of it. Granovetter's revelation was undoubtedly the inspiration for a generation of research examining the effect of social capital and social networks on status attainment, and it has had important implications for understanding chronic joblessness among the black poor.

To clarify, social capital is typically defined as the resources to which individuals have access by dint of their connection to others in their network of relations. Although many theorists are associated with the term, Pierre Bourdieu (1985) is usually credited with providing the first systematic discussion (Lin 2001; Portes 1998).[12] He used the term to describe the resources or profits to which individuals have access as a result of their membership or participation in groups such as families, parties, and associations. These resources or profits, which can be economic, cultural, or symbolic in form, are the product of the time and energy that members direct toward a series of material or symbolic exchanges with each other that help to reproduce social relationships with the conscious or unconscious objective of promoting long-term obligations from which tangible or intangible profits accrue.

Glenn Loury was one of the first to implicate social connections in the process of differential access to opportunities by race and gender; in doing so, he provided a framework within which to better understand racial inequalities in the labor market. In "A Dynamic Theory of Racial Income Differences" (1977), Loury drew from sociological research on intergenerational mobility and inheritance of race to assert that even if we could equalize racial differences in the quality and quantity of human capital, and even if we could encourage employers to eliminate their discrimination against blacks, racial inequalities would persist. Criticizing neoclassical theories of racial income inequality for being too individualistic and ignoring group processes, he asserted that blacks would continue to be disadvantaged in part because *blacks gen-*

erally have poorer connections to the labor market and lack information about job opportunities. Relative to whites, blacks lack social capital. Incorporating ideas behind the social capital theoretical framework into his analysis of persistent black joblessness, William Julius Wilson (1987) explained that when the black middle and working classes moved away from what were once vertically integrated black communities, those left behind became residents of neighborhoods steeped in poverty. As a result of their lack of regular and sustained contact with individuals who had strong attachments to mainstream institutions, residents have become socially isolated. Relative to poor residents of low-poverty neighborhoods, the number of people to whom residents of high-poverty neighborhoods are connected is small, and the connections they do have are also disadvantaged. Consequently, they know few who can act as role models, socializing them about appropriate workplace behavior and, most importantly, providing them with links to jobs. Thus, Wilson has argued, absent access to personal contacts who are able to provide job information—that is, absent social capital—even during strong economic times members of this group still have great difficulty finding work.

Wilson's thesis caused urban poverty scholars to begin to consider the role that personal relations play in the persistent joblessness crisis; this change of focus was an important breakthrough in urban poverty research since these largely quantitative approaches had done well in identifying the ways in which network structure and composition matter. For instance, all else being equal, larger, more diverse, and wider-ranging networks allow for greater efficiency in the flow of new and different kinds of information, whose quality, quantity, and timing increase individuals' edge in the competitive arena, thereby improving their attainment outcomes. Furthermore, networks higher in social status provide better resources since resources greater in quality and quantity inhere in positions located higher in social structure (Burt 1992, 1997; Campbell, Marsden, and Hurlbert 1986; Lin 1999; Lin and Dumin 1986).

This focus, however, has led scholars and researchers to neglect, within the context of embeddedness, the role of interpersonal relations and the intersubjective moments that inform the behaviors of the various actors who participate in the process. After all, access to job contacts does not guarantee that job information and influence will be mobilized on a job-seeker's behalf, as Nan Lin intimates when he states (2001, 92), "Not all persons accessed with rich social capital are expected to take advantage of or be able to mobilize social capital for the purpose of obtaining better socioeconomic status. An element of action and choice should also be significant." A job-seeker's decision to seek assistance or to accept it when offered and a job-holder's decision about whether to provide assistance depend in great part on interpersonal dynamics. And these dynamics do not always lead to cooperation between the actors occupying these positions. Indeed, as I will show, interpersonal relations and intersubjective moments are crucial for understanding persistent joblessness. This is not because they reveal the extent to which the black poor, especially those from high- and extreme-poverty neighborhoods, are disconnected from mainstream ties who could link them to job information and influence their hire. Indeed, similar to the findings reported in Newman's *No Shame in My Game* (1999), I found disconnection to be a rather rare occurrence.[13] Rather, interpersonal relations matter because it is through these interactions and engagements that the poor come to diagnose the problems of joblessness, theorizing about its primary causes and possible solutions. It is through these social interactions as well that joblessness discourses have their ultimate consequences, shaping how poor blacks engage with each other as actors, specifically as job-seekers and job-holders, in the economic realm, and thus affecting their labor market outcomes above and beyond the initiating factors deemed to cause joblessness (Pescosolido 1992). But only by examining the process of finding work and doing so in ethnographic detail do we gain insight into how black, poor job-seekers make sense of the process of finding work, the actions they take during the process, the motivations that underlie these actions, and how each of these is informed by their interactions with others in their social milieu. *Lone Pursuit* is an effort to address these empirical and theoretical shortcomings in the literature.

Anthony's Oversight

Although Anthony provided me with a fairly exhaustive list of factors to explain his joblessness, the one thing he failed to mention was an odd omission, I thought, given the extent to which it pervaded our conversations about his daily efforts at job finding. Specifically, even as days of unemployment multiplied into weeks, weeks rolled into months, and months approached a year, Anthony was strongly disinclined to seek assistance from his family members, friends, and acquaintances, not because he lacked contacts who could aid him during his search, but because he did not feel that he could or should mobilize his connections on his own behalf. When asked about the importance of using friends, relatives, and acquaintances for job information and influence, Anthony explained that while they were important to the process, he preferred not to employ this approach to finding work, stating somewhat defensively, "You ain't got to worry about me using your name to get in the door. Just give me an application; just turn it in for me. That's all I ask you. Because, you know, say if I do get a job and mess up on the job, I won't drag you down with me. So I prefer not to use your name."

Just as he resisted seeking assistance from his network of relations, save to the extent that they could give him information about job openings, so too was he unreceptive toward providing assistance to others. As he explained, "I'll use the same method on myself. I used to tell them, 'I get you an application, but don't use me at all. If you mess up a job, it won't fall back on me either.'" In other words, in a low-wage labor market where employers rely heavily on informal networks for recruitment and screening, Anthony, a man desperately seeking employment for some ten months, was so disinclined toward, even distrustful of, personal contact use that he approached the job-finding process as a defensive individualist, both in seeking a job and in being a potential job contact.

Had researchers examined in ethnographic detail Anthony's process of finding work, they would have discovered that although he believed that his prospects for finding work were made worse by employer discrimination and declining opportunities for lesser-skilled workers, he was even more convinced that ultimately his crisis of joblessness was of his own making and that only through his own efforts would he overcome his labor market difficulties. Moreover, researchers would have noted that Anthony's understanding of his situation and his resulting job search behavior—going it alone—derived from interactions he had with friends, relatives, acquaintances, and institutions, especially those who were positioned to assist him but chose not to because they blamed him for his own struggles. These labor market intermediaries were institutions and individuals who feared the effect that assisting him would have on their own well-being and who communicated these understandings and concerns to him in subtle but often obviously demeaning ways. It was these understandings, these tensions or conflicts between the roles of job-seeker and job-holder, that nurtured a pervasive distrust between them and Anthony and that primarily shaped his individualistic approach to job search; that approach, in turn, only disadvantaged him further because he was forsaking the use of personal contacts in a low-wage labor market that was heavily dependent on such referrals (Holzer 1996).

Job-holders' distrust and reluctance to assist their job-seeking friends and relatives have been noted in other qualitative studies. For instance, Newman (1999) observed that personal contacts were vital to the job-matching process among the low-wage workers she studied. However, assistance was not always forthcoming. Fearing that their referrals would prove unreliable and compromise their reputations with their employer, a few of her subjects, Newman observed, denied help to their job-seeking friends and relatives. In telling the story of a young black man struggling with the desire to be "decent" and the call of the "street," Elijah Anderson (1999) also noted that some in positions to provide job-finding assistance were often wary about doing so because they feared the negative consequences that a bad match might have on their own employment health and well-being. And in *Race and the Invisible Hand,* Deirdre Royster (2003) reported that a few of the black working-class men she interviewed felt that they had to use their positions as labor market intermediaries "carefully and sparingly" because they feared the negative consequences to their reputations if their referrals "messed up."

However, while these works are noteworthy, their reports are only suggestive of a pattern of distrust and noncooperation. In the absence of systematic investigations of job contacts' willingness to assist, it has been unclear to what extent those in possession of job information and influence have been disinclined to provide job-finding assistance. Nor has it been clear what conditions have had to be met for assistance to be forthcoming. Furthermore, previous research has not examined how job-holders' reluctance affects job-seekers' understanding of their own joblessness and thus the motivations behind their approaches to job search. *Lone Pursuit* does.

The Study

In collaboration with Alford Young Jr., a sociologist at the University of Michigan, and a small team of graduate students, between the fall of 1999 and the summer of 2002 I conducted in-depth interviews and a survey of 105 low-income, young, black men and women from "Southeast County," Michigan.[14] The purpose of the project was to collect data on the social experiences that helped shape the black poor's cognitive map of the world of work and their place in it. It was also designed to gain an understanding of how individuals' mental maps informed their labor market decisions, including information about their job referral networks and the process of finding work.

Research Design, Sample, and Data

As is often the case when studying low-income populations, we had great difficulty recruiting participants through random sampling techniques (Edin and Lein 1997). I catalog these difficulties in appendix A. More than one-quarter of the sample were recruited from one of the most socioeconomically disadvantaged neighborhoods in Southeast County through recruitment strategies that included direct calling, letter mailings, and door-to-door canvassing of the neighborhood's three public, low-income housing projects. Slightly fewer than three-quarters of the sample were recruited from two social service agencies. One of the agencies catered to residents experiencing various housing issues and provided them with some employment assistance as well. The other agency, the job center, yielded the bulk of our 105 interviews. In all, 72 percent of respondents were recruited at both social service agencies, and two-thirds at the job center alone.

The job center, a one-stop employment service center, offered a variety of programs to aid the transition to labor force participation and employment, including education, training, and employment programs, GED classes for high school dropouts, child-care referral services, and transportation services. Although the center was open to all of the county's residents, the majority of clients were black and poor. As a consequence of their participation in Michigan's Family Independence Program (FIP), the state's version of the federally funded TANF (Temporary Assistance for Needy Families) program, welfare recipients were required to take part in FIP's Work First program, which was housed at the job center. Work First clients were mandated to spend several hours each day looking for work, and many did so by browsing the employment section of local newspapers or surfing job bank websites on computers provided by the center. Work First also mandated that recipients take classes and workshops held at the center to increase their marketability and employability.

Because of welfare reforms that required welfare applicants to name the fathers of their children, young men were also being held accountable in ways that involved the job center. Court-ordered to pay child support, unemployed fathers were strongly encouraged by the state to visit the center to find work. Employed fathers stopped by hoping to find a better job than the one they already had. Both types of fathers were motivated by the desire to stop or, more realistically, slow their child support arrears. Childless young men and women also stopped by to browse local papers, surf the Internet, call employers, and submit résumés via fax or the Internet. All of these kinds of users also worked with staff members who recruited and screened applicants for local employers willing to hire from this low-skilled population and who encouraged job-seekers to attend weekly job fairs. It was largely from this general population of center clients that my sample was drawn.

Interviewers took up residence at the job center's office during regular business hours. With the assistance of center staff, interviewers identified subjects who fit the study criteria and recruited them for participation. We sought black men and women between the ages of twenty and forty who resided in Southeast County and who had no more than a high school diploma or GED. Respondents were asked about their family background, networks, employment history, and job-finding methods. They were also questioned in-depth about their childhood (including childhood impressions of work); marriage, relationships, and children; employment history, experiences, and impressions of work; job referral networks; philosophy of employment; and attitudes and opinions about the extent and nature of job opportunities for low-skilled workers like themselves. Interviews averaged between two and three hours and were conducted by African Americans. The reader should refer to appendices B and C for the in-depth interview protocol and survey instrument used to gather data. I also undertook an extensive examination of the job center while there. This examination included extensive interviews with center staff about their experiences assisting clients searching for work, observations of client and staff interactions, and a study of the center's physical space.

In table 1.1, I display the mean characteristics of respondents in the sample. (See table A.1 for mean characteristics by data collection strategies.) The average age of the sample was twenty-eight years, 78 percent had never married (though just under half reported living with a spouse or partner), and 75 percent had children—2.5 on average. Eighty-four percent were high school graduates (or had gotten a GED), and just over half were employed. On their current or most recent job, respondents' mean wages were $9.30 per hour (and the median was about $8.50). However, because median tenure was only eleven months—nearly one-third had not worked longer than six months—most families survived on poverty-level earnings. Indeed, one-third of respondents were receiving public assistance at the time of the interview—14 percent of the men and 47 percent of the women. Nearly half reported having ever received assistance—31 percent of the men and 68 percent of the women. (By and large, these figures are what we have come to expect in terms of the social and economic status of the black poor.) Finally, employing a variation of the categories of neighborhood poverty concentration typically used in urban poverty studies, I found that 69 percent of respondents lived in census tracts in which rates of family poverty were low to moderate (0 to 29.9 percent), and 31 percent resided in neighborhoods characterized by much of the urban underclass literature, with rates of family poverty that were high to extreme (30 percent and higher).

One of the novel approaches taken here is that I consulted with respondents about their roles as both job-seekers—individuals taking steps to find work on their own behalf—and job-holders—individuals in possession of information and influence and so in a good position to affect employers' hiring decisions on behalf of their personal relations. Regarding their role as job-seekers, I queried them about the level of difficulty they had finding any job; the obstacles they had faced in their attempts to find work; the extent to which friends, family members, and acquaintances were important to this process; and their experiences seeking help from others. I paid particular attention to why they asked others for assistance when they did; who they asked and why

Table 1.1   Mean Sample Characteristics

	Mean	Range
Age	28.4 (5.9)	17–43
Gender (females)	.52	0–1
Never married	.78	0–1
Have children	.75	0–1
Number of children (if parent)	2.5 (1.4)	1–7
High school graduate/GED	.84	0–1
Employed	.52	0–1
Hourly wages	$9.30 ($3.50)	$2.50–23.00
Public assistance		0–1
Currently receiving	.31	
Women	.47	
Men	.17	
Ever received	.46	
Women	.68	
Men	.31	
Neighborhood poverty rate		0–1
Low to moderate	.69	
High to extreme	.31	

Source: Author's compilation.
Note: N = 103.

they asked the people they did; what these contacts did for a living; whether or not they had influence on the job; what type of assistance they provided; whether or not they as job-seekers gained employment; and how they assessed the role that their ties played in the job-matching process. These questions were part of the effort to understand how respondents, as job-seekers, generally experienced the job search process, the role that their job-holding ties had played in the process, and how job-seekers made sense of job-holders' role.

I also asked them questions about their role as job-holders who were in a position to affect job matches between employers and job-seekers. What did they typically do when they heard about openings at their workplace? Had anyone ever come to them for help in finding or getting a job? How did they determine whether they would provide assistance, and what form did that assistance take? How did they assess the positive and negative aspects of helping others find work? My goal was to gauge how respondents, as job-holders, experienced the job-matching process and to understand the role that they saw for those in possession of information and influence vis-à-vis the job-seeker, the costs and benefits they associated with providing assistance, and the decisionmaking process they used to determine whether or not to assist.

Pervasive Distrust and Noncooperation

Interviews revealed that Anthony was hardly unique in his approach to job-finding assistance, whether as a potential contact or as a job-seeker. Although some job-seekers and job-holders were willing to receive and provide job-finding assistance, distrust between job-seekers and job-holders was pervasive, and it negatively affected their decisions to cooperate during the job search process. Specifically, when in possession of job information or influence, the overwhelming majority of job-holders expressed concern that job-seekers in their networks were too unmotivated to accept assistance, required great expenditures of time and emotional energy, or acted too irresponsibly on the job, thereby jeopardizing the job-holders' own reputations with their employers and harming their already tenuous labor market prospects. Consequently, they were generally reluctant to assist the job-seekers in their network. To justify their unwillingness, job-holders literally ranted about the importance of self-reliance, espousing individualistic tenets about finding a job.

Furthermore, job-holders' reluctance had consequences for job-seekers' search behavior. A substantial minority of job-seekers so feared falling short of expectations or being maligned by their personal contacts for being jobless that they were disinclined to seek assistance or to accept it when offered. To justify their reluctance to use personal contacts, job-seekers embraced individualism, choosing to forgo personal contact use in favor of much less effective job search methods.

But theirs was a *defensive individualism*. Within the context of poverty, friends, relatives, acquaintances, and institutions in their social milieu blamed the black poor and jobless for their persistent joblessness, deploying discourses of joblessness that privileged individuals' moral shortcomings and stressed personal responsibility and self-sufficiency as a panacea. Cognizant of how they were viewed and of how their joblessness was understood, job-seekers became defensive individualists. Their potential labor market intermediaries certainly pushed them into defensive individualism, but the black poor and jobless also embraced individualism and self-reliant approaches to job search as their own distrust toward themselves and intermediaries grew.[15]

A skeptical reader might argue that what I found were respondents' justifications for their joblessness rather than the motivations behind their job search. In other words, job-seekers who expressed a disinclination to seek assistance or accept it when offered did so to make excuses for their persistent joblessness. Such skepticism would be understandable if it were not for two things. First, respondents were asked a number of questions to gain insight into how they understood their labor market experiences. Unemployed job-seekers were asked to explain why they had such difficulty finding work. The whole sample was asked what made finding work difficult, to the extent that it was. In neither case did respondents offer that finding work was difficult because they chose to look for a job without the assistance of friends, relatives, and acquaintances. Instead, as I discuss in the following chapters, the overwhelming majority pointed to what they perceived to be personal obstacles to employment, such as human capital deficiencies, felony convictions, drug and alcohol abuse, lack of motivation, and familial obligations. A significant minority also pointed to structural constraints to employment, such as poor public transportation systems, employer discrimination, and the lack of jobs. Only four job-seekers in the entire sample explained persistent joblessness by pointing to a lack of relations who could help. No job-seekers explained their persistent joblessness in terms of their own unwillingness to seek assistance or to accept it when offered.

Second, one of the strengths of this study is that it attempts to understand the process of finding work from the perspective of both job-seekers and job-holders, those who are well positioned to provide information and influence hires. By adopting this strategy, I show that to the extent that job-seekers are disinclined to seek assistance or to accept it when offered for fear of losing face, they are doing so within the context of job-holding ties who express a great deal of distrust and reluctance to assist in ways that might harm their own labor market positions. In other words, job-holders' accounts of the job search process are very consistent with the accounts offered by job-seekers. Their stories jibe, providing further evidence that what I am referencing here is the actual job-seeking process and the motivations behind job search, not job-seekers' justifications for their own joblessness.

Readers may also wonder about the implications of my findings from having drawn the sample largely from a job center. Surely job-seekers who visit job centers do so because they lack access to social resources or are less likely to deploy the social resources they do have for job finding. These concerns are unwarranted, however, for the following reasons. Clients of the job center were often mandated to visit, sometimes as a consequence of Work First requirements. Others had been strongly encouraged by the state to visit the center to find work in order to pay down rising child support arrears. Also, the recently unemployed were required by the state to register at the job center in order to receive unemployment compensation. In other words, for many job center users their visits to the center were required and not the direct result of network dynamics.

Furthermore, center respondents were no more likely to express disfavor toward engaging a job referral network than their counterparts recruited by other strategies. I found that participants recruited from the job center were *far less reluctant* to use personal contacts than noncenter respondents. Whereas one-third of noncenter respondents claimed reluctance to use personal contacts, just one-fifth of center contacts did. And so it appears that visiting the center was less about the interpersonal dynamics of distrust and noncooperation than it was about being mandated to do so.

Overview of the Book

In *Lone Pursuit*, I engage current debates about persistent black joblessness by highlighting the process of finding work, which has often been neglected in prior research. In so doing, I show that interpersonal relations and intersubjective moments are crucial for understanding persistent joblessness. This is not because my analysis reveals the extent to which the black poor, especially those from high- and extreme-poverty neighborhoods, are disconnected from mainstream relations who could link them to job information and influence their hire. Rather, it reveals that the process of finding work is in great part a product of job-seekers' interactions with others in their social milieu, especially job-holders. Because the roles of job-seekers and job-holders are often in conflict, however, nurturing interpersonal relations characterized by distrust, these two fundamental nodes are often led to disengage from one another during the process of finding work, making all the more difficult the task of finding work in low-wage labor markets where employers rely heavily on job referral networks for recruitment and screening.

The arguments I put forward in *Lone Pursuit* about the interpersonal dynamics of (dis)trust, (non)cooperation, and individualism among black poor job-seekers and their job-holding relations contribute to these larger debates about the extent and nature of social support networks in poor black communities. In chapter 2, I engage this literature by asking two sets of questions. First, are poor blacks different? Are their interpersonal relations characterized by mutual trust and reciprocity, or are they more accurately described as distrusting and uncooperative, relative to other groups? Second, to the extent that the weight of the evidence supports the latter contention, how might we understand pervasive distrust and individualism among the black poor? To address the first set of questions, I draw from the extensive research on racial and ethnic differences in social support. To address the second, I draw from the expanding literature on trust and trustworthiness, elaborating on the conditions that must be met in order for the seeds of trust to be sown, grown, and harvested toward cooperative, mutually beneficial ends.

In chapter 3, I dive into the heart and soul of *Lone Pursuit* with an examination of the process of job-finding from the perspective of the jobholder, one of at least two crucial nodes in the job search process. I show that job-holders approach job-finding assistance with great distrust and reluctance and explain their general reluctance to assist in terms of jobseekers' reputations, their own reputations with their employers, and the strength of their relationships with job-seekers. Residing in a neighborhood characterized by concentrated disadvantage also helps to shape the extent to which job-holders understand job-seekers as risky investments and affects the extent and nature of the assistance they are willing to provide.

In chapter 4, I examine the process of finding work from the perspective of the job-seeker and show that a significant minority of jobseekers, cognizant of how they are perceived by others in their social milieu, refuse to seek or accept assistance from job-holders who have job information and influence. Instead, they choose to go it alone, adopting a defensive individualism that belies the central role of job referral networks for employers in low-wage labor markets. In this chapter, I also explore the reasons for their reluctance, linking it primarily to fears of falling short of expectations or being maligned by their jobholding ties for their state of joblessness. I also illustrate how and why men and women experienced these fears differently: the overwhelming majority of "reluctant" personal contact users were men, while the ranks of the "willing" were primarily women.

In chapter 5, I show that pervasive distrust and noncooperation are not unique to relationships between job-seekers and job-holders. They also characterize relationships between job-seekers and the job center employees charged with facilitating their clients' labor force participation and employment. I relate the dynamics between job-seekers and these institutional intermediaries to four key factors—the lack of institutional resources to effectively facilitate job-finding; the dominant institutional discourses of joblessness that define the problem of joblessness and provide a guide to addressing the problem, often quite insufficiently; the tenuousness of staff members' own positions as labor market intermediaries; and the behaviors of the poor and jobless, which largely result from the major barriers to employment they face but are interpreted as evidence of their moral and cultural deficiencies. I make the point that even within the context of institutional social capital, job-finding assistance is not necessarily forthcoming but instead is part of an elaborate decisionmaking process that rests on the interaction of these four factors, which also *inhibit* job finding among the black poor.

In chapter 6, I close *Lone Pursuit* by comparing and contrasting explanations for job-holders' and center staff's distrust toward and noncooperation with job-seekers. I make a broader statement about the conditions that facilitate distrust and noncooperation but that also aid in the reproduction of inequality at the micro level. I also identify those among the black poor who are most vulnerable under these conditions, and I suggest ways in which social policy might better address their issues.

Chapter 2

Pervasive Distrust and Noncooperation Among the Black Poor

In her highly influential ethnography, *All Our Kin* (1974), Carol Stack studied the coping strategies that families in one poor black community employed to survive persistent poverty and racism. In this three-year participant-observation of The Flats, the poorest section of a black community in fictitiously named "Jackson Harbor," Stack discovered that residents survived poverty by developing extensive networks of relationships with kin and nonkin alike and that these relationships were built on and characterized by ongoing obligations of typically generalized exchange. Within these networks, residents regularly gave to and received goods, services, and resources from family members and friends. They also proactively networked to increase the number of their exchange relationships in the hopes of building networks large enough and stable enough to receive a constant flow of resources that would sustain them through good times and bad.

What is more, residents trusted that their generosity would be reciprocated, even if they were uncertain about what they would receive in return and when their network partners would reciprocate.[1] Trust developed because residents who systematically failed to fulfill their obligations became the source of much gossip and were eventually excluded from the network's familial-based system of resource distribution; such exclusion often meant the difference between making ends meet and going hungry. With these potential costs for noncompliance, residents felt secure that others would abide by the rules of the exchange game. Thus, according to Stack, if only to cope with persistent poverty, poor black families developed relationships of trust and cooperation. They could not afford to do otherwise.

All Our Kin was more than an attempt to describe the tactics that poor black families develop to cope with the urgent needs produced by persistent poverty. Stack was also trying to counter the claims made by cultural deficiency theorists that black poor families and communi-

27

ties have responded to historic and contemporary disadvantage by adopting strategies that feed social disorganization and inhibit escape from poverty. With *All Our Kin*, then, Stack joined others (Aschenbrenner 1975; Billingsley 1968; Heiss 1975; Ladner 1972) in defining an alternative vision of social organization among the black poor, highlighting in particular patterns of social organization built on webs of kin-based relationships characterized by mutual trust and cooperation that make survival possible. Stack argued that these strategies for survival, though different from the forms of family and community organization typified by the mainstream, showed great resilience in the face of overwhelming obstacles through cooperation, which was not often seen among the middle class, black or white. Indeed, she maintained, "in contrast to the middle-class ethic of individualism and competition, the poor living in The Flats do not turn anyone down when they need help. The cooperative life style and the bonds created by the vast mass of moment-to-moment exchanges constitute an underlying element of black identity in The Flats. This powerful obligation of exchange is a profoundly creative adaptation to poverty" (43). In so arguing, Stack and others have also inspired what has come to be called the "superorganization" versus "disorganization" debates (see, for example, Sarkisian and Gerstel 2004), a line of research devoted to revealing the extent to which racial, ethnic, and class groupings differ in their embeddedness in social support systems that facilitate survival and economic advancement.

In part, the arguments I put forward in *Lone Pursuit* about the interpersonal dynamics of (dis)trust and (non)cooperation among black poor job-seekers and their job-holding relations contribute to these larger debates about the extent and nature of social support networks within poor black communities. In what follows, I engage this literature by asking two sets of questions. First, are poor blacks different? Are their interpersonal relations characterized by mutual trust and reciprocity, as Stack and others would argue? Or, as some have maintained, are they distrusting and uncooperative compared to other racial and ethnic groups? If so, how might we understand pervasive distrust and noncooperation among the black poor?

Are (Poor) Blacks Different?

To what extent do poor blacks receive social support from kith and kin, and how does this support compare to what is experienced by more affluent blacks and similarly situated nonblacks? After almost four decades of scholarly debate on this topic, there are no easy answers. While some researchers find evidence that the black poor do indeed rely heavily on their networks for social support, others find that blacks, and most especially the poor among them, are less engaged in extensive exchange networks. And of course, there are those who find support for both claims.

To explain the lack of consensus in the literature, some scholars point to a qualitative-quantitative divide (Brewster and Padavic 2002), arguing that while ethnographic work largely supports the "superorganization" perspective (see Aschenbrenner 1975; Hays and Mindel 1973; Ladner 1972; Stack 1974), findings drawn from quantitative analyses largely support the "disorganization" thesis (Eggebeen 1992; Eggebeen and Hogan 1990; Hofferth 1984; Hogan et al. 1993; Roschelle 1997). However, this distinction is far too simple. Instead, as Natalia Sarkisian and Naomi Gerstel (2004) note, there is so little consensus on these questions in part because there is considerable variation in how studies of social support are undertaken. Drawing from Peterson (1996), Sarkisian and Gerstel (2004, 816) point to five primary distinctions in studies on this topic. Studies vary in terms of the type of support being considered, who gives, who receives, the direction of the transfer, and the methodologies used.

Although these differences make consensus difficult to achieve, two things seem clear. First, extensive networks of social support are far less pervasive than previous research has suggested, a difference explained at least in part by a noteworthy decline in network-related support over the past thirty years (Brewster and Padavic 2002). Thus, a significant proportion of disadvantaged families do not receive enough assistance from friends and family to get by, and many do not receive any assistance at all. Second, blacks and the poor do appear less likely to give and receive than others, but this is not the case for all categories of exchange.

Exchanging the Basics

A number of studies have found that the extent and nature of the exchanges depicted by Stack (1974) and others occur only among a small minority of American families (Benin and Keith 1995; Brewster and Padavic 2002; Hogan et al. 1993; Jayakody et al. 1993). For instance, analyzing the National Survey of Families and Households, Dennis Hogan, David Eggebeen, and Clifford Clogg (1993) found that just over 10 percent were high-exchangers, people who gave and received many types of support. In contrast, over half were low-exchangers, people who had a low probability of giving or receiving assistance, care, advice, or money. And almost three-quarters of these low-exchangers did not take part in *any* type of exchange. Furthermore, compared to whites, blacks (including single mothers) and Latinos were far less likely to be high-exchangers and far more likely to be low-exchangers.

The poor were also less likely to give and receive than their more afflu-ent counterparts. Thus, among American families, extensive exchange networks appear uncommon, and contrary to Stack and others, they appear even more exceptional among blacks and the poor, suggesting that relationships of mutual trust and cooperation are not particular to the black poor. But even this last statement belies the complexity of the issue.

Although blacks and the poor appear less likely to give and receive than others, this is not true for all categories of exchange. When it comes to financial support, whites appear to have a distinct advantage over blacks, and the more affluent appear to have a measurable advan-tage over their more disadvantaged counterparts (Eggebeen 1992; Hof-ferth 1984; Lee and Aytac 1998; Parish, Hao, and Hogan 1991; Sarkisian and Gerstel 2004).[2] It also appears that blacks, and especially the poor among them, are less likely to receive emotional support, including ad-vice, from their network of relations (Eggebeen and Hogan 1990; Ka-plan 1997; Sarkisian and Gerstel 2004).

However, blacks appear more likely—far more likely in some in-stances—to take part in other forms of exchange. For instance, a num-ber of studies have found that they are more likely to exchange child care, including the care of sick children (Benin and Keith 1995; Hogan, Hao, and Parish 1990; Parish et al. 1991; Sarkisian and Gerstel 2004).[3] Previous research has also found that they are more likely to receive aid in the form of transportation from family members (Benin and Keith 1995; Sarkisian and Gerstel 2004), though whites appear more likely to get rides from friends. Furthermore, not only are blacks more likely to give and receive assistance with housework (Sarkisian and Gerstel 2004), but they are also far more likely to share a residence with other adult kin (Hofferth 1984; Hogan et al. 1990; Parish et al. 1991), an im-portant form of social support. In this regard, Sarkisian and Gerstel (2004, 823) are probably most accurate when they note that "[it] is im-possible to state whether black or white families are more integrated. Rather, whites and blacks both are actively involved in support trans-fers among kin. There are, however, racial differences in the relative prevalence of different types of support."

Most studies show a distinct social support disadvantage for the poor, however. For instance, the disadvantaged are less likely than their more affluent counterparts to receive child care (Benin and Keith 1995; but see Brewster and Padavic 2002), transportation (Benin and Keith 1995), and household assistance (Eggebeen 1992) from relatives. They are also less likely to give support to their adult children. Thus, the poor, black or white, do not generally appear to be more advantaged by extensive exchange relationships than their more affluent counterparts. On the contrary, they appear to be at a distinct disadvantage, and again, relatively few appear to get the assistance that they need to get by (Benin and Keith 1995; Hogan et al. 1993; Jayakody et al. 1993).

Providing Job Information and Influencing Hires

If we conceptualize job-finding assistance as a form of social support, quantitative research examining racial and ethnic differences in job search strategies, methods of job finding, and types of assistance received by job contacts is also worth noting. Previous research indicates that the overwhelming majority of blacks—roughly three-quarters—search for jobs through personal contacts, as do whites (Green, Tigges, and Diaz 1999). These rates are slightly higher among young blacks (Holzer 1987), poor blacks (Elliot and Sims 2001; Green, Tigges, and Browne 1995), and Latinos (Falcon 1995; Falcon and Melendez 2001; Green et al. 1999). Eight in ten of these job-seekers search through personal contacts.

However, although the overwhelming majority of job-seekers from each racial and ethnic group search for work through their personal contacts, they actually get jobs through friends and relatives at significantly different rates (Corcoran, Datcher, and Duncan 1980; Elliot and Sims 2001; Falcon 1995; Green et al. 1995; Green et al. 1999; Smith 2000).[4] Compare the experiences of blacks and Latinos, for instance. Recent research indicates that although 75 percent of blacks search for work through friends and relatives, fewer than half actually get matched to jobs through these informal channels. In contrast, whereas 85 percent of Latinos search through kith and kin, upwards of 75 percent find work this way. In other words, Latinos who search through personal networks are much more likely to be matched to jobs this way than their black counterparts, a gap that is most notable among black and Latino residents of poor neighborhoods (Elliot and Sims 2001).[5]

Finally, when personal relations do assist blacks during the matching process, they are less likely to do so proactively. According to Gary Green, Leann Tigges, and Daniel Diaz (1999), whereas 61 percent of blacks matched by personal contacts reported that their contact told them about the position for which they were hired—this being the least proactive of informal job-matching methods and the type of assistance offering no influence whatsoever (Granovetter 1974/1995)—only 44 and 41 percent of whites and Latinos who received job-matching assistance were aided in this way. In contrast, a significantly higher percentage of whites reported having been hired by their contact (18 versus 8 percent), and a significantly higher percentage of Latinos reported that their contact talked to the employer on their behalf (37 versus 25 percent).[6]

Furthermore, proactive assistance was associated with neighborhood poverty status, but in different ways for blacks and Latinos.

Among Latinos, a higher percentage of residents in high-poverty neighborhoods received proactive assistance from their personal contacts compared to their counterparts living in more affluent neighborhoods. The inverse was true for blacks. A lower percentage of black residents in high-poverty neighborhoods received proactive assistance from their job contacts, compared to their counterparts living in more affluent neighborhoods. Latino residents of high-poverty neighborhoods were also far more likely than black residents of high-poverty neighborhoods to receive proactive assistance (Elliot and Sims 2001). For Latinos, then, poverty appears to be positively associated with social support in the form of job-finding assistance (for a nice illustration of this, see Dohan 2003). However, among blacks the opposite appears to be true. Thus, quantitative research indicates that blacks, especially poor blacks, are less likely than whites and Latinos to receive the type of support that most effectively matches job-seekers to jobs.

Qualitative research also suggests lower levels of social support. In *Black Identities: West Indian Dreams and American Realities* (1999), Mary Waters introduces her readers to "American Food," a cafeteria located in the corporate headquarters of "a famous financial services company." With 170 native whites, blacks, and immigrants, including West Indians, employed to serve the company's 4,000 employees, the cafeteria provided an excellent opportunity to examine racial and ethnic differences in job-finding assistance on the same shop floor. After interviewing one-third of the cafeteria's workers and asking questions about recruitment and hiring practices, among other things, Waters learned that a significant shift in the demographic makeup of the workforce followed a change in how applicants were recruited and screened. Specifically, after the company began substituting employee referrals for newspaper advertisements and employment agencies as its primary source of applicant recruitment, in relatively short order the workforce was transformed from predominantly native black to predominantly foreign-born black. Of the small proportion of native blacks employed at American Food during the study period, the overwhelming majority had been hired *before* the company began using employee referrals. After informally institutionalizing employee referrals for recruitment, native blacks were largely excluded from the hiring process, while the proportion of West Indian workers in the cafeteria soared. Waters suggests that this pattern emerged because foreign-born blacks aggressively informed and recruited their ties. Native blacks did not.[7]

Although the studies summarized thus far indicate less cooperation among the black poor during the job search process, there is no evidence that this lack of cooperation is based in distrust, pervasive or otherwise. For a growing number of studies, however, distrust appears central. For instance, Katherine Newman (1999) notes that among the low-wage workers she studied, personal contacts were vital to the job-matching process, but assistance was not always forthcoming. Fearing that their referrals would prove unreliable and compromise their reputations with their employers, more than a few of her subjects denied help to their job-seeking ties. Elijah Anderson (1999) also finds that some blacks in a position to provide job-finding assistance were often reluctant to do so, fearing the negative consequences they would experience personally from a bad match. And in her interviews with working-class black men, Deirdre Royster (2003) learned that a few felt that they had to be careful and selective about how they used their position as a labor market intermediary because of the possible negative effect on their own reputation if their referrals "messed up."

Fears of being burned are hardly absent, however, within nonblack and nonpoor communities. Cecilia Menjivar (2000), for instance, finds distrust and noncooperation among the Salvadoran immigrants she studied. Although the majority of her respondents found out about their jobs through friends, relatives, or acquaintances, the job-holders among them were often hesitant to provide job recommendations. For example:

> Chentia A.'s husband, Don David M., an apartment manager, said that he often told people of job vacancies he knew about, but that he would never recommend anyone for a job, fearing that they would misbehave. Chentia told me, "It's too much responsibility to recommend someone you hardly know, especially how people behave here; if they do something bad, you're responsible. I never do that." Similarly, Victoria O. said that when she was out of work for four months, people would tell her about openings here and there, but it took a neighbor whom she had befriended and who knew of her situation to actually take her to an employer and recommend her. Otherwise, she admitted, no matter how many jobs she heard about, she would not have obtained one. (Menjivar 2000, 142)

Nancy DiTomaso (2006) also notes hesitation among some of the working- and middle-class white men she interviewed, based on their prior bad experiences. However, these accounts appear to be exceptions to the general norms of cooperativeness among these groups. The fear of making bad referrals and the consequent withholding of information and influence appear to be far more pervasive among and toward the black poor. Thus, prior research suggests that Latinos, whites, and even foreign-born blacks are far more likely to put their names on the line during the job-matching process than are native blacks, especially the poor among them.

Community-Level Observations of (Dis)Trust and (Non)Cooperation

Newman, Anderson, and Royster are not alone in their findings of pervasive distrust and resulting noncooperation. Among a number of the classic ethnographic studies of the black urban poor, a subtext of distrust and noncooperation also prevails (Liebow 1967; Suttles 1968). In *The Social Order of the Slum*, for instance, Gerald Suttles (1968) compared the level of ethnic solidarity among Italians, blacks, Mexicans, and Puerto Ricans in one of Chicago's oldest slums. He observed that blacks were far more likely to distrust each other than any of the other ethnic groups in the Addams area; in Suttles's (1968, 9) explanation, blacks "remain the most estranged from one another. Anonymity and distrust are pervasive, and well-established peer groups are present only among the adolescents." Because of this pervasive distrust, Suttles reasoned, even the most basic or mundane daily tasks were difficult to accomplish with assistance from others.

Observations from more recent qualitative research of poor urban communities also indicate that distrust and noncooperation are pervasive among the black poor. In *Code of the Street* (1999), for instance, Anderson contends that pervasive distrust among the black poor, specifically those residing in neighborhoods of concentrated disadvantage, has led to individualistic approaches to handling conflicts and gaining respect that are based on violence and retribution; these approaches have led to relatively high rates of violent crime. And in *Managing to Make It* (1999), Frank Furstenberg and his colleagues describe how pervasive distrust among neighbors led to individualistic approaches to child-rearing within poor black communities. The most "successful" inner-city parents were those who went outside of their communities to find the social and institutional supports they needed to raise well-adjusted children while isolating themselves from neighbors whose influence they feared would have a detrimental impact on their children. Less successful parents also tended to self-isolate, but they did so without seeking extra-community supports. Thus, pervasive distrust between parents fueled further isolation, noncooperation, and individualistic parenting strategies.

Finally, we might consider participation in rotating credit associations, defined by Shirley Ardener (1964, 201) as "an association formed upon a core of participants who agree to make regular contributions to a fund which is given, in whole or in part, to each contributor in rotation" (see also Geertz 1962). Ardener described one simple type: "Ten men meet every month and contribute one shilling each to a fund which is straightway handed over to one of their number. The following month another member receives the fund, and so it continues, members receiving in rotation, until at the end of ten months, each member will have put in ten shillings and received ten shillings" (201). This type of arrangement, or variations thereof, is used extensively among many ethnic groups in the United States (Bonnett 1981; Light 1972; Portes and Sensenbrenner 1993) and globally (Ardener 1964; Geertz 1962) to raise financial capital so as to increase participants' chances of social and economic integration into mainstream society in light of blocked opportunities to do so through mainstream financial institutions. Previous research indicates, however, that blacks are significantly less likely to organize this type of mutual-benefit association (Light 1972). The question is why.

Why Are (Poor) Blacks Different?

In prior work (Smith 2005), I proposed that the factors favorable to mobilizing one's social resources for assistance—to cooperate with others—operate on multiple levels, and I put forward a multilevel theoretical framework designed to take these into consideration. This baseline model, which centralizes the concepts of trust and trustworthiness, includes properties of the individuals involved in the potential exchange, properties of the dyad, properties of the network, and properties of the community. I build on this framework here to explain within-group pervasive distrust and noncooperation. In the concluding chapter of *Lone Pursuit*, I argue that these same factors provide us with some leverage for understanding why distrust and noncooperation seem to be heightened within poor black communities relative to those with whom they are often compared.

The Psychology of Trusting: "Low Trusters"

Previous research indicates that individuals differ in their propensity to trust others. According to Julian Rotter (1967, 1971, 1980), the prominent psychologist who conducted some of the earliest research on trust, while some have a "generalized expectancy . . . that the word, promise, oral or written statement of another individual or group can be relied on" (quoted in Cook, Hardin, and Levi 2005, 22), others tend to be rather suspicious. This predisposition to trust or not is not necessarily strictly rational, as James Coleman (1990) would conceive of it; it is not based on the knowledge of another's trustworthiness. Instead, this predisposition is psychological, a reflection of one's internal state (Aguilar 1984; Rotter 1967, 1971, 1980), which is largely assumed to be learned from previous experience with others, but most especially early life experiences with parents (Hardin 1993; King 2002; Rotenburg 1995;

Weissman and LaRue 1998). As Russell Hardin (1993, 508) so eloquently states:

> Experience molds the psychology of trust. If my past experience too heavily represented good grounds for trust or poor grounds, it may now take a long run of contrary experience to correct my assessments and, therefore, my actual psychological capacities. My capacity is constrained by the weight of past experience with all of the Bayesian reassessment and updating that this experience has stimulated. Trust has to be learned, just like any other kind of generalization.

There is nothing inherently good about being a "high" truster or bad about being a "low" truster. High trusters are vulnerable to being burned for trusting the untrustworthy, and in contexts where untrustworthiness abounds, being a low truster is probably the most prudent approach to adopt (Hardin 1993). However, there are serious downsides to being a low truster, including the lower likelihood of developing mutually beneficial, cooperative relationships. Why? First, low trusters, probably modeling the behaviors of others around them, are less likely than high trusters to be trustworthy themselves (Rotter 1967, 1971, 1980). Second, because the early past experiences of low trusters tend to be characterized by relationships warranting low trust, low trusters are less likely to "learn the contours of trusting relationships" (Cook et al. 2005, 25) and thus will find it difficult to assess accurately the trustworthiness of others. Indeed, Toshio Yamagishi (2001) finds that, compared to high trusters, low trusters are less able to distinguish between the trustworthy and untrustworthy because they are less sensitive to trust-relevant information and less accurate in judging others' trustworthiness (see also Rotter 1980; Yamagishi, Kikuchi, and Kosugi 1999). As a result, in dealings with strangers, low trusters are far more cautious (Yamagishi and Cook 1993; Rotter 1980) and far less likely to take risks (Rotter 1967, 1971, 1980). Kenneth Isaacs, James Alexander, and Ernest Haggard (1963) state:

> The fact of trusting or not trusting determines by itself large aspects of the subjective world of the individual. Expectations, anticipations, and hopes are influenced by it. Perceptions and conceptions of self and others, and the interpersonal possibilities are vastly different for the trusting and the nontrusting [who thus] live in different worlds. . . . The trustful person has less anxiety about inner or outer dangers; this thereby facilitates new experiences. He lives in a world which includes worthy persons. He experiences sympathy within himself and within others. The nontrusting person has expectations of harm. He is always at least a little wary. The common affective experience is fright, for the world is perceived as a dangerous place. (quoted in Aguilar 1984, 265)

For low trusters, this predisposition sets in motion a vicious cycle. It re-duces their willingness to engage in social interactions that might result in more rewarding, cooperative relationships, which might also im-prove their ability to distinguish accurately between the trustworthy and the untrustworthy, eventuating in an inclination to trust and coop-erate. Thus, the consequences of having a predisposition to distrust makes the possibility of developing mutually beneficial, cooperative re-lationships relatively low.

Moreover, some groups of people are more likely to be wary and to experience the world as a dangerous place. Trust has been linked to so-cioeconomic status and race, for instance. Those of low socioeconomic status are more inclined to distrust than their more affluent counter-parts (Bandura 1997; Brehm and Rahn 1997; Smith 1997; Wrightsman 1991; Yamagishi 2001), and blacks are also predisposed to be more dis-trustful than whites (Brehm and Rahn 1997; Smith 1997; Steel 1991; Wrightsman 1991), although this difference itself might be partially conditioned on class. John Aguilar (1984) contends that the predisposi-tion to distrust is more likely to develop as an adaptive strategy in com-munities struggling with chronic poverty and a history of exploitation, a direct contradiction of Carol Stack's (1974) thesis. Although Stack does acknowledge that relationships among kith and kin can be char-acterized by distrust as well as trust, she argues that the high level of exchange she observed could not occur within the context of pervasive distrust; as evidence, she highlights one subject's comments: "They say you shouldn't trust nobody, but that's wrong. You have to try to trust somebody, and somebody has to try to trust you, 'cause everybody need help in this world" (Stack 1974, 39–40).[8] However, this subject's comment only further highlights the tension that residents of neighbor-hoods characterized by concentrated disadvantage must resolve—how to trust anyone when the bulk of your prior experiences indicate that generalized distrust is the most prudent approach to take. To the extent that the black poor reside in communities characterized by "chronic poverty and a history of exploitation" (and that a substantial minority do is without question; see Jargowsky 1997; Massey and Denton 1993; Wilson 1987), these conditions might feed their predispositions to dis-trust, inhibiting the development of mutually beneficial cooperative re-lationships such as those that facilitate the job-matching process.

Rational Trust: Potential Exchange Partners Are More Untrustworthy

In *No Shame in My Game*, Newman (1999) notes that among the low-wage black and Latino workers of Harlem she studied, some job-holders feared that their referral would prove unreliable and compromise their reputation with their employer, and so they were hesitant to provide help. About one respondent Newman reports, "Larry trains a critical eye on the people in his own family and realizes that though he loves them, they are not always good bets as referrals. He thinks his sister is lazy and doesn't want to work. His mother doesn't work either and hasn't for as long as Larry can remember." (1999, 82) Thus, having assessed his sister and mother as untrustworthy, Larry denied them assistance. Unlike psychological trust, then, which relates to one's predisposition to trust, regardless of the attributes of the potential trusted, rational trust is based on one's cognitive assessment of another's trustworthiness.

Assessments of others' trustworthiness are typically based on reputation. When deciding whether or not to take part in an exchange, reputation is critical for determining action (see Granovetter 1985). According to Robert Wilson (1985, 27), "reputation is a characteristic or attribute ascribed to one person by another." In this sense, reputation is at least in part the product of one's network of relations, since it is through the network that knowledge about how an actor behaves in the context of one relationship spreads to others with whom the actor might deal. Furthermore, the quality of social judgments is itself conditioned on embeddedness, since the accuracy with which individuals are judged is only as good as allowed by the extent and nature of their network of relations.[9] Nonetheless, the opinions and actions of those making social judgments are largely attributable to the observations they have of actors' past actions or behaviors. One's good name may be determined by others, but others' determinations originate from one's own actions, by and large. Thus, reputation largely inheres in the individual. It is up to individual actors to either cultivate or destroy their own reputation (see Kreps 1996).

More important, however, is the role that reputation plays in facilitating social capital activation. Because of information asymmetries, quality is not often known before an exchange occurs (Podolny 1993; Shapiro 1982), and this lack of knowledge contributes to the uncertainty and riskiness of the situation. To assess risk, then, actors look to reputation on the assumption that past behavior is indicative of how individuals will act in the future. All else being equal, the greater one's reputation, the lower the perceived risk of loss, the greater one's trust, and the greater others' willingness to partake in reciprocal exchanges. Reputation thus acts as a signal, in the formal economic sense (Spence 1974). It leads to an expectation of quality from which calculations of risk can be made and decisions about whether and how to act determined.[10]

What I have laid out thus far assumes a two-party exchange in which the reputation of the potential beneficiary is of central concern. The effect of reputation on decisions to exchange is complicated further in three-party exchanges where one party, B, acts as an intermediary between two others, A and C. In such situations, B's decision to assist A by matching him with C is not only based on whether or not A is reputable. Attention to short- and longer-run consequences requires that B consider the state of his own reputation with C as well. As Robert Wilson (1985, 28) states succinctly:

> To be optimal, the player's strategy must take into consideration the following chain of reasoning. First, his current reputation affects others' predictions of his current behavior and thereby affects their current actions; so he must take account of his own current reputation to anticipate their current actions and therefore to determine his best response. Second, if he is likely to have choices to make in the future, then he must realize that whatever the immediate consequences of his current decision, there will also be longer-term consequences due to the effect of his current decision to his future reputation, and others' anticipation that he will take these longer-term consequences into account affects their current actions as well.

The context of providing job-finding assistance is consistent with such a three-party exchange. Here, job contacts (B) act as intermediaries—as lobbyists for job-seekers (A) and advisers to employers (C).[11] Based on job contacts' own reputations, employers make predictions about whether or not job contacts' referrals will pay off, and so job contacts' decisions about whether or not to act as advisers to employers, or how to approach the advisory role, hinge on their own reputations with employers. When job-holders have sterling reputations, employers are likely to look upon their referrals favorably, assuming their judgments to be sound. Job contacts, perceiving this, are more likely to refer their job-seeking relations. Among those with subpar reputations, employers are likely to think twice, correlating contacts' past behavior and actions with that of any referrals they make. Job contacts in this position are less likely to refer their personal contacts. However, these are only the short-term considerations.

Job-holders concerned with the long-term consequences of their behavior also consider job-seekers' reputations because the outcome of matches will undoubtedly affect their own reputations and thus their future opportunities. Whether or not job contacts are allowed to assist again, whether they receive promotions, or whether they get raises may all hinge on the reputations they develop as a result of the matches they broker. Thus, if a job-seeker is of known ill repute—for instance, he or she is profoundly unreliable—then the job contact is not likely to refer that person to his or her employer for employment. However, if the word is that the job-seeker is reliable, the job contact is more willing to assist.

Interaction effects must be considered as well. Job contacts with reputations built on a long history of positive behavior may very well suffer little from a botched referral and thus may be more willing to assist job-seekers whose reputations are shaky, perceiving that their own future reputation, and thus future opportunities, will be unharmed by one or two blemishes. Ill-reputed job contacts concerned with long-term consequences, however, have a narrower range of options. Bad referrals will only weaken their standing in the firm, reducing the likelihood that they will be able to take advantage of opportunities that arise in the future. To optimize outcomes, then, those held in low regard can hope to improve their reputation, and thus their competitive edge, by aiding only job-seekers who are themselves held in high regard.

Another factor worth noting, since it is likely to affect job-holders' decisions, is the general reputation among employers—the generalized trust, we might say—of the groups with which job-seekers are identified. Job-holders who perceive that their employer has a distaste for hiring members of certain groups, such as inner-city blacks, may be even more stringent in their criteria for determining who to assist in an effort to reduce the risk of making a bad match. This consideration is consistent with Elijah Anderson's interpretation of black job-holders' reluctance to assist. In telling "John Turner's Story," a tale of a young black man trying to turn away from the call of the street, Anderson (1999, 252) speaks of Curtis, whom he describes as "a sixty-year-old black union steward at a local hospital whom I had known for about five years." Anderson approached Curtis for job-placement assistance on John Turner's behalf. Anderson describes this interaction:

> Curtis said much by saying only, "Tell that boy not to mess me up!" Black people like Curtis who consider sponsoring someone like John Turner may be concerned on several levels. Because of their understanding of the history of racial prejudice in our society, they may sense that their hold on their own position is somewhat tenuous. They have often had to wage a vigorous campaign for the trust of employers and fellow workers. For them to sponsor someone for a job, they must be able to view him or her as fully trustworthy. Furthermore, a common feeling is that a black person who is judged incompetent on the job may easily make other black people look bad. Curtis, as a union steward, was not seriously afraid of losing his job. But he was concerned about being messed up, about looking bad, particularly to relatively powerful whites. In response to these insecurities, black men like Curtis are usually extremely careful when recommending other blacks for jobs. (253–54)

According to Anderson, then, the careful deliberations of black job-holders are at least in part a reflection of their understanding that, for blacks, trust is difficult to earn from employers and, in the face of black job-seekers who "mess up," easy to lose.

Drawing from Deirdre Royster's (2003) study, we can contrast the reluctance expressed by some of the black men she interviewed with the willingness expressed by their white counterparts. In spite of problematic reputations resulting from poor school performance and run-ins with the law that would have concerned most black intermediaries and weakened their desire to provide assistance to their job-seeking relations, white intermediaries interpreted white job-seekers' prior "bad behavior" differently—as "early mistakes and mischievous adolescent antics." By framing their behavior in this way, friends, family members, and acquaintances diminished its seriousness and affirmed job-seekers' worth, an interpretation that made assistance possible. Royster illustrates this point by highlighting the experiences of one young man she called Oscar. Oscar, Royster (2003, 161–62) explains,

> [had] been in trouble with the police while in high school, yet still managed to get extensive help from members of [his] networks. Oscar, a printing student, had managed to land on his feet, after being arrested a number of times and serving some jail time, by relying on friends, neighbors, and family members. His first job, with an insulation company, came as a result of his brother's and uncle's help: "my brother and uncle worked there and they just needed a helper and they just got me the job and I started going to work with them." Oscar had run-ins with the boss's brother at the insulation job, which he left and then returned to after serving a short sentence for assault with a deadly weapon and malicious destruction. I asked Oscar how he managed to stay employed given his bad record. He explained: "Brothers uncles, friends—I know about fifteen people from this neighborhood—a lot of them are cousins, people's kids."

Thus, faced with the option of helping job-seekers with similarly negative reputations, previous research suggests that white job-holders appear far more reluctant to do so than their black job-holding counterparts.

This difference might be explained by white intermediaries' more forgiving nature. It is more likely the case, however, that the consequences faced by whites for facilitating bad matches are less damaging to their own status and reputation than such consequences are for blacks. Nor will poor performance on the job by whites' job referrals be interpreted as an indication of the state of all white job-seekers' work ethic and worth. In other words, because employers assess and value the reputations of workers from different racial and ethnic backgrounds differently, and because black workers are typically assessed most negatively (Neckerman and Kirschenman 1991), black job-holders positioned to influence the matching process are likely to face an additional "tax" on their status and reputation if the matches they influence end badly, and this additional tax makes black job-holders more critical than their white counterparts when assessing the risks to their reputation of assisting their job-seeking relations.

We might think of this as a response to stereotype threat, a term coined by the social psychologists Claude Steele and Joshua Aronson (1995, 1998) to describe individuals' fear that their behavior will confirm a negative stereotype held about their group. To the extent that individuals care about doing well in the area about which their group has been negatively stereotyped, their fear often leads to poorer performance than they might have had in a neutral context. It also leads them to distance themselves from activities and associations related to the negative stereotype.

Importantly, this formulation suggests that the intermediary's decisionmaking process is not only informed by the effect on the potential beneficiary's reputation, the intermediary's own reputation, and the interaction between the two, but also motivated by the third party's general perception of (psychological trust toward) the group with which the potential beneficiary is associated. While the third party's assessment might not necessarily be rational trust, the intermediary is indeed following a rational course of action by taking this information into consideration when assessing risks to his or her own status and reputation before deciding to assist the potential beneficiary. In the end, however, each of these factors motivates a view of the black poor as untrustworthy and too risky to assist.

The Strength (or Fragility) of Close Ties

In *Tally's Corner* (1967, 175), an account of friends and networks among black street-corner men, Elliot Liebow suggests that although his subjects were embedded in networks of relations in which they frequently exchanged material and social support ("Leroy watches Malvina's children while she goes out to have a few drinks with a friend. Tonk and Stanton help Budder move the old refrigerator he just bought into his apartment. Robert spends an evening giving Richard a home process"), close relationships were still highly volatile—one moment romanticized, the next disavowed as a source of any benefit whatsoever. To account for this volatility, Liebow proposed examining the structure and character of the men's network of personal ties. He hypothesized that many of his subjects' relationships were doomed to fail because they tended to develop intimate relationships very quickly, publicly declaring their commitment to one another by "going for brothers" or "going for cousins," for example, and offering the requisite material and social support assumed to exist between individuals occupying these formal roles without learning the personal history of their "brother" or "cousin" and without establishing through a series of ever-increasing exchanges the mutual trust and displays of trustworthiness needed. As a result, Liebow explained, friendships did "not often stand up well to the stress of crisis or conflict of interest, when demands tend to be heaviest and most insistent. Everyone knows this. Extravagant pledges of aid and comfort between friends are, at one level, made and received in good faith. But at another level, fully aware of his friends' limited resources and the demands of their self-interest, each person is ultimately prepared to look to himself alone" (180).

John Aguilar (1984) also observed volatility in relationships among the Indians he studied in one Mexican community. The volatility resulted in part because people had unrealistic expectations about what others could and would do for them, even during the early stages of new relationships. Because expectations were unrealistic, "friends" almost always failed to live up to each other's expectations, and these failures led to feelings of "bitterness and disillusionment" (Aguilar 1984, 19). The result, Aguilar found, was an "idealistic bifurcation of friendship into absolutely true and absolutely false [that allowed] no room for degrees of intimacy and strength of loyalty and little, if any, sense of a condition of a growing relationship. Therefore, both the emotional intensity and cognitive rigidity of expectations put too great a burden upon the new friendship when it is in its most delicate phase of development" (19).

Given Liebow's and Aguilar's insights, we might also locate pervasive distrust and noncooperation among the black poor in the health and well-being of dyadic relationships because, independent of the reputations individuals have developed outside of the context of the relationship, trust and trustworthiness can develop between potential exchange partners in a way that facilitates instrumental aid (Burt 2001; Cook and Hardin 2001). It is well known that trust and trustworthiness in dyadic relationships emerge from a history of successful reciprocal exchanges (Blau 1964; Cook and Hardin 2001; Cook et al. 2005; Hardin 1993, 2002, 2004). The initiation of informal exchange relationships is typically characterized by relatively small-scale exchanges, such as borrowing or lending a book. As these smaller obligations are honored and riskier exchanges are undertaken with success, uncertainty about the exchange partners' reliability declines and trust between the partners grows (Kollock 1994). Iterated exchanges also have a tendency to breed stronger, more cohesive and affective bonds (Lawler and Yoon 1996, 1998). For both of these reasons, the likelihood increases that future exchanges will be made (Molm, Takahashi, and Peterson 2000). Unpaid obligations, on the other hand, lead to distrust and erode the chances of long-term exchanges, since actors whose credits go unpaid are likely either to withdraw from future exchanges or to change the extent and nature of the exchanges to which they do commit. As Burt (2001, 33) explains, "Where people have little history together, or an erratic history of cooperation mixed with exploitation, or a consistent history of failure to cooperate, people will distrust one another, avoiding collaborative endeavors without guarantees on the other's behavior." Under these conditions, the likelihood of partaking in obligations of exchange declines precipitously, and with it so too does the likelihood of activating one's social capital—that is, getting assistance when needed.

Research by Edward Lawler and Jeongkoo Yoon (1996, 1998) has shown that network structures also affect the strength, cohesion, and affect of the dyadic relations embedded in them. Certain network structures facilitate repeated exchanges between members of similar power. To the extent that these are successful, trust, cohesion, and emotional affect between the members grow, and these feelings promote commitment to the dyad, even when superior exchange options become available. Thus, network structures are not inconsequential to dyad cohesion or closeness and the reciprocity that often results. This is the point to which I now turn.

Social Closure and Norms of Cooperativeness

In Aubrey Bonnett's (1981) study of rotating credit associations among West Indians of Brooklyn, he notes that defaults by members were so infrequent that organizers were uncertain how they would respond if placed in that situation. How could this be? According to Bonnett, organizers essentially instituted "structures of trustworthiness" that ensured contributors' compliance. Organizers, for instance, often limited participation to members of their own social networks, that is, those they knew well and could trust. To the extent that organizers were uncertain about a contributor's trustworthiness, they would schedule the contributor in question to receive his or her payout in the final rotation, leaving no incentive for him or her to default. In rare cases when contributors did default, community members penalized them by damaging their reputations. Word spread fast. According to Bonnett (1981, 351), "In one instance, it was reported that a defaulting member was employed as a nurse at a local hospital in Brooklyn. After several unsuccessful attempts to get her to pay, the organizers passed the word around that she was financially irresponsible. It is felt that this caused her to be passed over for promotion to the post of a nursing supervisor." It was not only other West Indians in New York who were informed when contributors defaulted. Those in London and the West Indies were informed as well. By tainting defaulters' reputations in this way, community members reduced the likelihood that others in the community would trust and thus cooperate with those who failed to fulfill their obligations and comply with group norms. The organizers also lowered the risk that others would default in the future.

These informal credit or savings associations are not unique to Brooklyn's West Indian residents. Alejandro Portes and Julia Sensenbrenner (1993) describe other such associations among New York City's Dominicans and Miami's Cuban population. About the former, they note the existence of "networks of informal loan operations" that were primarily used to fund new businesses. Decisions to loan were based solely on the borrower's reputation, and there was no question that the debtor would repay the loan in full because, as Portes and Sensenbrenner explain, retribution against defaulters was swift, including coercion and ostracism, and Dominicans had few other means for economic advancement outside the Dominican community. In Miami's Cuban community, character loans were employed (until the early 1970s) with great success. No one defaulted. As with the Dominicans' informal loan operations, character loans were secured for business start-ups based solely on debtors' personal reputation. If debtors had defaulted, they would have been excluded from the Cuban community with no other source of support upon which to rely.

These three examples of informal credit and savings associations highlight the importance of what Coleman termed the "trustworthiness of social structures" for facilitating cooperation among members of a community. Specifically, Coleman (1988, 1990) proposed that actors are not likely to activate social capital unless embedded in a trustworthy network of relations. However, Coleman argued, some network structures, such as those characterized by social closure, are superior to others in promoting trustworthiness. Typically found in smaller communities, social closure describes network relations that are dense, overlapping, and close-knit. Everyone is either directly or indirectly connected to all others through short chains, and the information channels created by these connections pass news and gossip quickly throughout the network. As a result, there is little that anyone can do without having others in the network discover it, a monitoring capacity that encourages trustworthy behavior. Thus, the trust that emerges in this context is not trust in the encapsulated-interest sense that Russell Hardin endorses (Cook and Hardin 2001; Cook et al. 2005; Hardin 2002, 2004). Instead, it is the *enforceable trust* proposed by Portes and Sensenbrenner (1993): embeddedness in networks characterized by social closure provides actors with community-backed assurances that potential exchange partners will honor obligations or face appropriate sanctions, such as shunning or social exclusion. These assurances reduce the risks associated with reciprocal exchanges, and they pave the way for extensive and long-term obligations—fertile ground for social capital activation (see also Granovetter 1985).[12]

A wonderful empirical example is Edwina Uehara's (1990) examination of the effect of network structures on the ability and willingness of poor black women who have recently lost their jobs to mobilize their ties for instrumental aid, with network structures characterized by social closure that facilitates this type of assistance. She discovered that women embedded in high-density, high-intensity networks were more likely to engage in generalized exchanges than women embedded in networks low in both because the former were better able to control each other's behavior through tracking, monitoring, and sanctioning, which created an environment of trustworthiness that promoted extensive exchanges.

Gerald Suttles's (1968) rich ethnographic account of racial and ethnic differences in ethnic solidarity in one "slum" community also implicates loose network structures and relatively poor monitoring capacities in explaining the pervasive distrust and noncooperation among its black residents. In this regard, blacks were most distinct from Italians, whose community was nothing if not provincial. An inward society, the Italian community, by Suttles's account, was one in which everyone knew everyone else and had known everyone for some time. These strong, overlapping, and intertwined associations were linked through kinship, close friendships, and local associations, which provided an "intricate communication network" that enabled residents to spread "gossip, slander, invective, and confidentiality"; this information allowed them to monitor each other's activities and, along with effective sanctions, keep behaviors in check. Structures of trustworthiness undoubtedly afforded Italians in the Addams area a great foundation for building social capital. As Suttles (1968, 102) explained, "They handle grievances, contracts, and exchanges in a very informal manner, usually limited to the immediate parties. If in need, they exact aid in the form of favors and generally ignore sources available to the general public." Suttles did not observe the same structures, however, among the black residents of the Addams area. Unlike the Italians, who knew each other well and trusted each other very much, blacks in the area were characterized by Suttles as a "highly fluid population in which acquaintances are temporary or, at least, expected to be temporary" (124).[13]

However, for Suttles and others, network structures are a mediating factor and not the driving force behind distrust and noncooperation. Instead, many scholars have pointed to the community and the extent and nature of its institutional resources to understand pervasive distrust and noncooperation, because, as Portes and Sensenbrenner (1993, 1335) argue, "enforceable trust varies greatly with the characteristics of the community."

Enforcing Trustworthiness in Communities of Concentrated Disadvantage

To explain poor blacks' difficulty in creating and maintaining stable, long-lasting, trusting relationships, Suttles (1968) pointed to their residence in public housing projects. These relationships, he argued, were inherently unstable because housing regulations required families to move once their household incomes exceeded a certain level. Thus, housing regulations created such high turnover among black residents that trust between residents was difficult if not impossible to develop and nurture over time. Anderson (1999) attributed pervasive distrust and resulting individualism to declining job opportunities and a reduction in city services, most notably law enforcement. Without such services, residents of ghetto neighborhoods constantly feared victimization; as a result, few residents related amicably, and fewer still assisted others in need. Furstenberg and his colleagues (1999) located the distrust and noncooperation they observed among parents in disadvantaged communities in the deterioration of city services and the loss of key community institutions that had brought families together in the past in ways that built trust and facilitated cooperative efforts.

The common thread linking these studies is their analysis of the role of key community institutions, private and public, in facilitating the development of trust and cooperation among residents. Because poor communities are less likely than their more affluent counterparts to have a stock of private and public institutions that meet residents' basic needs, provide opportunities for residents to come together and build relationships of trust and cooperation, and help to integrate residents into the larger society (Sampson and Groves 1989; Sampson et al. 1999; Shaw and McKay 1942/1969; Wacquant 1998; but see Small 2004), they are more likely to be socially isolated, and their interpersonal relationships are more likely to be characterized by pervasive distrust and noncooperation.

Or are they? The seminal work of William Julius Wilson suggests that they are. In *The Truly Disadvantaged* (1987), Wilson argued that as a result of deindustrialization and the exodus of the black middle and working classes from what were once vertically integrated communities, many of the institutions that these stably employed residents helped to support disappeared as well. What they left behind were neighborhoods of concentrated poverty in which a significant minority, if not the majority, of residents were poor and institutions of social and economic support were at best marginally effective but often absent. Lacking regular and sustained interaction with mainstream ties and institutions, then, residents of such neighborhoods became socially isolated from those who would have been best equipped to provide opportunities for mobility during strong economic times and best able to buffer them from the worst effects of economic downturns.

Furthermore, chronic economic hardship diminishes both individual (Pearlin et al. 1981) and collective efficacy (Sampson et al. 1999; Morenoff, Sampson, and Raudenbush 2001). Because they lack the material resources to support the development and maintenance of community organizations themselves, they have few opportunities to come together and collaborate to define common problems and values, to build trust and structures of trustworthiness, to develop effective social controls, and to achieve common goals. It is within this context of high poverty, low levels of community institutional resources, and high degrees of social isolation not only from mainstream ties and institutions but from each other that destructive forces, such as crime, substance abuse, violence, and neglect, become all-encompassing (Wacquant and Wilson 1989; Sampson et al. 1999; Sampson and Wilson 1995), breeding further pervasive and generalized interpersonal distrust. The acute vulnerability that residents experience in this context fuels uncooperativeness and gives birth to individualistic approaches to getting things done, as illustrated in more recent accounts, such as Anderson's *Code of the Street* (1999) and Furstenberg's co-authored *Managing to Make It* (1999). Thus, it is argued, relative to poor residents of comparatively affluent communities, the likelihood of individuals mobilizing their network of social relations in the neighborhoods characterized by concentrated disadvantage is low because high rates of poverty have a negative effect on the density of community institutional resources, the dwindling of which then feeds social isolation, diminishes trust, and fuels noncooperation.[14]

Mario Luis Small (2004) makes an alternative argument in his ethnographic case study of Villa Victoria, a poor, predominantly Puerto Rican housing complex in Boston's tony South End. Small's observations lead him to assert that the relationship between poverty, social isolation, and social capital depends on the context. In Villa Victoria, Small finds, high poverty resulted in an *increase* in the density of community resources, not a decline. He explains this paradox by noting that politically liberal Boston responds to the needs of its poor by providing a wealth of institutional resources that the poor need to survive and that it does so in and around the neighborhoods in which they live, thus facilitating access. Furthermore, Small finds that the high density of resources led to an *increase* in social isolation, not a decrease. He explains this apparent paradox by noting that residents of neighborhoods with a high density of resources did not need to leave the neighborhood to get their needs met. Although this might have reduced their opportunities to develop relationships outside of the Villa, residents nurtured relationships with others from the neighborhood. Small concludes that high-poverty neighborhoods do not have to be associated with low-density resources. Nor is the relationship between resource density and social isolation inherently negative. Indeed, as with the Villa, the opposite can be true.

Small's quantitative analysis of this question, with co-author Monica McDermott, bears this out. In their study of organizational resources in poor urban neighborhoods, Small and McDermott (2006) report that as the proportion of poor residents in a community increases, the number of establishments in that neighborhood—hardware stores, grocery stores, convenience stores, pharmacies, savings banks, credit unions, child care centers, restaurants, laundries, and grooming stores—increases as well, if only slightly. The same is true with regard to the proportion of foreign-born residents. However, they find that as the proportion *of black residents* in a neighborhood increases, the number of establishments declines significantly. Furthermore, the interaction between the proportion of poor residents and the proportion of black residents is significant for a number of establishments—convenience stores, pharmacies, restaurants, and laundries—indicating that poor black neighborhoods have even fewer institutional resources than both more affluent neighborhoods and poor neighborhoods in which other racial and ethnic groups predominate. Why are poor black communities different? Why is it that institutions intended to meet the basic needs of residents tend to be weak or absent in poor black communities?

Loic Wacquant (1998, 25) convincingly and passionately indicts state structures and policies:

> The major social-organizational cause of the continued degradation of social conditions and life chances in the black America's ghetto [is] the erosion of "state social capital," that is, organizations presumed to provide civic goods and services—physical safety, legal protection, welfare, education, housing, and health care—which have turned into instruments of surveillance, suspicion, and exclusion rather than vehicles of social integration and trust-building. The near-total breakdown of public institutions, combined with and abetting the withdrawal of the wage-labor economy in the context of extreme and unyielding racial segregation (Massey and Denton 1993), has accelerated the shrinking of the ghetto's indigenous organizational basis and helped concentrate in it the most dispossessed segments of the urban (sub)proletariat, thereby further depreciating the informal social capital available within it.

Key for Wacquant is the remarkable decline of public authority, a decline he attributes to a lack of organizational resources, including financial capital, manpower, motivation, and skilled and competent personnel. These shortages, he contends, have led to a prolific decline in public services, including those related to safety and legal protections. And as Anderson has argued, this reduction in public authority has also led to individualistic approaches to handling conflicts and gaining respect that are based in violence and retribution, further feeding distrust and noncooperation. For Wacquant, then, it makes little sense to examine interpersonal relations among the black poor without also investigating the role played by state structures and policies because the processes associated with state structures and processes "become locked in an apparently self-sustaining cycle that gives all appearances of being internally determined and takes on the appearance of 'collective pathology,' all the better to make outsiders (and even insiders) forget about the causal role of the breakdown of public institutions in triggering and sustaining them" (34–35).

Where public institutions have generally failed, private institutions might succeed. It is unclear, however, to what extent these are able or willing to engage the black poor in ways that might help to establish structures of trustworthiness that breed trust and facilitate cooperation. With regard to this question, a look at the black church is revealing because it is a community institution in which the seeds of trust can be planted and cultivated in ways that benefit the whole. Historically, the black church has been one of the most important and influential of all the institutions in the black community, in great part because it has served multiple functions. In addition to its role as a religious institution, it has acted as an educational institution by providing schools and educational programs to serve its members (Drake and Cayton 1945/1993). At times it has acted like the press, disseminating to church and community members the relevant news of the day (Drake and Cayton 1945/1993). The church has served as a labor market intermediary, facilitating job matches between workers and local industry (Sugrue 1996). Well known, too, is the black church's role as a political or "race" institution that mobilizes church and community members to achieve goals of black uplift by making claims on the state (Du Bois 1899/1996).[15] Indeed, according to St. Clair Drake and Horace Cayton (1993, 398), "separate Negro churches came into being as protest organizations and have always been associated in the popular mind with 'racial advancement.'"

The black church has also served the function of social service provider, identifying the needs of its members as well as those of members of the larger community and putting into place programs to help to meet those needs (Lincoln and Mamiya 1990). Furthermore, because the black church and its leaders have earned a great deal of respect and honor both inside and outside the community, the black church has become a central avenue through which resources from outside of the community are funneled. In other words, the black church has been perfectly situated for both intra- and extra-community linkages that can help to make things happen. Indeed, according to Michael Foley, John McCarthy, and Mark Chaves (2001, 215), "churches are often the last to leave deteriorating neighborhoods and dwindling communities and the first to return. Religiously based social service efforts carry an important part of the burden of providing for the needs of poor communities. Congregations and local denominational bodies frequently build broad community coalitions on behalf of policy change and to strengthen both private and public social services for the poor."

Given these multiple and intersecting roles, the black church has been a fairly stabilizing force within the black community. Not only do members benefit from regular and frequent contact and interaction with other congregants that helps to build relations of trust and cooperation, they also sometimes benefit from the relationships that their churches develop with other intra-community and extra-community institutions. Consequently, the black church has the potential to plant the seeds of trust in communities of concentrated disadvantage where trust does not already exist, providing the foundation for cooperation and positive change.

I would contend, however, that by and large the black church is not the stabilizing, trust-building force within communities of concentrated disadvantage that it has the power to be or that it seems to have been in times past. Church membership and participation among the black urban poor is marginal at best and certainly well below national averages. Recent reports bear this out. For instance, Rev. Dr. R. Drew Smith (2001) examined church attendance and membership among black residents of three low-income public housing complexes in Indianapolis. He found that six in ten residents were "unchurched": they not only were not members of a church, but attended church infrequently, at best. This level of engagement with the church contrasts sharply with national averages. According to George Gallup and Michael Lindsay (1999), just 19 percent of blacks, 24 percent of Latinos, and 32 percent of whites could be described as unchurched.

Nor does the black poor's engagement with church appear to have changed much over time. In *Black Metropolis* (1945/1993), Drake and Cayton's pre–World War II study of Chicago's South Side black population, we learn that among its 100,000 lower-class residents, roughly half reported church membership, but in reality fewer than one-third of lower-class South Side residents paid membership dues, and fewer than one-tenth attended church with any regularity. The "faithful few," as Drake and Cayton called them, represented just a small fraction. Why?

Through open-ended interviews, Smith and his team (2001, 311–2) learned that low-income public housing project residents were not church members because "they were not spiritually ready to make the lifestyle adjustments that would be expected of them, or that they would expect of themselves, if involved with church life. Others were more openly antagonistic to the idea of involvement with churches— often without citing the reasons for their antagonism." Among those with whom Drake and Cayton (1945/1993) spoke, nonmembers and members alike also criticized the church strongly.[16]

The poor's lack of engagement might also result from the black church's disinterest in engaging the poor among them. This is my second point. According to Foley, McCarthy, and Chaves (2001, 219), "Congregations are as well represented in the poorest neighborhoods as in better-off ones, and . . . whatever the truth to claims that there has been an institutional flight from the poorest neighborhoods over the last twenty or thirty years (Wilson 1996), many congregations remain as sources of social capital within those communities." But their own data also indicate that the presence of these institutions does not mean that the poor are actually engaged with them. Indeed, they go on to report, the overwhelming majority of congregants who attend churches in the poorest of neighborhoods are not poor themselves. Eighty percent or more are middle- and upper-income.

Smith's work suggests that churches in these communities do not make much of an effort to reach out to the most disadvantaged in their communities. When he asked residents of the low-income housing projects in Indianapolis whether they had been approached by any church asking if they would participate in services or seek membership, two-thirds of his respondents indicated that they had not been contacted at all. Drawing from the University of Chicago sociologist Omar McRoberts, we can make an educated guess as to why. In his well-written and insightful study *Streets of Glory* (2003), an examination of black churches in Boston's Four Corners neighborhood, McRoberts explains that different churches engaged with residents of the poor communities in which they were located to different degrees depending on their conceptualization of "the street." Some churches viewed the street as a "recruiting ground" and "felt it was their duty as people in possession of Truth to transfigure that space by carrying the Good News into it" (86). Among these churches, proselytizing was key. Other churches viewed the street as the "point of contact with people at risk" (91). According to McRoberts, because "the street was the place where Jesus tested the commitment of the faithful to those poor and vulnerable," members "felt called to engage the street on its own apparent terms rather than proselytize or avoid it altogether" (91). Another set of churches conceived of the street as both a recruitment ground and a point of contact. Members of these churches "attempted circuitously to attract people to church by offering social services and championing abstract social causes such as violence and drug use prevention" (94). The overwhelming majority of churches in the Four Corners section of Boston, however, did none of the above. Instead, viewing the street as "the evil other," they avoided it altogether. According to McRoberts (2003, 83):

> [These churches] drew a thick line between themselves and the street and avoided all superfluous contact with the latter. Ministers did not preach on street corners or go door-to-door seeking recruits. After services, even on the loveliest spring afternoons, congregants moved quickly to cars and church vans to avoid exposure to danger. The "evil other" perspective, however, was not just about fear of danger. It took fear a step further, posing the street as the cosmic nemesis of the church.

Thus, although some focus solely on the black church's inability to address effectively the overwhelming problems faced by the black poor in their struggles to survive, I would contend that the black church, as a community institution, is no longer a stabilizing, trust-building force, because of its tendency to disengage from the black poor and to judge the street and the people of it to be the moral equivalents of Satan.[17] Here again, even within the context of access, mobilization of a great many black churches and the resources to which they have access appears unlikely because of the meanings that the church ascribes to those who live in poor black communities.

Conclusion

Was Carol Stack wrong? Does a subtext of distrust and noncooperation prevail where she observed trusting, cooperative, and mutually beneficial relationships? There seems to be little question that relationships in The Flats were characterized by trust, enforceable trust (Portes and Sensenbrenner 1993), and cooperation that made survival possible. More recent work suggests, however, that within poor black communities kin-based support has declined substantially over time in response to macrostructural changes in the larger society that have affected its availability and nature (Brewster and Padavic 2002).[18] These accounts explain declining cooperation, but they do not explain the emergence of distrust. Why are poor blacks' interpersonal relations characterized by pervasive distrust, which feeds noncooperation?

There is no simple answer to this question, because the conditions favorable for trust and cooperation operate on multiple levels. Furthermore, while each factor may directly and independently create and nurture trust and trustworthiness, each also probably acts indirectly through factors operating on other levels. For instance, while we may conceive of pervasive distrust and noncooperation among poor blacks in terms of a psychology of distrust—poor blacks are predisposed to not trust—predispositions to trust or not are largely considered to be learned behavior, that is, they are a function of having had past relationships characterized by trust or the lack thereof. But having past relationships characterized by trust or distrust is itself a function of embeddedness in a larger social context—the social network and the community.

We might also conceive of pervasive distrust and noncooperation in a community of poor blacks in terms of the trustworthiness of its members. To the extent that community members are deemed untrustworthy, often based on reputation, cooperation is unlikely. The ability to develop reputations of trust is contingent, however, on being embedded in social contexts that are supportive of trustworthy behavior. For instance, it makes little sense to expect a worker to arrive at work on time each day when she does not have access to safe, dependable, and affordable transportation and child care. Here again, the larger social context is implicated. However, and importantly, rational assessments of trustworthiness are not solely a function of the trusted's reputation. The more that is at stake for the truster because of his or her own social and economic circumstances or because of third-party concerns, the more stringent the criteria for determining the trusted's trustworthiness, and the lower the likelihood of taking part in cooperative efforts.

We might also understand pervasive distrust and noncooperation among the black poor in terms of the strength or fragility of their dyadic relations. The stronger the bonds of trust, developed over time through a series of iterated exchanges, the greater the likelihood of mobilizing this social resource for getting things done. The likelihood of having strong relationships based on trust and reciprocity, however, appears at least in part contingent on the structure of the network (open or closed), which itself is at least in part conditioned on the organization and resources of the larger community in which individuals are embedded. Thus, because the factors that affect the creation and nurturance of trust operate at multiple levels, there are multiple avenues to travel to understand why the black poor's interpersonal relations are characterized by pervasive distrust and noncooperation.

What I have outlined in this chapter provides an overview for how we might come to understand this phenomenon generally, as well as how it plays out during the process of finding work. I now move on to the heart of *Lone Pursuit*, where I analyze at length the nuances of these dynamics as they play out during the process of finding work. My analyses reveal that during the job search process, jobholders and job-seekers' pervasive distrust, non-cooperation, and embrace of individualism is primarily a function of individuals' psychologies of distrust and cognitive assessments of jobseekers' and jobholders' untrustworthiness. However, these two factors cannot be understood without also taking into consideration the structural context (neighborhoods and labor markets) within which black poor job-holders and job-seekers express distrust of each other and reluctance to engage in the job matching process with each others, espousing tenets of individualism instead.

Chapter 3

The Job-Holder: Espousing American Individualism

After years spent in a series of low-wage jobs, Diana Ellsworth, a twenty-nine-year-old single mother of one, hit the proverbial jackpot, landing a job as a meter reader for the water company, a position that paid $19 per hour, offered great benefits, and included union membership. Because of her work history and current employment status, Diana would be a great social resource for job information and influence, and she knew this.[1] Indeed, when asked how important it was to use friends, relatives, and acquaintances to find out about job opportunities, Diana indicated that it was very important and that she was quite proactive in collecting and disseminating job information. She explained:

> The job that I am [in], when I go out and read [meters], I ask, you know what they pay and, you know, if I go to a business to read or whatever, I always ask, "Ya'll hiring?" and what they paying, you know. And then I'll pass the information along to somebody else I know in need of a job or looking for a job, especially my boyfriend. I'll say, "Go over there and apply to so and so, and they're making this kind of money," you know. If I think it's in their range or something that they might be interested in doing, I pass the information along, and I always ask people just, you know, so that you have a resource package of information along.

Diana's inquiries were motivated at least in part by her desire to find a steady, well-paying job for her "off and on" boyfriend, the father of her eight-year-old son. Because her boyfriend lacked the "proper skills to get a decent job" or "the motivation to get out and just go find something better," Diana resolved to do so for him, inquiring whenever possible about the availability of decent opportunities in the hopes of securing the future of her own family. However, Diana also rationalized that by collecting and then disseminating job information to others, she was actually serving the whole community as well. As she put it, "You don't want to see nobody out of work. And like I say, once people start working or people work, it enhances the community, the whole aspect, that somebody else is employed that can contribute to the taxes, that can contribute to whatever, that might help save somebody from getting on welfare or that might impact whatever it might be, you know. So it's always a help. I look at it as a whole community-wide [benefit]." Thus, Diana embraced the role of labor market intermediary in her family and in her community in an effort to uplift both.

Further probing revealed, however, that Diana's role as intermediary was much more circumscribed than one would expect given her seemingly proactive stance and her strong desire to promote group uplift. Specifically, although Diana was not categorically against recommending her job-seeking relations for jobs, the assistance she provided primarily took the form of information dissemination, which is no more effective than walk-in strategies of job search at securing employment, especially in low-wage labor markets where employers rely heavily on informal recommendations to make hires (see Holzer 1996; Kasinitz and Rosenberg 1996; Kirschenman and Neckerman 1991; Neckerman and Kirschenman 1991).[2] And her job-seeking relations often pointed this out to her. As she explained:

Sometimes people, they don't be appreciative, or they think you trying to bum-steer them or give them wrong information or something like that, you know. But, you know, I just tell them, I said, "Look, I ain't no magical genie," you know. Like, "I can't get you a job," you know. "I don't own the company, nothing like that." But, you know, sometimes people be disgusted. Like I know a couple of people have asked me, "Well, why can't you just put your name on the application and say you recommend?" And I say, "Wait, it don't work like that! You have to go to extremes like everybody else." But, you know, I always tell them, "Hey, go apply." That's all you can do, you know. And then after that it's up to the people that want to hire you.

Why the reluctance to recommend? Diana had one central concern—that she might vouch for job-seekers who would later reveal themselves to be "bad workers," workers "that might have some effect on, you know, me as a person." This concern, however, did not stop Diana from assisting. She did so, but primarily as a disseminator of information, since this form of assistance allowed her to contribute without negatively affecting her own reputation. In the few instances when she did "put her name on the line," she did so only for job-seekers she believed to have solid reputations on the job that would not pose a risk to her own.

As indicated in the introduction, mine is not the first study to report that job-holders express distrust toward job-seekers and thus are disinclined to assist them. In *No Shame in My Game* (1999), Katherine Newman notes that among the low-wage workers she studied, personal contacts were vital to the job-matching process, but assistance was not always forthcoming because job-holders feared that their referrals would compromise their reputations with their employers by behaving inappropriately. Newman (1999, 82) explains, "A bad call can jeopardize a good worker's reputation and damage his credibility should he want to foster another friend's chances someday." Elijah Anderson (1999) and Deirdre Royster (2003) also observed that job-holders positioned to assist were often tired of doing so and provided job-finding assistance "carefully and sparingly." Despite these contributions, however, in none of these studies do we gain a sense of just how pervasive this distrust and corresponding noncooperation is. Nor are we made privy to the depth of experiences and understandings that motivate job-holders' distrust and unwillingness to cooperate.

By systematically examining the job-finding process, I found that Diana was hardly alone in her approach to providing assistance. Although most of my respondents saw value in using personal contacts to find work, when actually in a position to assist with job information or influence, job-holders were not so enthusiastic.[3] Indeed, *reluctant personal contacts*—that is, job-holders who usually chose not to assist or who limited the assistance they provided—were in the majority in my sample, constituting some six in ten job-holders. Comments indicative of reluctance included, "I kind of even limit my helping people out to where it won't affect me," and, "First of all, I don't know a lot of people that have really looked for employment, and I question the people that I do know. I don't think they would take it serious, and I don't want to put my name on it." *Open personal contacts*—job-holders willing to help almost anyone who asked—were in the minority, representing just two-fifths of job-holders. Comments indicative of openness included, "I never turn nobody down," and, "If they come to me, of course I will tell them."

Why were reluctant personal contacts in the majority? When queried about their reluctance, these job-holders raised three concerns (see table 3.1). One-fifth of them had come to believe that those without jobs lacked the motivation and determination to follow through on offers of assistance and thus would waste their time and frustrate them. One-tenth expressed concern that their referrals were too needy and that by taking on job-finding obligations they would become responsible not only for job-getting but for helping their referrals stay employed, thus compounding the stresses in their own overburdened lives. Finally, 70 percent of these job-holders feared that, once hired, those they had assisted would act irresponsibly on the job and thus compromise their reputations and labor market stability. In all, eight in ten expressed one or more of these concerns and perceived job-seekers as too risky and perhaps too undeserving to trust with assistance.[4]

Table 3.1   Job-Holders' Concerns About Job-Seekers

Concern Type	Expressing Concern
Job-seekers are too unmotivated	20%
Job-seekers are too needy	10
Job-seekers are too irresponsible	70
Total expressing one or more concerns	81

Source: Author's compilation.

Job-holders' perceptions of untrustworthiness were not without consequences. Figure 3.1 displays, by concern type, the percentage of jobholders who expressed reluctance to assist. Among those who believed that job-seekers generally lacked motivation, 78 percent were reluctant to assist. Just 56 percent of those who did not express this concern were reluctant to assist. Eighty percent of those who feared that job-seekers would be too needy were reluctant to provide assistance. Just 58 percent of job-holders without this concern were reluctant to assist. Finally, among those who feared that their referrals would be too irresponsible on the job, 73 percent were reluctant to provide assistance compared to just 35 percent of job-holders who did not express this concern. In all, 71 percent of those who expressed one or more of these three concerns

Figure 3.1   Job-Holders Reluctant to Assist, by Concern Type

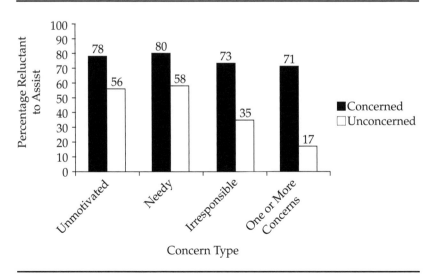

Source: Author's compilation.

were reluctant to provide job-finding assistance compared to just 17 percent of job-holders who expressed none of these concerns.

Given the extent to which concerns about motivation, neediness, and irresponsibility shaped job-holders' perceptions of risk and affected their willingness to assist, it is a wonder that they assisted at all. But they did. Some 87 percent reported that at some point in the past they had assisted family members, friends, acquaintances, or even strangers who had approached them for job-finding assistance, and most said they would probably do so again. However, as with Diana, the extent and nature of the assistance they provided depended on a number of key factors. In this chapter, I explicate these factors, explaining job-holders' willingness to assist primarily in terms of their assessments of the job-seeker's reputation, their own reputation with their employer, and the strength of their relationship with the job-seeker. The structural context within which job-holders made decisions also mattered. Access to social capital interacted with neighborhood poverty status to affect their willingness to assist, as did local labor market conditions. Job-holders were also making decisions in a labor market context in which soft skills were rising in importance. This factor helped to shape the extent to which they understood job-seekers as risky investments and affected the extent and nature of the assistance they were willing to provide. Assessments of high risk in helping some job-seekers caused job-holders routinely to deny assistance, and in its stead they espoused tenets of individualism to job-seekers. In what follows, I outline the criteria upon which job-holders made their assessments of risk.

The Job-Seeker's Reputation

Without question, job-holders determined whether or not to assist based on job-seekers' reputations. Indeed, 75 percent of my respondents reported that when in possession of job information and influence, they largely based their decisions on what they knew of a job-seeker's prior actions and behaviors, both on the job and in his or her personal life. This knowledge signaled to job-holders the likelihood that the job-seeker would act responsibly throughout the employment process, and particularly whether the job-seeker would do anything that could have a negative effect on the job-holder's own reputation (see figure 3.2).

Work History and Work Ethic

Thirty-eight percent of respondents considered job-seekers' *work reputations* when deciding whether to assist. Like employers, they were concerned with whether job-seekers had been stably employed, the circumstances under which they had left their last job, the frequency with which they had moved from one job to the next, and how they typically behaved at work. As one respondent proclaimed, "You're doing the same thing an employer would do. Like a reference check." Job-seekers known for having integrity on the job—by being dependable, dedicated, and productive—were held in high regard and readily given assistance. Indeed, this was the primary reason why Jessica Bernard, a twenty-eight-year-old unemployed mother of three, aided her cousin. She explained:

> I have a little cousin. She's fifteen or sixteen years old, and when I was working for the university—you know, they have the students that do work, a couple of hours for lunch and a couple of hours for dinner—and I know she's a good worker, so I told her that they were hiring, and I talked to my supervisor and he told me to tell her to come in, and she filled out the application and she started working that day. She was working at McDonald's, but she had been at McDonald's for a long time, so I knew that she would work, especially by her being young. I knew she would go to work everyday, and she gets upset when she can't be on time, because her mom's got problems. So I told him about her, because I knew she was somebody who was going to be there.

Jessica determined that her cousin would be of little risk to her own reputation because, even at such a young age and with enormous obstacles, her cousin had accumulated a solid record of employment. That she had been employed at McDonald's for some time and had taken great pains to arrive at work punctually, in spite of a troubled mother, was evidence enough of her strong work ethnic and general trustworthiness. When job-seekers presented a steady record of employment, their job contacts calculated the risk of helping as minimal and thus were willing to do so.

Whereas job-seekers with stellar reputations were embraced, those deemed to have a poor work ethic—for transitioning in and out of jobs frequently, being habitually absent or tardy, or having a poor work attitude—were summarily denied assistance or given weak referrals to other jobs. In a typical comment, Shirley Wyatt, a twenty-seven-year-old, unemployed single mother of four, exclaimed, "If I know what type of person they is, if I know whether they actually going to get the job and stay at the job, or they one of them people that, you know, I know after the first two little paychecks, they going to be quitting, ain't even no need for me to be telling you because you ain't going to be staying there." This was how Cynthia Wilson viewed her own brother's relationship to employment. Because of his past behavior in the labor market, she was skeptical that he would be consistent and dependable if she were to facilitate his hire at her job. At the time, she worked full-

Figure 3.2   Job-Seeker-Related Attributes Affecting Job-Holders' Decisions to Assist, by Gender

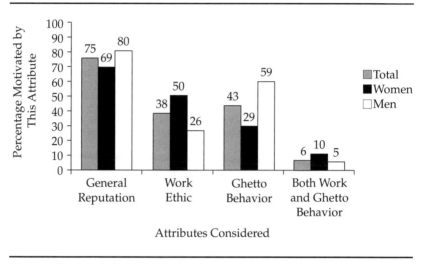

Source: Author's compilation.

time at a calling card company making $9 per hour and learning computer skills. She explained:

> First of all, figure out what type of work history they already have, you know, versus someone like my brother, for instance. He wanted to get [a job]. I'm like no, 'cause you jump from job to job to job. Can't do that. Well, he finally found a job that he liked. He's been there, I think, for two years now. *Now* if he came and said, well, Cynthia, is [your employer] hiring? No problem, no problem.

Even though her job-seeking relation was her brother, with whom she presumably had had a long history, the strength and nature of their relationship was somewhat inconsequential. Instead, the history of his behavior on the job interested Cynthia most, providing her with information from which to deduce his future conduct. Once he repaired his reputation by working steadily with one employer, Cynthia was willing to provide assistance.

Women were far more likely than men to assess trustworthiness by considering job-seekers' history of employment experiences. Whereas only 26 percent of the men mentioned work history, half of the women did. (Possible explanations for this gender difference are explored in the next section.) Not all contacts, however, assessed trustworthiness in terms of work history. For some, job-seekers' behavior in the personal realm was most significant.

Acting Ghetto: Bringing the Street to the Job

Forty-three percent of job-holders considered how job-seekers carried themselves outside of the employment arena when deciding whether to assist. Of special concern were those whom respondents described as "real ghetto"—individuals whose behavior included being loud and raucous, abusing illicit drugs and alcohol, and taking part in criminal behaviors such as robbing and stealing—because such inclinations would almost certainly destroy the job-holder's reputation. The drug and alcohol abuse and criminal aspects of ghetto behavior were little tolerated. As Cynthia Wilson explained in reference to another job-seeking friend, Cornelia, "She was like real ghetto, you know. She was heavy off into drugs, and I was like, I don't think so. You're not going to make me look bad." Each time Cornelia would inquire about job openings at Cynthia's place of employment, Cynthia would lie to save face. She recounted, "I just said they're not hiring. Every time. I know one point in time that job got to be hiring, but I was like, 'They're not hiring.' [She laughs.] It's a freeze!" Because of Cornelia's drug addiction, Cynthia could not bring herself to inform her friend that her employer was hiring. Since that time, Cynthia and Cornelia have become best friends, and Cornelia now knows that Cynthia misled her about past job opportunities. However, Cynthia still refuses to assist her best friend, who has yet to overcome her addiction.

For some job-holders who were embedded in networks of relations in which a number of people had problematic reputations, the thought of providing job-finding assistance caused great concern. This was Robert Randolph's issue. Robert was a thirty-two-year-old, unmarried, and unemployed father of three. When asked how he determined whether or not to assist, he said:

> You know, because I know a lot of people that smoke rocks [crack], you know, and do drugs and not really serious about getting out here and finding a job. Those are the people that, you know, I would say, "Well, there's a person out here that may have something for you, you know, you go talk to." I will put 'em in contact with somebody, you know, but I wouldn't put my name out there and recommend 'em, you know. I wouldn't do that, no.

Since so many of his friends regularly committed theft and larceny, Monroe Laschley expressed similar concerns. A thirty-five-year-old single father of three, Monroe justified, "I got friends, you know, that's thieves, that want to rob and steal, you know what I'm saying? How would I be like trying to get them a job where I'm working at, you know what I'm saying? Then, the boss's car come up missing or something, or you know a computer come up missing." In situations like these, the prospect of providing assistance was inherently risky because so many of their friends, family members, and acquaintances were known to be of such ill repute that job-holders felt that they could not trust them to behave appropriately.

Lee Boswell had very similar concerns. At thirty-seven years of age, Lee had recently completed a five-year sentence for assault with intent to do great bodily harm. He explained that multiple factors—drug and alcohol abuse, immaturity, and jealousy—converged into murderous rage one evening in which he had beaten his girlfriend until she was close to death. Since his release, he had committed a great deal of time to his own rehabilitation. He was in therapy and had been taking part in Alcoholics and Narcotics Anonymous programs, and through a temporary employment agency he was working. His primary goal, he explained, was to learn how to spend time with himself and to make himself happy. So, when asked how he determined whether to assist his job-seeking relations—several of the inmates with whom he had been incarcerated had contacted him to gain job-finding assistance upon their release—he explained, "I would know they character and what they doing, and if I know they still messing around or drinking and stuff, then I wouldn't be able to do it and I would let 'em know, you know, once you get yourself together, holler at me then. But if I know that they using or got sticky fingers and stuff like that, I wouldn't give no recommendation." These job-seekers constituted huge risks to job-holders' reputations and labor market stability. As a result, they garnered little or no consideration among job-holders.

Job-holders had a greater range of responses toward job-seekers known for their raucous or "ghetto" behavior. Some found ghetto behavior offensive at all times; to Henry Wilson, for instance, such behavior was a sure sign that the offender did not share his values and attitudes and thus could not be counted on to represent him well on the job. At thirty-two years of age, Henry was married with two children, steadily employed, and churchgoing. He was proud of the various roles he played and took his responsibilities very seriously. When asked why he was reluctant to provide assistance to job-seekers in his network, he explained:

> The conversations that they have. Uh, I'm a very entrepreneurial-minded person, try to be a spiritual person, responsible. [This is] not to say that you gotta be like me, but when you're talking outside. . . . I'm a married man. I like to look at a beautiful woman—you're an attractive woman. I like looking at you, but, you know, I don't feel like going beyond that. [Mocking those in question . . .] "Oh, let me see if I can sneak around," you know, and these people that are consistently talking about drinking,

partying. And I talk about investments or things of that nature or just general family stuff. They don't get it. . . . It's over their head, so I just leave it alone.

Similarly, Gary Hanson, a thirty-one-year-old, unemployed single father of seven, expressed concerned about how job-seekers would represent him, explaining, "If they would be the type of person [to say], 'Oh man, fuck that bitch, man!' you know, that's not the person I would want to put my name on the line for." Statements such as the one Gary cited, while far from innocuous, might be interpreted as such in the context of a private conversation. However, for job-holders making decisions about whom to trust with their names and reputations in the labor market, statements such as these are a sure sign of job-seekers' vulgarity and boorishness, attributes that job-holders do not want associated with their names. And this was of no small consequence for Gary. He had once assisted a good friend only to have his employer dismiss the friend for frequent absences, cursing, and intimidating others. As Gary understood it, "he brought the street to the job, you know, and you don't just bring the street to the job. That's a total separation." While they have remained friends, Gary would not contemplate working with his friend again.

Other job-holders were offended by raucous behavior only when the individuals engaging in it seemed oblivious to context. For these job-holders, acting ghetto itself was not to be scorned. Indeed, when socializing with kith and kin, it was quite enjoyable. Problems would arise, however, when individuals did not take their social context into consideration. Job-seekers' inability to discern the proper context for acting ghetto was the primary reason Brenda Bowen gave for refusing assistance. So, like Cynthia Wilson, she often lied about job openings at her place of employment to job-seeking ties who behaved in this way in order to save face—theirs and her own—as well as to preserve opportunities to receive assistance in the future. A thirty-six-year-old separated, unemployed mother of two, Brenda said:

I hate to be judgmental, but I look at the way this person is reacting. If you can't control yourself in public, no matter that you're not at a job, you're out in public and these are people that you really don't know and they're judging you and the only thing they can judge you by is what they see and you don't know how to act, you know, you're speaking ignorant, you know. Because I been around people like that, you know. Say, for instance, I don't know you and you're walking past and I'm standing here with this girl and she's just cussing and just saying all kinds of ignorant things. I might say it, but when you're walking past, I'll stop.

In addition, job-holders like Brenda worried that once hired, these job-seekers would undoubtedly reveal something about their own private lives that they would prefer to remain private.

Interestingly, a higher percentage of men looked to these personal habits outside of the work arena for signs of trustworthiness; women prioritized work history as a criterion for assessing trustworthiness. Compared to only 29 percent of women, 59 percent of men considered the extent to which their job-seeking ties acted ghetto when deciding whether and how to assist. Although it is difficult to determine with these data why men and women diverge in the criteria they use to assess reputation—and thus trustworthiness—this gender difference may be attributable to the frequency with which male job-holders are presented with these issues relative to their female counterparts. Given the large extent to which networks, particularly job referral networks, are segregated by gender (Drentea 1998; Hanson and Pratt 1991; Smith 2000), male job-holders are likely to encounter male job-seekers more often, and thus they run a higher risk of assisting those who are known for deviant or criminal behavior. Female job-holders, on the other hand, are likely to come into contact more often with female job-seekers and thus run a higher risk of assisting those for whom family responsibilities make it more difficult to get to work regularly and punctually. This explanation is consistent with prior research that has revealed the different ways in which inner-city employers perceive black men relative to black women. Whereas employers often fear that black men will rob and steal from their business and thus are less willing to hire them relative to men of other racial and ethnic groups, inner-city employers' concerns about black women as employees appear to center largely on the pattern of absences and tardiness that they attribute to their extensive familial responsibilities (see Browne and Kennelly 1999; Kasinitz and Rosenberg 1996; Kirschenman and Neckerman 1991; Neckerman and Kirschenman 1991; Wilson 1996). Gender differences in assessments of trustworthiness, then, may be linked to differences in the types of risks that male and female job-seekers present to job-holders.

The Job-Holder's Reputation

Although job-holders relied heavily on job-seekers' personal and professional reputations when deciding whether to assist them, their own reputations, experiences, and status mattered as well and affected the likelihood that they could be mobilized for help. Specifically, they were far less likely to assist anyone if their own reputations were sullied or if they had a history of assisting unmotivated job-seekers. Their assistance was also contingent on their own social and economic stability, or lack thereof. These results are displayed in figure 3.3.

Figure 3.3   Job-Holder-Related Attributes Affecting Their Decisions to
Assist, by Gender

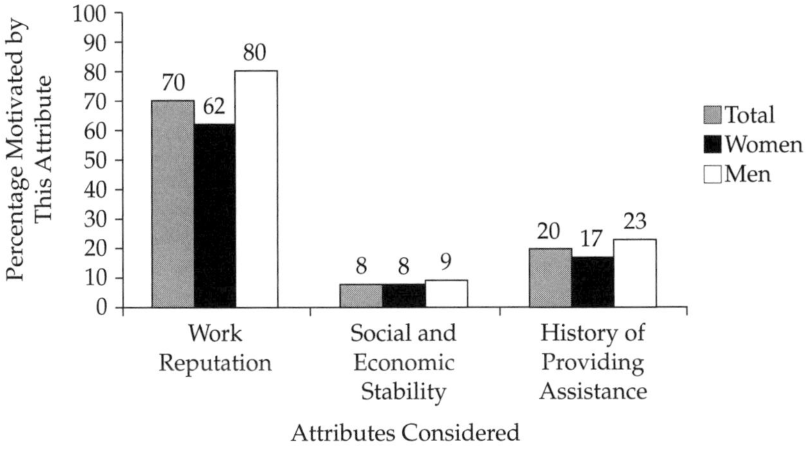

Source: Author's compilation.

The Job-Holder's Reputation with the Employer

Why were job-holders so concerned about job-seekers' reputations? Overwhelmingly, job-holders feared making bad referrals that might tarnish their own reputation and threaten their own labor market stability. Roughly 70 percent—62 percent of women and 80 percent of men—feared that if they personally vouched for a referral, there was no way to ensure that that person would show up to work, work beyond the first paycheck, be prompt and regular, be productive on the job, and not steal, curse, fight, or disrespect authority. At the very least, job-holders would be embarrassed for having provided a disreputable referral; at most, they could lose their own jobs as well as future employment opportunities.

Jackie York, a twenty-seven-year-old single mother of five children, was one such example. Although receiving public assistance, she supplemented her income by caring for other children in her home, one of only a few positions she could envision given that she had small children of her own. She had recently become certified by the state to provide in-home day care and hoped to obtain an advanced license in order to open her own center.

Previously, Jackie had worked in a yearlong part-time position making $10 per hour supervising a cleaning crew. As supervisor, she could influence hiring, and she described how she helped three friends get jobs. Unfortunately, none of them worked out. She first assisted her eldest son's great-uncle. Although she suspected he had a drug habit, she believed that employment would get him on the track to recovery. At the very least, she reasoned, it would do no harm because there was nothing on the job site that he could steal. Hired on a Tuesday, the uncle worked Wednesday and Thursday, but he did not show up for work on Friday; nor did he call. Because he had worked so well his first two days, helping the crew to complete their tasks one hour earlier than the norm, Jackie gave him the benefit of the doubt and decided to guarantee his presence by picking him up before work. On Monday and Tuesday, this approach worked; by Wednesday, however, it did not. Within one week of his hire, the uncle was let go, and Jackie described herself as "looking a little foolish." In trying to assist the uncle in getting to work on time, she had arrived at work late as well. In the process, she began to lose her employer's trust. Jackie explained, "She's looking at me like, 'You ain't picking up your pieces too well.'"

Her employer's perception only worsened with Jackie's next two referrals. She aided the girlfriend of her eldest son's father, reasoning that because their sons were half-brothers, the extended family would benefit. Her ex's girlfriend, however, was also unreliable. She worked the first day, arrived out of uniform the second day (which meant that she could not work), and did not show at all the third day or thereafter. Although Jackie believed that her third referral, an ex-boyfriend, was a good worker, her employer found him too slow and fired him without her knowledge, confirming that her employer had lost confidence in her.

To get her referrals to see these consequences, Jackie reminded them of her own poor socioeconomic status; she described pleading with them to behave responsibly so as not to harm her reputation. Perceiving this approach as ineffective, however, she changed tactics. "I did get smart. I did get a little bit smart. I said, 'Look, don't tell them you know me. Just go on in there and get the job.'" However, Jackie now declines to partake in obligations of exchange around job-finding at all. When asked about the positive aspects of helping others to find work, she responded:

I'm not the right one to ask that question. I would just have to say that that's something you got to do on your own. I don't see anything positive right now. I can't be objective anymore. "No, I ain't heard nothing about no job." You know, I have to say that because if I say, "Well, I do know some . . ." [job-seekers respond,] "Oh, for real, girl!" [and so I say,] "I ain't heard nothing, you know, about your situation."

Self-preservation now dictated that Jackie remove herself from the process, and as with Cynthia Wilson and Brenda Bowen, that included concealing her knowledge of job opportunities.

Terrance Blackburn, a twenty-two-year-old high school graduate, also refused to vouch for job-seekers after getting burned by several referrals, a pattern that ruined his reputation in the eyes of his employer. He justified not helping a previous referral again:

> Because I got a bad reputation from that guy. You know, my manager said, "You bringing me all these people and they don't want to work." So, no, I wouldn't stick my neck out there. I'm going to get my head chopped off. I mean, if they ain't going to stay, why not put your two weeks in. I mean, just so I won't look bad. So [you] quit on the people, [and] they asking me, "Where your friend at?"

Although job-holders like Jackie and Terrance were not at risk of losing their jobs, developing a pattern of bad referrals had diminished their reputations with their employers. A pattern of bad referrals indicates that one may be a poor judge of character, thus limiting the possibility that the employer will consider one's future referrals. It may also reduce one's prospects for promotions. By distancing themselves from job-seekers during the matching process, job-holders shield themselves from the stain of bad behavior and the stigma associated with common, negative stereotypes of the black poor—what several respondents described as "ghetto" behavior.

Job loss, however, is possible. When a referral steals or is very unproductive, for example, a job-holder may become implicated by association, diminishing the trust the employer has in him or her. Such was the case for Jeremy Jessup. Jeremy was forty-two years old, and although unemployed when we interviewed him, he survived by making $7.50 to $8.00 an hour working short stints through temporary employment agencies. When asked about the importance of using friends, relatives, and acquaintances during this process, Jeremy appeared unimpressed. Although he thought that personal contacts were helpful for job finding, he explained that he preferred to find employment on his own because, if he failed, his actions would not reflect badly on the person who had assisted him. He did not want anyone to be held accountable for his actions. As it turned out, Jeremy's hesitation about providing job-finding assistance was not based on having abused the trust of previous contacts; he had been burned by previous referrals himself. As a supervisor for a construction company contracted to build several homes in the area, Jeremy was in the position to hire many friends he thought needed employment. He told me what happened:

I had worked for [the construction company], and they're building brand-new houses, and I hired a couple of my friends, and when they came to work, all they wanted to do was sit down and get paid for it. They felt like they didn't have to work. They figured, like, you know, instead of taking a half-hour lunch, you could take an hour-and-a-half lunch and everything was okay. I was supposed to just let that go. [But] we all got fired because the work wasn't getting done. I couldn't do it all by myself. So, no thanks. No thanks. Now I call [the construction company] trying to get back, and they won't even return my calls.

Jeremy has since helped a nephew get a job, but he is wary of assisting others. Neglecting to determine the reliability of his friends cost him his job as a supervisor with the construction company and any future employment opportunities with that firm.

The disinclination to assist job-seekers expressed by Jackie, Terrance, and Jeremy contrasts sharply with the orientation of job-holders, like Wilson Smith, whose reputations were still very much untarnished. Wilson, a twenty-one-year-old high school dropout, linked his ability and willingness to assist in the past to his good standing on the job. As he explained it, "The jobs that I did work at, like, you know, *the ones that I was doing good at*, like [a fast-food chain] or the one with [another fast-food chain], I could just pull people in there, because either the boss was cool with me or I just was taking care of business." With an unsullied reputation, he was willing to act on his job-seeking ties' behalf, knowing that his own positive standing in the firm would facilitate the hiring of any referrals he made. Once job-holders ceased "taking care of business," however, and made referrals that led to their own loss in reputation and status, the likelihood that they would provide job-finding assistance diminished substantially. First, as with Jackie, Terrance, and Jeremy, employers were less likely to allow employees with tarnished reputations to make referrals, questioning their ability to discern trustworthiness and employability in job-seekers. Second, job-holders began to question their own ability to distinguish between the trustworthy and the negligent and unreliable. Their experiences fed a psychology of distrust. With little confidence that their job matches would turn out well, job-holders with tarnished reputations either avoided providing assistance altogether or only offered assistance that did not link them to the applicant in the minds of employers. For instance, when they did pass along information about job openings, they often added the caveat, ". . . but don't put my name on it," so that the job-seekers were clear that they could not refer to their relationships as a signal of their credibility on the job.

Drawing from Fernandez and Fernandez-Mateo (2006), however, to the extent that employers do not favor informal referrals over other applicant recruitment strategies, the costs *and* pecuniary benefits of producing referrals may be reduced to nothing, thus increasing the likelihood that employees will make referrals because their risk of loss declines to nothing. Indeed, I found that job-holders who worked at firms where the hiring process was formalized had fewer concerns about their own reputations or the reputations of those they assisted, primarily because they were not held responsible for screening their referrals or held accountable for negative outcomes. For these job-holders, it was a win-win situation. After referring job-seekers, their work was done. Job-seekers then had to pass the firm's hiring criteria, including drug tests and proficiency tests. If they failed and were not hired, the job-holders were not implicated. If a job-seeker was hired but did not work out, the job-holder who made the initial referral was not faulted. Again, job-holders did not need to be concerned about their reputation and the reputation of their referral because a formalized system reduced their personal responsibility and accountability.

Social and Economic Stability

Under certain circumstances, job-holders would assist job-seekers of ill repute. Indeed, a few respondents (roughly 8 percent) indicated that they would assist almost anyone, regardless of reputation, because they could not afford to do otherwise, a finding that differed little by gender. Their social and economic circumstances were so dire that they felt they could not shun any opportunity to partake in the obligations of exchange that might serve them in the future. Take Laura Odoms, a thirty-three-year-old single mother of four who, at the time of the interview, supported her children with public assistance. When asked about prior occasions when she had helped others secure jobs with her former employer, she recounted the following experience:

> I used to work at Days Inn, and I helped a friend of mines get a job. But instead of her wanting to help to clean the room, she knew people that stayed in the room where she wanted to go and just sit around and hang out. And you can't do that. So the lady, the supervisor, kept saying, "Well, I'm going to let you handle this. You brought her in. . . . I'm going to let you either handle it or fire her." And I had to let her go because it was either me or her, and I had to keep my little job.

Before her referral was hired, Laura had counseled this woman, her best friend, about responsible workplace behavior. However, her friend broke the rules anyway and suffered the consequences, at Laura's hands. This outcome is hardly unique given other respondents' accounts of their referrals' betrayals. What is unique about this situation, however, is that Laura was still willing to assist her friend—she remained her best friend even after Laura fired her—if presented with a future opportunity to do so. The overwhelming majority of job-holders in similar situations were adamant that, at the very least, they would not assist the individual who had acted inappropriately.

Is Laura's response irrational? Why continue to assist another person, even a best friend, who shows little interest in respecting the terms, in this case clearly stated, of the exchange? Laura explained her willingness to assist her best friend in the future—indeed, her willingness to help anyone—by pointing to her own precarious economic situation. Because she herself was struggling to care for her family and would almost certainly require assistance from others, her friend included, with various tasks in the future, she refused to close any door to a potential future exchange. When asked why she would be willing to give her best friend job-finding assistance in the future, she explained:

> Because the majority of my friends are in situations like me, and we try to help each other. Besides, if I need the help as far as money or a ride or if I need her to watch my ten-year-old, she's there. And I feel people, especially in my situation, I don't have much, and I'm trying to get much because I want my kids to be dependable. That is, when you get old enough to be on your own, this is what you got to do.

Laura's explanation indicates that her willingness to assist was intricately tied to her own social and economic vulnerability. Would her disposition toward providing future job-finding assistance survive if she had access to stable and safe child care, a steady income, and reliable transportation, all in-kind support that her friend did provide? It seems very unlikely. Lacking these, however, she felt that she could not burn the bridges she did have in the form of support from her job-seeking ties, even if their behaviors were unpredictable and often irresponsible, because they did provide some in-kind assistance that she could not do without.

For those who struggled but with less desperation, providing job-finding assistance required more time and energy than they wished to expend given their already overburdened lives. Such was the case for Steve Jackson. Downwardly mobile at twenty-one, Steve earned $7.50 per hour working full-time as a delivery truck driver. Both of his parents had an advanced degree, and they had raised their two children in middle-class, racially mixed neighborhoods. Steve himself was working toward a college degree at a major state university when he learned that he had gotten his girlfriend pregnant. He returned home, planning to work full-time to support his child while taking classes at a local university. Overwhelmed by his responsibilities, however, he fell behind academically and then dropped out. After leaving school, he worked as a sales representative with a telecommunications company earning $15 per hour. In his next two positions he earned $12 per hour selling cellular phones. Because of conflicts with management, however, he quit. With a downturn in the economy, there were few jobs at his preferred wage rate, and pressed to pay off $2,500 in rising child support arrears, he settled for $7.50 per hour driving a delivery truck.

Given the major stresses in his life, Steve found the task of helping others emotionally daunting, particularly when close friends were involved.

> It could be a lot of stress, and if you take it seriously to the point where you're really trying to get this person some help, it could be stressful for you. You might meet with them and give them some ideas and that could be extra things to do, and you know, you got your own problems without dealing with someone else's job problems.

This was especially true for Steve considering that the majority of job-seekers who had approached him had few marketable skills. He now refused to assist unless the job-seeker had a résumé in hand with which to work. To Steve, a résumé signaled that the job-seeker would not require more time and emotional energy than he could afford. After all, he too was struggling to keep his head above water. Absent assurances that the job-seeker would not overburden him, his assistance was unlikely. Besides, he could imagine making it without the help of others, particularly from those who sought help from him. Although struggling, he was far from the level of desperation that Laura experienced constantly. In his position, Steve was clear that assistance was more a hindrance than a possible help.

A History of Providing Job-Finding Assistance

Job-holders' willingness to assist was also decisively shaped by their history of prior referrals. Indeed, one-fifth of job-holders (17 percent of job-holding women and 23 percent of job-holding men) suggested that they were less likely to provide assistance because they had all too often come across job-seekers they perceived to be unmotivated. They described situations in which their job-seeking relatives, friends, and associates would complain about their labor market detachment and ask for help finding work. Once presented with assistance—typically information about job openings—these job-seekers would express interest but not follow through. They would either fail to call the job-holders or neglect to complete the application. A few days later, the cycle of complaining and requests for assistance would continue. These experiences fed a generalized distrust among job-holders.

Many, like Leah Arnold, found this cycle of requests and inaction vexing. At the time of the interview, Leah was twenty-five years old and working full-time, earning $8.25 per hour providing client assistance in a disabled care facility. When asked about the negative aspects of trying to help others find work, she responded:

> It's their enthusiasm. The negative aspects is, you tell them about it, they sound like, "Oh, for real!" like that, and then the next thing you know, two weeks later you done told them about five jobs. Two weeks later, "Girl, I still need a job." You're like, okay. Girl, you better look. You better go look, 'cause I done told you, and after so many times, hey. So that's the negative aspect is when they don't have the motivation or the enthusiasm to go out there and get it even after it's right there.

Rolanda Douglass was a thirty-nine-year-old mother of four who had recently been hired full-time as a dietary aide at a convalescent home. Having been employed at six different jobs over the past three years in various service occupations, she knew the low-wage labor market fairly well. Furthermore, her goal of finding "the job" that would take her into retirement kept her actively engaged in her job referral network. Her most recent job, although fine for the moment, did not offer benefits and paid only $7.50 per hour—about $4.00 per hour less than she estimated she needed for financial security. Constantly searching newspapers and working her network, she had learned of many opportunities and passed these on to those in need. As a result, Rolanda fashioned herself as a major source of job information and influence for her network of family and friends.

Rolanda had begun to feel, however, that her efforts at disseminating information about jobs and her offers to intercede were in vain because all too often job-seekers would not follow through. She recounted a recent conversation with a neighbor, a young single mother on public assistance who was on her way to the welfare office to find work. Rolanda informed her neighbor that her employer was hiring, and she provided a job description, including the hours needed, the type of work required, and the wage rate. Rolanda strongly encouraged her neighbor to apply, offering to provide an application and to return it when completed. She herself had a great incentive to be so encouraging. Her employer paid at least $200 for every referral brought in, and given her low wages, Rolanda had hoped to augment her annual income through the referral process. Days after that conversation, however, her neighbor had still not initiated further contact. Rolanda explained disappointedly, "Even though you tell 'em about it and they be like, 'Okay,' it's like I'm wasting my breath." Although she was disappointed by the loss of the referral bonus, she also felt less valuable. If few wanted the resources she had to offer, why bother?

Another job-holder collected rental and job applications to supply to those she deemed in need. Tylea Bond was a twenty-five-year-old mother of an eight-year-old and infant daughters. Although she had first given birth when she was just seventeen years old and had been on public assistance within a year, by the time of the interview she had accumulated four years of full-time work experience. She was earning almost $9 per hour at the local university working in student services. Having worked her way up to what she considered a "pretty good" job with "good benefits," Tylea believed that anyone could find a good job, with patience and resolve. With this in mind, she was keen on assisting others. She collected information about housing and jobs and would offer it, often unsolicited, in the hopes that other women would use it to better their own lives. More often than not, however, recipients of her attention would not respond, and their inaction infuriated her. She complained about one such person:

> I told this girl at my church, she has six kids, and I don't know what her living is like, but I keep telling her about this housing up here and stuff. I don't like my area that I live in now, but there are low-income housing areas that are nice in this area, and she will not come up here. And so I just got totally mad. I got mad, because I'm like, "You're just stupid," you know what I'm saying, "because I'm trying to help you out. I'm trying to get you ahead, expose you to some things, and you're not even thinking about none of that stuff. I'm telling you how much money you could be making, and you're not even going to try." So, it's just frustrating.

Frustrated by their perception that the persistently jobless were unwilling to better their circumstances by drawing from the resources they offered, these job-holders had become discouraged. In a manner similar to that of discouraged workers who have had such difficulty finding work that they stop searching altogether, discouraged job-holders were no longer willing to help because the jobless did not participate in obligations of exchange around job information and influence. Tylea threw away her folder of job and housing information. Rolanda came to believe that the job-seekers she knew so lacked initiative that she eventually required evidence that they were committed to employment before she would participate in obligations of exchange. Leah denied her associates' requests for job-finding assistance, instructing them to look for work themselves. Thus, as with reputational concerns, job-holders' inclination to assist was historically constituted, and outcomes often fed a psychology of distrust. The likelihood that they would offer their job-finding assistance as a social resource declined as the number of their failed attempts to assist accumulated.

The Strength of Ties

In addition to the attributes and positions of job-holders and job-seekers, assistance was also contingent on the strength of the relationship between them. One-tenth of job-holders considered the strength of their relationships with job-seekers when deciding whether to assist. Typical were comments such as: "It's gotta be a family member," "I think I'd keep it in the family," or, conversely, "It depends on how much I know the person. If I don't know them, then I don't really care too much about them." Job-holders were more motivated to assist those with whom they had had long-standing relationships, such as relatives and close friends, for two reasons. First, these relationships tended to be founded on a history of successful exchanges that reduced job-holders' uncertainty about their exchange partners' reliability, thereby nurturing feelings of deep mutual trust. Second, with a history of successful exchanges, stronger, more cohesive, and more affective bonds had developed that further facilitated reciprocal exchanges.

These two reasons partly explain why Yvonne O'Neill, a thirty-year-old single mother of two, devoted so much time and energy to securing employment for her best friend, Danielle. At the time of the interview, Yvonne was making $190 every two weeks working part-time at a family-owned portrait studio. Over the previous six years, she had held five jobs averaging ten months each, most often in health care assisting with and monitoring clients' personal care. Even with her spotty work history, she had gained quite a bit of work experience. When asked how she had helped job-seekers, Yvonne provided the following example:

> I helped [Danielle] get a job through [a health care center] I used to work. She was not too familiar with more technical medical things, far as personal life care. Like she is not comfortable with bathing a person's private areas and things of that nature, so they try to get her things that didn't require that. But at times some of her assignments required that she bathe this person or clean their ostomy bags and things of that nature. She'll call me. For example, we are going to go out for the evening or whatever, and she had to do a client, and she told me who it was, and I already done that client, and I knew what this entailed. So what I did, I said, "I will meet you over there, and I will give her a bath and shower, you can cook, and we'll be out of there in half the time." I helped in that manner. Or sometimes I've had to talk her through ostomy care or urine ostomy bag. "I don't know how to change it. I'm going to kill him." "Oh no you're not. What you do, put your gloves on, make your sterile field, dah . . . dah . . . dah . . . dah . . . dah." So I've talked her through it over the phone. Still

had to go over there, make sure she didn't put the bag on wrong, but it seems like that helps her become more comfortable with it, and now she can do it if she has to.

Essentially, Yvonne provided a recommendation and then trained her unskilled friend, performed some of her work tasks, encouraged her regularly, and probably shielded her from job loss. However, even with such a high level of involvement, Yvonne never spoke about assisting Danielle as a sacrifice or a burden. Instead, it was a continuation of a series of material and symbolic exchanges between the two that had helped to reproduce the long-term obligations of support and encouragement they provided each other. During Yvonne's own spells of unemployment, Danielle would call Yvonne regularly with reports of employment opportunities after having scoured local newspapers for job listings that matched Yvonne's skill set. She would also provide encouragement to ensure that Yvonne would act. Yvonne continued:

> When I am looking for work and I already have a job . . . like say now, I have like three or four little things I do, keep me busy. If I am looking for something else, she'll call me up. She works for [the utility company], midnight [shift]. She'll call me at three in the morning. "I'm looking through the paper. I want you to write this down. Okay, call this person in the morning, they're doing office work," or, "They're doing housecleaning work," or, "They're doing private care." This, that and the other. "They will need some help. Call. . . ." You know, she will go down the list, and I'm like, "Danielle, it's four in the morning." [Danielle replies,] "I don't care. Write it down." You know, she is very helpful. If I see something, I'll leave it on her answering machine or her voice mail, or I'll call her up and, you know, always, whether it be looking for a better car, looking for an apartment, or see something in the paper far as like household items, you know, like a garage sale.

Evident is the mutual trust and affection that Yvonne and Danielle share as a result of their history of successful reciprocal exchanges. Furthermore, that their exchanges were not limited to the realm of work probably cemented the strength of their tie and facilitated Yvonne's willingness to aid Danielle in the ways that she did. In other words, in the context of relationships characterized by such mutual trust and affection, assistance, often unsolicited, is undertaken with little forethought, even at the relatively high levels of time, energy, and commitment that Yvonne described.

Close relationships hardly guaranteed, however, that job contacts would assist their job-seeking ties. Job contacts frequently denied assistance to job-seekers they considered close. Cynthia Wilson, the twenty-nine-year-old married mother of three, declined to aid her brother and her best friend, judging both to be unfit for employment. Monroe Laschley, the thirty-five-year-old single father of three, refused to help his close friends, fearing that his employer would inevitably become a victim of their relentless thievery. And although he was very sympathetic about his close friends' joblessness, Steve Jackson, the twenty-one-year-old, downwardly mobile university dropout, avoided requests for assistance because he was overwhelmed by the extent and nature of the assistance often required. Even Yvonne, who with no hesitation did more than most job-holders would probably do to aid her best friend, intimated that job-seekers' reputations mattered most.[5] In other words, those in possession of job information and influence were by far more motivated by concerns about job-seekers' reputations when determining whether to assist them than by the strength of their relationships with them.

This finding does not negate the significance of close ties. Instead, it suggests that tie strength serves another function. As Vincent Roberts explained when asked how he determines whether to assist, "I would say family members, you know, because I know them better. Be around them. You know, it's more easier, okay." In other words, job-holders most preferred to assist close relations not so much because there had been reciprocity between them in the past as because closeness provided access to firsthand knowledge about job-seekers' past actions and behaviors outside the context of the relationship, reducing the information asymmetries that made it difficult to ascertain the level of risk they were exposing themselves to by providing assistance. Thus, although important, the strength of the relationship was secondary. Decisions to assist were overwhelmingly based on how job contacts perceived the job-seekers' reputations.

The Structural Context of Social Resource Mobilization

The decisions that job-holders made about the extent and nature of the assistance they would provide was not only contingent on the interaction between job-holders' and job-seekers' reputations and the strength of the relationship between these two sets of actors. It was also contingent on the structural context within which this decisionmaking process was undertaken. Although social closure seemed to matter little, job-holders' willingness to assist was also affected by the interaction between their access to social capital and their neighborhood poverty status. Local labor market conditions mattered as well. And their decisions to assist were also being made in a labor market context in which soft skills were of increasing importance to employers.

Figure 3.4   Job-Holders' Primary Concerns About Job-Seekers, by Neighborhood Poverty Status

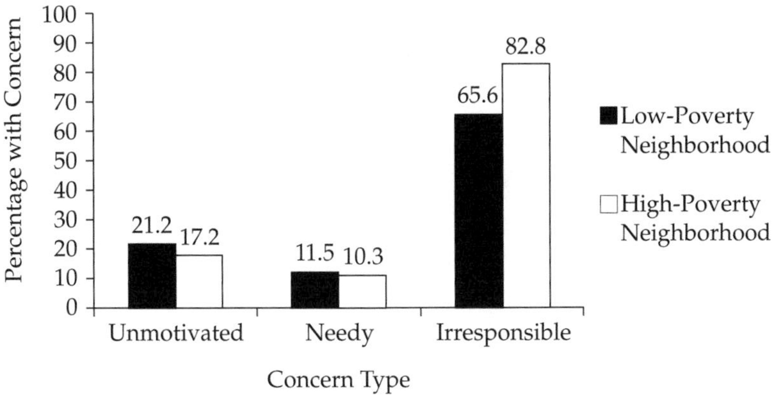

Source: Author's compilation.

Access to Social Capital and Neighborhood Poverty Status

We can see the impact of the interaction of neighborhood poverty status with access to social capital on job-holders' willingness to assist in the fact that 53 percent of job-holders from low-poverty neighborhoods expressed reluctance to assist their job-seeking relations whereas 77 percent of job-holders from high-poverty neighborhoods expressed such reluctance. Although job-holders differed little with regard to their concerns about job-seekers' motivation and neediness, there were noteworthy differences with regard to their concerns about job-seekers' irresponsibility. As shown in figure 3.4, 21 percent of job-holders from low-poverty neighborhoods and 17 percent of job-holders from high-poverty neighborhoods expressed concern about job-seekers' lack of motivation. Also, 11 percent of job-holders from both low- and high-poverty neighborhoods were concerned about job-seekers' neediness. However, whereas 66 percent of job-holders from low-poverty neighborhoods expressed concern about job-seekers' irresponsibility on the job, 83 percent of job-holders from high-poverty neighborhoods did.

What's more, residents of high-poverty neighborhoods appeared far less inclined to provide assistance in the face of concerns than were residents of low-poverty neighborhoods, especially with regard to questions of irresponsibility. Figure 3.5 shows the percentage of job-holders

Figure 3.5   Job-Holders Who Were Reluctant to Assist, by Concern Type and Neighborhood Poverty Status

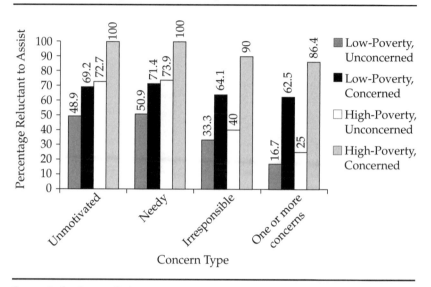

Source: Author's compilation.

who were reluctant to assist by concern type and neighborhood poverty status. The relationship between reluctance and neighborhood poverty status was similar with regard to concerns about job-seekers' motivation and neediness. In both instances, a lower percentage of job-holders from low-poverty neighborhoods were reluctant to assist (50 percent among those without these concerns and 70 percent among those who did have these concerns) than was the case for job-holders from high-poverty neighborhoods (73 percent among those without these concerns and 100 percent among those who did have these concerns). And while those with concerns expressed reluctance to a greater degree than those without these concerns, differences are minor and cannot be attributed to the concern effect.

Shifting the focus to the question of irresponsibility reveals that those with concerns are far more likely to express reluctance than those without concerns, whether in low- or high-poverty neighborhoods. The effect for job-holders from high-poverty neighborhoods, however, appears larger. When faced with suggestions of job-seekers' irresponsibility, job-holders from high-poverty neighborhoods appear more likely to express reluctance. This is also true when we compare job-holders with no concerns at all to those with one or more concerns. In other words, not only does living in a high-poverty neighborhood increase the percentage of job-holders who are concerned about irresponsibility, but it leads more of those with these concerns to express reluctance.

Among residents of high-poverty neighborhoods, could the greater reluctance to assist be attributed to inferior access to social capital compared to their counterparts residing in low-poverty neighborhoods? To gain a sense of job-holders' access to working relations, I used a survey instrument called a position generator (see section E of appendix C for the position generator instrument that I used). Following the lead of Nan Lin (2001), I randomly selected a set of fifteen occupations and asked respondents if they knew anyone who held any of these positions. If they did, for each I asked if the nature of the relationship was professional, personal, or both, and I asked how frequently they were in contact with the relation. The occupations, which ranged in skill level, included five unskilled or semi-skilled workers (cashier, child care worker, nursing aide, machine operator, and taxicab driver/chauffeur), five skilled or semi-professional workers (electrician, high school teacher, police officer, secretary, and social worker), and five professional workers (accountant, computer programmer, lawyer, physician, and registered nurse).[6]

As shown in figure 3.6, I found no difference between residents of low- and high-poverty neighborhoods in access to social capital, as measured by the number of positions to which respondents reported

Figure 3.6   Access to Social Capital, by Neighborhood Poverty Status

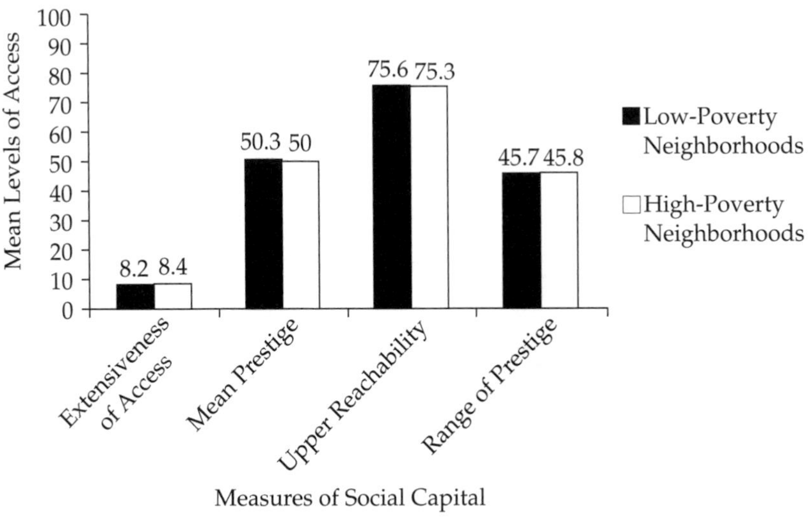

Measures of Social Capital

Source: Author's compilation.

access (8.2 versus 8.4, respectively), the average prestige score of the positions to which respondents reported access (50.3 versus 50.0, respectively), the highest prestige score to which respondents reported access (75.6 versus 75.3, respectively), and the difference between highest and lowest prestige scores (45.7 versus 45.8, respectively).[7]

Differences emerge, however, when I distinguish residents by employment status. Employed residents of high-poverty neighborhoods look little different from residents of low-poverty neighborhoods in terms of the number of positions they have access to (figure 3.7), the mean prestige of the positions their contacts hold (figure 3.8), contacts' upper reachability (figure 3.9), and contacts' range of prestige (figure 3.10). In fact, in some cases employed residents of high-poverty neighborhoods had *greater* access to social capital compared to low-income residents of low-poverty neighborhoods.[8] Although this finding seems counterintuitive, it makes sense if we consider that the institutional resources in predominantly black, high-poverty neighborhoods tend to be inadequate to meet residents' needs (see Small and McDermott 2006). Highly "competent" residents of these low-resource communities probably have to make connections with individuals and institutions outside of their neighborhoods to effectively manage their work and family lives (Furstenberg et al. 1999).[9] This probably explains why employed residents of high-poverty neighborhoods have levels of social capital access equivalent to the social capital of low-poverty neighborhood residents, whether employed or unemployed.[10]

The reader who has reviewed figures 3.7 through 3.10 may have noted that it is not residence in high-poverty neighborhoods per se that

Figure 3.7   Access to Social Capital (Extensiveness of Access), by Neighborhood Poverty and Employment Status

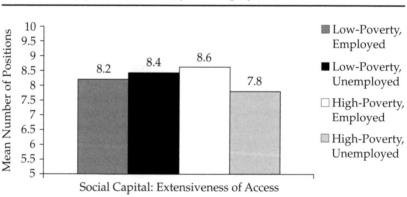

Source: Author's compilation.

Figure 3.8   Access to Social Capital (Mean Prestige), by Neighborhood Poverty and Employment Status

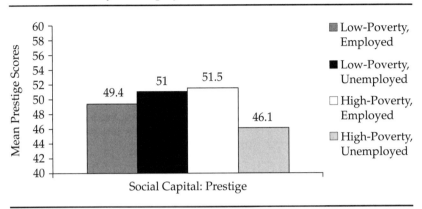

Source: Author's compilation.

is negatively associated with access to social capital, but residence in high-poverty neighborhoods *while unemployed.* Relative to the employed in their own neighborhoods and residents of low-poverty neighborhoods (both employed and unemployed), the unemployed in high-poverty neighborhoods reported access to substantially fewer positions, the positions they had access to had substantially lower average prestige scores, the average highest prestige score to which they reported access was noticeably lower than that of the other three groups, and the contacts' range of prestige was also narrower than for em-

Figure 3.9   Access to Social Capital (Upper Reachability), by Neighborhood Poverty and Employment Status

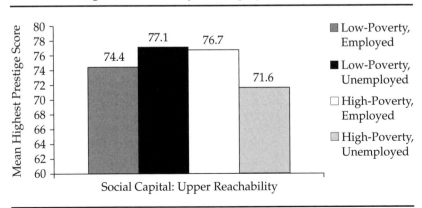

Source: Author's compilation.

Figure 3.10   Access to Social Capital (Range of Prestige), by Neighborhood Poverty and Employment Status

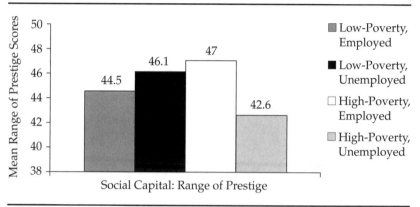

Source: Author's compilation.

ployed residents in their own neighborhoods and residents of low-poverty neighborhoods.

The irony here is that while unemployed residents of high-poverty neighborhoods have relatively inferior access to social capital, they live in neighborhoods in which their employed neighbors have substantially greater access and these potential social resources are less likely to be mobilized on job-seekers' behalf.[11] By focusing on working respondents—those in a position to provide information about job opportunities and influence hires—I found that in low-poverty neighborhoods job-holders willing to provide assistance had greater access to social capital than their reluctant counterparts. Whereas willing job-holders reported access to 8.9 positions, those reluctant to assist had access to 7.9. In high-poverty neighborhoods, however, the reverse was true— willing job-holders had less access to social capital than their reluctant counterparts. Whereas willing job-holders reported access to 7.7 contacts, job-holders disinclined to provide assistance reported, on average, 9.3 contacts (figure 3.11). In other words, the relationship between access to social capital and orientation toward assisting appears highly contingent on the poverty status of the neighborhoods in which job-holders reside. Why is this?

Compared to those living in low-poverty neighborhoods, a higher percentage of job-holders who resided in high-poverty neighborhoods had been burned by job-seekers in the past. Indeed, although one-fifth of residents of low-poverty neighborhoods had been negatively affected by providing assistance, almost half of residents of high-poverty neighborhoods had been burned. Consistent with concerns about being

Figure 3.11   Access to Social Capital, by Neighborhood Poverty Status and Orientation Toward Providing Job-Finding Assistance

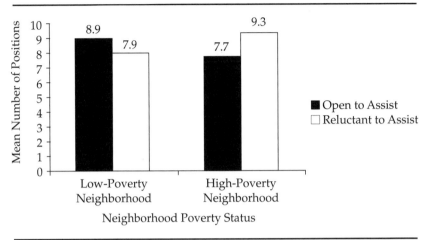

Source: Author's compilation.

burned, when asked how they determined whether to assist their job-seeking ties, a higher percentage of job-holders from high-poverty neighborhoods made determinations based on job-seekers' personal reputation—specifically, on whether they were "ghetto." Whereas 54 percent assessed whether they would assist using this criterion, just 37 percent of those from low-poverty neighborhoods did. However, job-holders in high-poverty neighborhoods were no more concerned than residents of low-poverty neighborhoods about their job-seeking ties' work reputation. Whereas 39 percent of the latter used this criterion to judge their job-seeking ties, 42 percent of the former did.

Residents of neighborhoods of concentrated poverty were far more concerned about ghetto behavior than were those whose neighborhoods were less uniformly disadvantaged. But it would be hasty to assume that poorer neighborhoods naturally house people who are inherently less trustworthy. As Elijah Anderson (1990, 1999) has shown, in neighborhoods in which rates of poverty are high and a significant minority of residents are unemployed or out of the labor market altogether, ghetto behavior is more prevalent and perceived to be so. And while the majority of residents in such neighborhoods do not act ghetto, residents undoubtedly employ this distinction to ferret out, in various contexts, those who can and cannot be trusted. Residents of neighborhoods in which rates of poverty are high are likely to encounter these behaviors more often than do residents of other neighborhoods, and thus are more likely to employ this criterion to assess whether they would assist. Job-holders' cognitive assessments of trustworthiness will be based on whether or not job-seekers exhibit this behavior. However, within the context of concentrated disadvantage, a psychology of distrust also develops as a disproportionate share of negative experiences feeds a belief that others cannot be trusted. In other words, because they reside in riskier social environments, they are more likely to perceive job-finding assistance as a risky endeavor.

The Rising Importance of Soft Skills

Job-holders also have to make determinations about the extent and nature of the assistance they would provide in a labor market context where soft skills have reportedly been rising in importance. In *Stories Employers Tell: Race, Skill, and Hiring in America* (2001, 44), Philip Moss and Chris Tilly distinguish between hard skills, which are "cognitive and technical abilities," and soft skills, which they define as "skills, abilities, and traits that pertain to personality, attitude, and behavior rather then to formal or technical knowledge." They then distinguish between two categories of soft skills. The first category, *interaction skills*, is a set of personal characteristics such as "friendliness, teamwork, ability to fit in, and appropriate affect, grooming, and attire" (44) that allow employers to assess how well individuals will "interact with customers, coworkers, and supervisors." The second category, *motivation skills*, includes characteristics such as "enthusiasm, positive work attitude, commitment, dependability, integrity, and willingness to learn," all of which add to an individual's capacity for productivity. And, the economist Harry Holzer (1996) contends, employers are seeking these skill sets—interaction and motivation—with greater frequency (Cappelli 1995; Holzer 1996). Indeed, Moss and Tilly report that when employers were asked about the most important qualities they looked for in entry-level applicants, 54 percent mentioned hard skills, but 84 percent mentioned one or both types of soft skills.[12] Seventy-five percent mentioned soft skills first. Furthermore, employers often point to blacks' lack of these sought-after skills to justify their greater preference for white, Latino, and Asian workers (Kirschenman and Neckerman 1991; Wilson 1996).

The problem, of course, is accurately and objectively assessing workers' soft skills. As Moss and Tilly point out, while it may be a relatively simple matter to test an individual's mathematical ability or typing speed, it is much more difficult to determine accurately that person's friendliness, propensity for teamwork, and ability to fit in, not to mention his or her enthusiasm, positive work attitude, commitment, dependability, integrity, and willingness to learn. And because accurate assessments of these attributes are so difficult to make, employers often do so based on their own judgments, which are highly subjective, culturally contingent, and strongly affected by their own class, race, and gender stereotypes. These crude assessments often work to blacks' disadvantage during the hiring process; indeed, blacks are sometimes excluded from serious consideration almost as soon as they walk through the door, if not before (Kirschenman and Neckerman 1991; Browne and Kennelly 1999; Moss and Tilly 2001).

Assessing soft skills is also problematic because the social environment in which workers find themselves strongly determines their motivation to work and ability to interact well with others. According to Moss and Tilly (2001, 45):

> Soft skills are profoundly dependent on context. How successfully a worker interacts with customers, coworkers, and supervisors depends decisively on how these other parties view and treat the worker. Pay level and his or her treatment by managers shape a worker's level of motivation. We would argue that for these dimensions of worker performance, the worker's context is *at least as important* as any intrinsic characteristics of the worker. (emphasis in original)

Thus, judgments that blacks lack soft skills relative to others may be explained at least in part by the self-fulfilling prophecies that are at play in the working environment. Employers expect certain types of behaviors from their black workers based on racial and gender stereotypes, then interact with blacks and interpret their behaviors through the lens of these stereotypes; in this interaction, blacks produce the very behaviors that then provide evidence justifying employers' fears. It is within this labor market context in which employers see soft skill sets as the most important qualities that workers can have (and that, generally speaking, they believe blacks do not have) that job-holders in my sample expressed a great deal of concern about job-seekers' interaction style and motivation.

Given this, some might wonder whether job-holders' disinclination to assist was less a function of their assessment of job-seekers' work and personal reputations than a reflection of their concern that, because of racial stereotyping about soft skills, employers would tend to assess black referrals negatively, creating a less rewarding job referral process for black job-holders. This is not an unreasonable proposition. Indeed, in *Race and the Invisible Hand* (2003), Deirdre Royster intimates that some of her blue-collar workers were disinclined to influence the job-matching process because they perceived that, because of employer discrimination, their attempts to influence the hire of black applicants would only reduce the likelihood that these applicants would be hired.[13] However, while Royster's suggestion may be accurate among the blue-collar workers she studied, I found no evidence in my data to support the contention that low-income job-holders *consciously* chose not to influence the hiring process because they believed that employer discrimination would cause their attempts to influence the job-matching process to have a negative effect on their referrals' chances of getting a job. Nor did they indicate that employers' negative stereotyping of blacks negatively affected their willingness to assist their job-seeking relations. Insofar as job-holders' disinclination is a product of employers' negative stereotyping and discrimination, I suspect that this effect is an indirect and unconscious one. To the extent that employers discriminate against blacks under the guise of soft skills discourses, justifying personnel decisions in ways that disadvantage black workers by pointing to workers' stock (or lack) of this special skill set, I contend that it is through their own experiences with employers that job-holders learn to invest in soft skills themselves and assess others based on these criteria. In contrast to what Royster found, the overwhelming majority of my respondents seemed convinced that information *and* influence greatly improved job-seekers' chances of finding work, a perception borne out by prior research. They also firmly located their unwillingness to assist their job-seeking relations in the latter's problematic reputations and the effect that such a reputation might have on the firm's health and well-being as well as on their own reputation with the employer.

Local Labor Market Conditions

If only a little, local labor market conditions mattered as well. The first two years of data collection coincided with the tail end of the period of economic expansion. In 1999 and 2000, the average monthly unemployment rates in Michigan were 3.9 and 3.7 percent, respectively. By 2001 the period of great prosperity had clearly ended. That year Michigan's average monthly unemployment rate had risen to 5.2 percent and increased again in 2002 to 6.2 percent.[14]

It is possible that job-holders' decisions to assist were affected by these changes in the economic cycle. To address this question, I selected out of my sample those who resided in high-poverty neighborhoods, because job-holders from low-poverty neighborhoods were not interviewed until after the downturn in the economy, and so there was no variation there to examine. When I compare orientation to providing job-finding assistance and distrust toward job-seeking relations, I find that both changed somewhat in line with cyclical changes in the economy. Seventy-one percent of job-holders from high-poverty neighborhoods interviewed between 1999 and 2000 were reluctant to provide job-finding assistance. Among those interviewed in 2001–2002, 80 percent were disinclined to assist. A higher percentage of respondents interviewed during the economic downturn also expressed distrust (again, 80 percent versus 92 percent). A good economy offering lots of jobs for less-skilled workers does appear to loosen job-holders' concerns enough to distrust less and assist more. However, with the economic downturn a greater percentage of job-holders were concerned about the risk that job-seekers posed, a concern that led to higher rates of distrust and reluctance to assist.

There is ample research considering the effect of labor market conditions on personal contact use. While some argue that word-of-mouth increases during recession because employers do not have to use any other method to find qualified candidates (Jenkins et al. 1983; Licht 1992; Wial 1991; Wood 1985), others argue the opposite, finding that tight labor markets are associated with greater word-of-mouth recruitment (Fevre 1989). It may very well be the case that employers rely more on word-of-mouth recruitment during economic downturns, but their criteria for recruitment undoubtedly become more stringent as their ability to hire workers declines and the number of available applicants grows. And employers' greater stringency no doubt affects job-holders' own screening process as they determine whom they might assist. It is this relationship between employers' hiring practices and job-holders' response to it that is likely to explain why job-holders' distrust and disinclination to assist grow during economic decline.

Social Closure

Whether or not job-holders are willing to assist might depend not just on how many workers they know and what types of jobs these workers have held. It might also depend on the structure of the networks in which job-holders are embedded. Drawing from James Coleman (1988, 1990), we can say that actors are not likely to cooperate unless embedded in networks characterized by social closure. Typically found in smaller communities, social closure describes network relations that are dense, overlapping, and close-knit. According to Coleman, closed communities facilitate cooperation by promoting trustworthiness— what he calls trustworthiness in structures. Such a network structure allows for the emergence of effective social norms and sanctions that regulate behavior. Because ties are dense, overlapping, and close, everyone is either directly or indirectly connected to all others through short chains. The information channels that these connections create pass news and gossip throughout the network. As a result, there is little that anyone can do without having others in the network discover it. This monitoring capacity is key if sanctions are to be imposed for noncompliance and members are to be kept in line. While not necessarily trust in others in the encapsulated-interest sense of the term (Cook and Hardin 2001; Hardin 2002), embeddedness in networks characterized by social closure provides actors with community-backed assurances that potential exchange partners will honor obligations or face appropriate sanctions, such as shunning or social exclusion. These assurances reduce the risks associated with reciprocal exchanges, and they pave the way for extensive and long-term obligations, which provide fertile ground for social capital activation (Granovetter 1985).[15]

Unfortunately, these data do not allow for such a rigorous examination. Drawing from prior research, however, it is possible to distinguish, in at least two ways, embeddedness in closed networks from embeddedness in structures in which connections are far more loose and free-floating. First, within closed structures information flows through an intricate communication network in the form of "gossip, slander, invective, and confidentiality." Within more free-floating networks, information flow is decidedly less elaborate. Individuals know of their potential exchange partners' habits and behaviors in large part because they see these themselves or their partners inform them in one-on-one conversations. A trustor is much less likely to have other sources to confirm or deny a trustee's presentation of self and thus is less likely to have the information needed to make well-informed decisions regarding who to trust and assist.

Interestingly, there was very little variation in how job-holders received information concerning their job-seeking ties' reputations. The overwhelming majority based their decisions on information they had gleaned in two ways. They either knew of a job-seeker's past behaviors and actions because they had observed these firsthand or, when they had little information to go on, they would engage a job-seeker in a lengthy conversation in order to gather bits of information they believed would provide a more accurate picture of that person's character. In other words, through one-on-one encounters, job-holders sought to reduce information asymmetries. In these data, information about the job-seeker's reputation rarely filtered through an intricate communication system. When queried about how they knew what they did or how they would go about finding the information they needed, just one other respondent replied in the way that Yvonne O'Neill did. Yvonne explained that her information was "based on knowing them personally. Or, uh, asking about them, like, 'Does she go to work? What does she do? What did she do all day? What did she do with her time?'" In other words, she would refer to others in her network for information about a job-seeker's past actions and behaviors if she lacked firsthand knowledge.

This was not the case, however, for the overwhelming majority of job-holders. Instead, the majority most often limited their assistance to close friends and family members because these were the people about whom they had firsthand knowledge upon which to make reasonable assessments of trustworthiness. Recall Vincent Roberts's declaration, "I would say family members, you know, because I know them better. Be around them. You know, it's more easier, okay." Job contacts most preferred to assist close relations because closeness provided access to firsthand knowledge about these job-seekers' past actions and behaviors outside the context of the relationship, thus reducing information asymmetries that made it difficult to ascertain the level of risk they were exposing themselves to by providing assistance.

When job-holders did not have firsthand knowledge of a job-seeking tie's reputation, they would seek out the information they needed to determine trustworthiness—and thus whether to assist—not by contacting interconnected and trusted friends, family members, and acquaintances but by engaging the job-seeker in a lengthy conversation. Typical were comments such as, "Ask the person," and, "I just asked a lot of questions [of the job-seeker]." By engaging job-seekers in lengthy conversations that resembled in many ways a job interview, job-holders believed that they could ascertain job-seekers' trustworthiness and thus accurately calculate the risk they might incur if they were to assist.

This is how Annette Charles approached this dilemma. At the time of her interview, Annette was twenty-eight years old, unmarried, without children, and working part-time doing clerical work at a community college. Not only was Annette concerned about the effect that a bad referral might have on her reputation, but she was also concerned about whether or not she would enjoy having the job-seeker on the job with her. For both of these reasons, she felt that it was important to ascertain as much about job-seekers' reputations as possible, and she did so by engaging them in conversations that elicited bits of information that would provide her with a more accurate picture of their character and intentions. She explained, "I'll get to talking to them, and if they have a good, you know, standing, then, you know, I'll go up to somebody and say, 'You know, for this position, I know somebody who can do this.'"

Similarly, Sally Lowe, a twenty-four-year-old high school dropout and single mother of a toddler, was very concerned about job-seekers' reputations, especially after having been burned by a previous referral, the sister of her son's father. After this experience, she reported, "I'm still going to help people, [but] I'll get into your background a little more and all that." When asked how she planned to delve more into job-seekers' backgrounds, she did not refer to others in her network as a primary source of information. Instead, she said, she would just talk, openly talk to them, and open the conversation, you know. Talk about myself, and hey, if you got something similar to it, open your mouth and let me know. Let me know what's going on with you, because I'd rather know if you're my friend, or you're my buddy, I'd rather know how your life was and how your life is now, than to be trying to go and guess, you know. Because, a friend, if you're my friend and I'm trying to be your friend, I need to know as much as I can about you because we have this friendship. And, if something goes wrong, I want to be able, if you don't have anybody else, to come and say, "Yeah, you know, this is my friend. I'm here to help her. I'm here to give her the strength she needs, you know." I would rather you open up to me than for me to have to wait and see and find out later on that you're just not right.

Here again one is struck by the lack of reference to a network of ties that could provide Sally with the information she requires in order to make determinations about who to assist. Instead, she makes assessments based on one-on-one conversations with potential exchange partners, recognizing that these conversations, while potentially illuminating, are also potentially rife with disingenuousness and exploitation. Indeed, this is why one seeks the counsel of others so as to gain additional information that either confirms or disproves characterizations that people make of themselves. However, like Sally, job-holders in this position rarely mentioned the counsel they received from others in their network.

What this pattern indicates is that, to a great extent, job-holders are largely determining the trustworthiness of others in isolation and outside of the context of a vibrant or intricate information network. What rarely showed up in these data were references to knowing or determining others' reputations by chatting, gossiping, or sharing information with others in their network or community. Instead, communication most often occurred between job-seeker and job-holder. The sheer absence of intricate communication networks was most salient, indicating that people relied relatively little on others to monitor the behavior of those with whom they had dealings. This pattern is not indicative of embeddedness in closed networks, as there was little evidence of a flow of information from dense, overlapping, or close-knit relations.

Moreover, within closed structures *sanctions* for noncompliance occur on the collective level, including social exclusion from all things social and economic. Outside of closed networks, sanctions take place within the dyad, in the form of withdrawal from future exchanges or from the relationship. Although examinations of information flows and sanctioning methods may not be the ideal way of determining whether respondents are embedded in networks characterized by social closure, they do provide us with some sense, albeit incomplete, of the role that social closure plays in facilitating social capital activation vis-à-vis other factors deemed important for the same.

Without an intricate communication network, community- or network-backed sanctions were unlikely, and this is what the data suggest as well. Although these data provide overwhelming evidence that sanctioning occurred within the dyad, there was absolutely no indication that sanctioning was backed by the collective, be that the network of relations or the community of relations. When job-seekers failed to fulfill their obligations, as happened frequently, job-holders most often responded by withdrawing from future exchanges of that type, refusing to provide job-finding assistance to job-seekers who had forsaken them and, as with Jackie York and Terrance Blackburn, eventually refusing to assist anyone at all. As evidence, one-fourth of job-holders reported having been burned by previous referrals when they, for instance, failed to show after a few days, acted boorishly on the job, or stole from the employer. All but one of these job-holders—Laura Odom—managed their referrals' transgressions by pledging not to assist these particular individuals again with job information and influence. However, most maintained relations on some terms, even if more guarded than before—no job-holders reported ending relationships for their relations' misdeeds. For instance, Gary Hanson shared that, after his referral "brought the street to the job," he would no longer consider working with him but they were still good friends.

This form of sanctioning is consistent with what occurs within a dyad, not in a community in which norms of cooperativeness prevail. If sanctioning had occurred in the latter context, we would expect job-holders to discuss how the job-seeker had been excluded from social functions and economic opportunities by the network or the community. No one shared this type of information. There appeared to be no sanctions backed by the community that the debtor had to bear. Only the less severe sanction of withdrawal from the relationship with the job-holder was enforced. Here again, informal structures supporting trustworthiness appear weak, if not absent.

In summary, these data indicate that in the context of job-finding cooperation among the black poor is not a function of social closure. That there was so little variation in how job-holders learned of their job-seeking ties' reputations and in how they appeared to sanction those who failed to behave as expected—both indications of the extent to which job-holders were embedded in closed networks—strongly suggests that this was not a defining factor in whether job-holders would provide assistance.

Conclusion

Job-holders represent a major conduit of employment information and influence in the United States: they match roughly half of all job-seekers to employers. Conventional wisdom now has it that the black poor are less efficacious in this regard because job-seekers, suffering from social isolation, have very limited access to job-holders of social worth (Wacquant and Wilson 1989; Wilson 1987). The findings presented here suggest, however, that access, at best, explains only one part of the puzzle. Instead, the social capital deficiencies apparent among the black poor seem to have as much if not more to do with job-holders' willingness to assist than with access. In other words, even when information is available and job-holders can influence hires, they often choose not to do so. That job-holders expressed such great reluctance to provide the type of job-finding assistance that facilitates employment adds a layer of understanding to this complex and persistent problem.

When job-holders did assist, their assistance was contingent on a number of key factors: the job-seeker's reputation, the job-holder's reputation and status, the strength of the relationship between the job-holder and the job-seeker, and the job-holder's structural embeddedness. Job-holders were displeased by job-seekers who transitioned in and out of jobs frequently, who were habitually absent or tardy, or who had poor work attitudes. They were also concerned about whether their job-seeking ties would "bring the street to the job," a possibility that included, among other behaviors, showing the effects of alcohol and drug abuse, acting raucously and boisterously, stealing, and intimidating authority figures and coworkers. As a result, job-holders overwhelmingly made determinations about whether to assist based on their job-seeking relations' reputations, both at work and at home, since these provided them with some indication of how the job-seeker might behave on the job. Their decisions were based at least in part on their assessments of others' trustworthiness.

Job-holders paid this much attention to the reputations of their job-seeking ties because of the potential damage that job-seekers might do to their own reputations. Indeed, it was the interaction between the two—job-holders' and job-seekers' reputations—that seemed to matter most in their determinations. It was noteworthy that job-holders with a stellar reputation on the job, like Wilson Smith, were generally open to providing job-finding assistance, while those who had tarnished their reputation with their employer, like Terrance Blackburn, were patently against providing assistance. What was striking, however, were the narratives provided by job-holders like Jackie York and Jeremy Jessup. Both began providing referrals when they were in good standing with their employers, and because they were held in high regard initially, they were willing to influence a few questionable hires. As these hires failed to work out, both of their reputations became tarnished, and they became increasingly reluctant to recommend any of their friends for jobs, deeming the process inherently risky. Jackie eventually lost the confidence of her employer, and Jeremy lost his job. As a result of potential outcomes like these, both job-seekers' and job-holders' reputations dominated job-holders' concerns about whether to assist.

There was one contingency, however, to reputational concerns. Even for job-seekers of ill repute, job-holders could be mobilized if their own levels of social and economic stability were very low and they felt they had nothing to lose. Those who perceived their situation to be dire, like Laura Odoms, were willing to provide assistance to almost anyone who came along, regardless of reputation, hoping that those assisted would quickly become sources of social and material support in turn. For instance, even though Laura's close friend had a bad reputation as a worker, she was also a major source of in-kind assistance to Laura, who was not willing to forsake her friend with regard to job information and influence because their friendship and the resources she gained as a result of it were more valuable to her than her low-wage, dead-end job. Job-holders who were less overwhelmed by their circumstances because they had greater personal, social, or material sources to draw upon were less likely to come to the aid of others without regard to reputation.

Whether or not job-holders could be mobilized for job-finding assistance was also affected by their history of prior attempts to assist. Specifically, job-holders whose attempts to intercede had been met with job-seekers' disengagement were far less open to providing assistance than those whose history of assistance included successful matches of motivated job-seekers. After a time, the former became like discouraged workers—they eventually stopped trying to assist, perceiving the activity to be a waste of time because, in their judgment, job-seekers were too unmotivated to take advantage of the information they had to offer or the influence they could wield. In these cases, a psychology of distrust prevailed.

The structural context mattered as well. Job-holders' access to social capital and neighborhood poverty status interacted to affect their willingness to assist. Among the employed of low-poverty neighborhoods, willingness to assist was associated with greater access to social capital. However, among the employed of high-poverty neighborhoods, reluctance to assist was associated with greater access to social capital—this relationship is unfortunate, even if understandable, given that these job-holders reside in neighborhoods where access to social capital among the unemployed appears inferior. Furthermore, job-holders are making decisions in a labor market context in which soft skills are growing in significance to employers and cyclical changes in the economy affect employers' hiring practices.

Finally, findings from recent research on the hiring process appear to call into question the notion that the black poor might be reluctant to provide assistance to their job-seeking relations. Specifically, using a unique dataset of one racially diverse job site, Fernandez and Fernandez-Mateo (2006) investigated racial and ethnic differences in referring behavior and found that, compared to white employees, black employees were more likely to produce referrals. Asians and Hispanics, however, were the employees most likely to produce referrals. Given this, Fernandez and Fernandez-Mateo conclude (2006, 66), "in contrast with expectations of certain theories, which suggest that minorities might be reluctant to engage in networking activities, we found that African Americans, Asians, and Hispanics are significantly more likely to produce referrals than are whites."

Fernandez and Fernandez-Mateo's work is compelling and insightful, but their evidence does not contradict the findings reported here and in related work on this topic (Smith 2005), primarily because they investigated the referral and screening processes in a context where the employer did not prefer referrals to any other method of applicant recruitment. As evidence, they did not offer any incentives to employees for helping to make successful matches; presumably, they also did not sanction employees who made bad matches.[16] This is crucial. In a context where there are no costs (or pecuniary benefits) to making referrals, employees can produce referrals without risk of ruining their own reputation or making more tenuous their own position. In the very few cases in my data where job-holders worked at firms that did not favor referrals over nonreferrals, job-holders were more than willing to make referrals—and to do so frequently—primarily because they were not held responsible for inviting a bad candidate to apply or for negative outcomes. At these firms, after producing a referral, a job-holder's work was done. If the job-seeker failed to make it through any stage of the hiring process, or if that person subsequently left the job, the referrer was not implicated and indeed could continue to produce referrals with impunity. However, the overwhelming majority of job-holders worked in environments where job referrals were prized by employers as a primary source of recruitment; in this context, a decision to assist could not be made without also taking into consideration both the costs and benefits of making the referral. In the next chapter, I explore the impact that job-holders' reluctance has on the search methods employed by job-seekers.

Chapter 4

The Job-Seeker: Embracing Individualism Defensively

Job-holders' calls for personal responsibility and self-sufficiency were not without consequence. Instead, they had a profound effect on the job search strategies deployed by job-seekers.[1] Consider the words of Robert Randolph, a thirty-two-year-old unemployed father of three. When asked how important it was to use friends and relatives to find out about jobs, Robert responded:

> It's very important. I mean, 'cause if you use all the options that you have, it's always good to go to somebody you know [and say,] "Well, you know, what's going on? You know anything that's open?" You know. But sometimes you have to be careful who you call friend and associate. You know what I'm saying? 'Cause a lot of people will [say,], "*We ain't got nottin', la la la.*" It's, you know, strange. Like I say, you know, I usually find [jobs] myself.

Elizabeth Macon expressed a similar concern. When asked if there were any negative aspects of helping people to find work, the twenty-three-year-old high school graduate replied, "It's a lot of people that make it negative. They keep it to their selves. It's ridiculous. You don't supposed to do that. I feel that if you know something, you know, share it." Not surprisingly, Elizabeth maintained that she had never sought job-finding assistance from anyone she knew. Judith Wesley maintained the same, and the following explains why. When asked how important it was to use friends, relatives, and acquaintances to find out about job opportunities and to get jobs, the twenty-four-year-old food service worker hesitated and then replied:

> You got some people who can probably get you in and some people who probably can't get you in. So, the ones who can get you in, it's more easier to get in that way, but you're representing that person who got you in, so you got to be on good behavior because they can get fired and you're giving that person a bad name, and that person can't get nobody in no more because you messed up his reputation on the job. It's not that

important to use friends, but if you try to do it on your own instead of
using somebody else to get you in, it's better if you can get in on your
own, just your name and don't put that person's name as your reference
or nothing.

Robert, Elizabeth, and Judith were not alone. As shown in table 4.1,
although nine out of ten job-seekers had mobilized friends and relatives
for help in finding work at some point in the past, and although more
than half had found their current or most recent job through a personal
contact, a significant minority of job-seekers were disinclined to use personal contacts. For instance, one-quarter (26 percent) of all job-seekers
expressed great reluctance about relying on friends or relatives for help
finding work. Also, when job-seekers were asked what advice they
would give young people entering the labor market about how to find
jobs—an open-ended question for which they could provide any response—just one-third recommended that young job-seekers use personal contacts at all. Roughly four in ten pointed to institutional sources,
such as temporary employment agencies, welfare-to-work transition
programs, and the like. Four in ten also advised walk-ins as a viable
strategy of job search, but the majority (three-quarters) strongly encouraged new entrants to check local newspapers daily and to surf Internet
job banks for job postings—the last recommendation something of a
paradox given that no job-seeker who searched and submitted a résumé
via the Internet ever found employment this way. Few employers even
acknowledged receipt of these applications.[2] What is most telling here,
however, is that personal contact use was suggested least often.[3] Finally,
when asked what search strategies they were employing to find work,
slightly more than one in four *unemployed* job-seekers said that they
were actively seeking job-finding assistance from friends and relatives.
Four in ten sought assistance from formal institutions that provided
links to employers, six in ten checked the want ads and other media
sources, and more than two-thirds were walk-ins.[4] Clearly these figures
are not mutually exclusive. On average, unemployed job-seekers listed
two search strategies.[5] Among those using just one job search strategy,
half were walk-ins, one-quarter sought assistance from formal institutions, and another one-quarter sought information from media sources.
No unemployed job-seeker relied solely on personal contacts to find work.
   This chapter is devoted to understanding job-seekers' ambivalence
toward personal contact use in a labor market context where employers
rely heavily on informal job referral networks for hiring (Holzer 1996)
by comparing the job-finding experiences of willing and reluctant personal contact users. *Willing personal contact users* were job-seekers for
whom assistance from personal contacts was almost always welcome.
They represented 74 percent of all respondents and were distinguished

Table 4.1   Views of and Engagement with Personal Contact Use as a Job
Search Strategy

Views/Personal Contact Use	
Personal contacts used for finding work in the past	89%
Found current or most recent job through personal contact	50
Job search strategies that respondents would recommend to young job-seekers	
Personal contacts	33
Employment agencies	37
Walk-in	37
Local newspapers or Internet	77
Job search strategies of unemployed job-seekers (N = 37)	
Personal contacts	27
Employment agencies	38
Local newspapers or Internet	60
Walk-in	68
Reluctant to use personal contacts to find work	26

Source: Author's compilation.

by comments like the following: "I always use people that I know, you know, if they have a way to get in or whatever. They're the first ones I go to actually." And "[Using friends, relatives, and acquaintances is] very important, because they usually have the inside scoop. So, yeah, I use all the resources I can." These comments contrast sharply with those of *reluctant personal contact users*, the 26 percent of job-seekers who were against relying on friends and family members for help finding work. These job-seekers made comments such as, "I try not to use people to get a job mostly," and, "I mean, if you can network like that you can get a plug in that way. That's fine, but I wouldn't necessarily say that that would be my way of getting a job, you know. Because I like doing things on my own." Or, "I'm usually out on my own doing my own thing, trying to find my own line of work. I'm not saying they input won't help, but I'm usually on my own."

When queried about their reluctance, two concerns emerged as central. As with job-holders, both concerns implicated reputation and trust, or the lack thereof. First, reluctant job-seekers expressed concern that they would be unable to fulfill the obligations associated with receiving job information, but they were especially concerned about influence. Specifically, they were concerned that their behavior on the job would almost certainly have a negative effect on the status and reputation of their job-holding relations and that in the end such an outcome would highlight the extent and nature of their own untrustworthiness and incompetence. In a similar vein, in *Tally's Corner* (1967), Elliot Liebow described how the low-income black men he observed had so little faith in their skills as working men, believing themselves to be ignorant and incompetent, that they often either refused to seek better job opportunities for which they were qualified or declined to accept such offers when they did arise. In essence, like Liebow's subjects, some of my reluctant personal contact users held such a deep distrust of themselves that it affected their willingness to seek assistance or accept it when offered.

Second, reluctant personal contact users expressed great concern that their requests for assistance would be met with rejection and that such rejection would again call into question their trustworthiness and competence. In this sense, job-seekers sensed their job-holding relations' deep distrust of them, and this perception had led to a disinclination to seek assistance from them. Some reluctant job-seekers feared both. Taken together, two-thirds of reluctant personal contact users described one instance after another in which their ability to meet obligations had been called into question or their requests for assistance had been met with scorn. Put simply, they feared losing face.[6] Among willing personal contact users, just 22 percent raised such concerns.

These were not the only concerns that reluctant contact users shared. One job-seeker located her disinclination to use personal contacts in the heavy competition for decent jobs, which, she reasoned, would increase the costs associated with assistance.[7] Four job-seekers indicated that personal contacts were simply less effective than other methods of job search.[8] And although we generally assume that people prefer to work with friends and relatives, one job-seeker also explained his disinclination to seek or accept assistance in terms of his unwillingness to work with his relations, stating, "Usually I don't get off on that, 'cause it's a bad mix to work with your friends generally. Because, you know, work pressure and things of that nature usually brings out the worst in us, you know." Finally, one job-seeker indicated that she preferred not to use personal contacts to find work because she felt that the cost of the exchange was too high, especially when the terms of the exchange had not been clearly articulated beforehand.[9]

Each of these four sets of concerns implied distrust and caused job-seekers to avoid assistance from friends, relatives, and acquaintances. Reluctant personal contact users primarily avoided using personal contacts, however, because they feared falling short of expectations or having their requests for assistance met with scorn. Thus, when they declared, "I like doing things on my own," they were showcasing their *defensive individualism*. Their declarations of autonomy and self-sufficiency and their concomitant avoidance of personal contact use emerged *only after* they perceived that help would not be forthcoming and that, in some cases, it should not have been forthcoming, less because their ties were unable to assist them than because their ties would (and in some cases should) have been unwilling to do so. By embracing individualism—avoiding informal assistance from friends and relatives and pursuing self-reliant, though relatively unsuccessful, job search strategies—not only did they attempt to protect the reputations of their friends and relatives and shield their own from further ridicule and disparagement, but they also sought to repair their reputation by demonstrating evidence, through their self-reliant approach, of their autonomous, self-sufficient, and driven nature. This is an almost tragic and ironic turn, since such performances of autonomy and self-sufficiency only served to disadvantage reluctant personal contact users further in a low-wage labor market where employers rely heavily on job referral networks for applicant recruitment and screening.

By comparing the job-finding experiences of the reluctant personal contact users to those of the willing, however, I not only reveal the sources of the former's reluctance but also identify important factors that shape whether and to what extent job-seekers, even those who are hesitant, will mobilize their social resources to find work. Job-seekers' willingness to seek or accept assistance was contingent on three key factors. First, based on their own reputation, they assessed their ability to fulfill obligations toward job-holders who were willing and able to assist. To the extent that they assessed themselves as risky prospects, they were unwilling to mobilize their social resources on their own behalf. Second, they considered the history of responses to their requests for assistance. If they perceived themselves to have been rebuffed in the past, especially by those close to them, job-seekers were generally disinclined to reach out or accept help. Third, the structural context within which job-seekers made decisions mattered. Specifically, their willingness to seek or accept assistance was contingent on gender: men were far more likely than women to express great reluctance to seek assistance or accept help when offered. Reluctance to use personal contacts was also associated with access to social capital, neighborhood poverty status, and local labor market conditions. In what follows, I elaborate on the significance of each of these three factors.

Reputations on the Job and Off

As shown in the preceding chapter, it was not unusual for matches made by job-holders to end badly and have a negative effect on their standing on the job. Some job-seekers were very sensitive to this issue and so were reluctant to use personal contacts to find work. In large part, they were reluctant because they had so little trust in their own ability to carry out an often-explicit component of the exchange to avoid trouble that would embarrass or hurt their job-holding contact. Instead, they considered themselves magnets for the very situations they wanted and tried so desperately to steer clear of. And their concerns were not unwarranted. Their reputations had been so sullied by a series of personal and labor market failures and disappointments that their sense of personal efficacy in both realms had been profoundly diminished, assuming it had developed at all.[10] Whereas 15 percent of willing personal contact users explained that past delinquency, such as drug or alcohol abuse and felony convictions, made finding work difficult for them, 26 percent of reluctant personal contact users provided this explanation. Also, reluctant contact users were far more likely to have been *fired* from their last job than were willing contact users. Whereas 20 percent of willing personal contact users reported that they had been fired from their last job, 42 percent of reluctant contact users did. Among those who had used a friend or relative to find their last job, 30 percent of the willing had been fired, compared to 57 percent of the reluctant. Although none of the willing shared doubts about their ability to fulfill their obligations, one-quarter of the reluctant (six) expressed concern about their ability to fulfill obligations toward their personal contacts, pointing to their own sullied personal and work reputations to explain (see table 4.2). Not surprisingly then, reluctant contact users were less likely to feel that their job-holding ties would *or should* put their names and reputations on the line for them, and so they would not ask. Given the pervasive distrust and noncooperation reported in the previous chapter, even if these job-seekers had been willing to accept assistance, their reputations were so problematic that it is

Table 4.2   Orientation Toward Personal Contact Use, by Reputational Concerns

	Total	Willing Personal Contact Users	Reluctant Personal Contact Users
Concerned about ability to fulfill obligations	6	0%	25%
Past delinquency made finding work difficult	18	15	26
Fired from last job	26	20	42
Fired from job a relation assisted with	34	30	57

Source: Author's compilation.

not clear that job-holders would even offer assistance. Jeremy Jessup is a prime example.

Troubled Pasts, Hopeless Futures

Jeremy was forty-two years old. Although unemployed when interviewed, he survived by making between $7.50 and $8.00 an hour working short stints through temporary employment agencies. Jeremy began working when he was fourteen years old, performing janitorial tasks at a local junior high school. After graduating, he immediately went to work at an auto plant making $18 per hour. He held this job for almost ten years until his longtime abuse of the plant's medical leave policy backfired and he was fired from his job.

During his tenure at the plant, Jeremy had developed carpal tunnel syndrome, which required four surgeries to resolve. Overcome by a great love of sport and by his injudiciousness, Jeremy used his disability to apply for medical leave every summer for several years so that he could play league softball. After each season's completion, he would return to work. Because the plant's fairly generous medical leave policy allowed him to take home 95 percent of his pay, he had almost no financial disincentive to stop taking advantage of that policy, and he ended up taking off several summers. By so brazenly playing the system, however, he alienated not only his employer but also the union, which refused to represent him after he was fired. He was twenty-nine years old and, for all intents and purposes, had gambled away his only chance at economic stability. Thirteen years later, he was still mourning the loss of this job, viewing it as a major and negative turning point in his life.

Having held various jobs since then, Jeremy explained his difficulty finding and keeping steady work in terms of bad luck, racial discrimination, nepotism, and, burdened by a drug addiction, his own unreliability. The last factor was of greatest relevance to him. Indeed, when asked what type of person had the best chance of getting a good job, Jeremy did not list those positioned in the right place at the right time. Nor did he discuss white privilege or the benefits of having great connections. Instead, he explained that those who get good jobs are "the people that are dependable people. Like they can count on you to be there every day when you supposed to be there. They don't have to worry about you. [You'll] do a good job when you're there, and you're willing to help others." For this reason, he believed that his sister had done well for herself, having developed a stellar record of service driving a city bus for over twenty years. About her, he said, "They know when she's supposed to be there, she will be there, you know. And I guess [she] could be my role model there, because I look up to her for that, and I always say I wish I could change my life, get another chance somewhere else, and be just like her, you know. Be reliable." For Jeremy, reliability had become the highest of virtues. It was what he desired most but had the greatest difficulty achieving.

By the time I met Jeremy, he had so little confidence in his own capacity for reliability that he would not allow others to be held responsible for his actions. Thus, when asked about the importance of using friends, relatives, and acquaintances while looking for work, Jeremy explained that while he thought personal contacts were helpful, he preferred to find employment on his own, because if he failed—indeed, when he failed—his actions would not reflect badly on those who had assisted him. He reasoned, "I think I should do it myself. Say you get me a good job, then I blow it. It makes you look bad. So if I get it myself, then I make myself look bad and not you, so." By finding work himself, Jeremy preserved his relationships so that he might be able to draw support or assistance in the future in contexts where he might be better able to fulfill his obligations.

This was the case as well for Anthony Redmond, whom I introduced in chapter 1. Recall that Anthony was a thirty-six-year-old black man, a high school dropout, and a convicted felon. Given these individual characteristics, one could not understate his low probability of gaining employment. In the search for employment, there are few, if any, attributes that cripple job-seekers' chances more. Indeed, when I met Anthony, he had been without steady work for just short of one year. Still, that day he was hopeful, almost upbeat. Only moments before our meeting he had interviewed with TJ Maxx and UPS at the center's weekly jobs fair. Both employers had promised to call him within days with their hiring decision, and both expressed optimism about his chances. This was the closest that Anthony had come in months to finding employment. However, it was not to be. His race, criminal record, and lack of education probably remained barriers, because neither employer called.

By the age of twenty-one, Anthony had been convicted of breaking and entering and felonious assault; he described the lawbreaking that led to his incarceration as "stupid kid stuff." With time, his circumstances only worsened. Although he was sentenced to serve five years, Anthony's prison term was lengthened to fourteen years after he got into a serious altercation with two associates from his neighborhood who were also incarcerated. According to Anthony, these inmates decided to settle their long-standing antagonism by stabbing him. Unfortunately for them, Anthony got the upper hand and stabbed them instead, an act for which he received an extended sentence almost ten years longer than the original.

After his release from prison, Anthony initiated a new start, and for a short while he succeeded. With the help of a friend, he eventually landed a job as a porter, cleaning and test-driving cars for a dealership, an ironic position given that one of his earlier convictions was for grand theft auto. Once settled in his new job, for which he was paid $320 a week, he bought himself a mobile home and a car and seemed well on his way to achieving the American dream—or so he thought. Soon after making these major purchases, Anthony was fired. He had been employed no more than seven months when he lost consciousness behind the wheel of a company car, crashed it, and totaled his future. Anthony explained that he had been working fifty-two hours per week on average but was eating no more than one meal a day. Doing so, he reasoned, took its toll. Not only did he lose his job, but his driver's license was revoked as well. Almost immediately after, he exclaimed, "I lost my home, I lost my car, I lost everything."

Anthony had not worked steadily since, even though he said he was willing to accept almost any job and had gone to great lengths to find work.[11] In part, he explained his difficulty getting a job in terms of his two strikes. As a black felon, he believed that few employers would entertain the idea of hiring him.[12] And although he expressed a great deal of frustration regarding employers' refusal to give him another opportunity to prove his worth, much of his anger about the state of his life was self-directed. It was clear that no one frustrated Anthony more than he frustrated himself. In his mind, he was his own greatest obstacle and, in some ways, deserved to be cast aside; the distrust he had inspired in others had largely been warranted. After all, he had little, if any, trust in himself. Thus, when asked about the importance of using friends, relatives, and acquaintances to find out about job opportunities, Anthony explained that while they were important to the process, he preferred not to rely on this essential source of job-finding. He explained, "You ain't got to worry about me using your name to get in the door. Just give me an application; just turn it in for me. That's all I ask you." When I asked why, Anthony, like Jeremy, replied, "Because, you know, say if I do get a job and mess up on the job, I won't drag you down with me. So I prefer not to use your name. 'You got any friends? [mimicking what an employer might say]' No. I heard about it on the website, or, you know, Work First." Probing further, I asked whether Anthony had ever been in a position in which he had botched a job that a personal contact had found for him. When he explained that he had not, I pressed further still, asking why he assessed himself as such a high risk. To that he answered, "Because things just happen. I'm like bad slip rock. I don't have no luck. None. That's a fact. None." As happened with Jeremy, Anthony had come to believe that he had little power to determine the course that his life would take. His life experiences had almost completely crushed his sense of self-efficacy and weakened his spirit. In that psychological state, he deemed it irresponsible to subject anyone else to his unpredictability and untrustworthiness. He alone owned the task of finding a job—a very lonely pursuit for someone with so many individual and structural barriers to overcome and so few tools with which to do so.[13]

And just as he perceived himself as untrustworthy, so too did he perceive his friends. Consequently, not only was he opposed to receiving job-finding assistance from friends and relatives, except for receiving information about job openings, he was also reluctant to assist friends in their quest for work. He explained, "I'll use the same method [on others that I use] on myself. I used to tell them, 'I get you a application, but don't use me at all. If you mess up a job, it won't fall back on me either.'" When I asked why he and his friends did not provide more proactive assistance, he provided the following justification:

> See, my friends . . . I can't speak for no other people friends, but my friends, they not like that. See, we roughnecks. You see, you all call us thugs, and, you know, ghetto. We just call ourselves roughnecks, because we not thugs. We used to be like that. We just, just different from most people. We see somebody that we know, if they need some help, we give some support, help them out, and we'll let him know or her know—don't use my name. Because you know how you is. You know, your temper or your attitude.

This is a telling comment for a number of reasons. Anthony clearly perceived himself and his friends as outcasts—members of a group stigmatized by their delinquent past but also distinguished, at least among themselves, by their attempts at redemption. Anthony revealed to me the promise he had made to avoid at all costs the illegal activities that eventually led to his incarceration, a promise he found increasingly difficult to honor as months of unemployment approached a year. The redemptive process itself was pursued largely in isolation, because although members of his group provided some assistance and support, the dominant discourse they deployed was one of self-sufficiency. In other words, even among Anthony's "roughneck" friends, the stigma of thuggery and untrustworthiness prevailed, and so job-seekers could not expect that others would be willing to go to bat for them. This, coupled with their unwillingness to seek aid for themselves from personal contacts, forced job-seekers of Anthony's ilk into self-sufficiency. They were pulled into self-reliance by their distrust of themselves and their desire to protect or salvage reputations, theirs and others, and they were pushed into the same by their distrusting peers who, as Anthony indicated (and I illustrated in the previous chapter), were too reluctant to assist for fear of the negative consequences. This consistency between their expectations of themselves and the expectations of their job-holding relations produced an exaggerated independence, a defensive individualism that informed their job search behaviors.

Unlike Jeremy and Anthony, who were concerned with both protecting job-holders' reputations and rehabilitating their own, John Richards's desire to forgo personal contact use was mostly concerned with protecting his own reputation. John was a thirty-six-year-old high school graduate who, although unemployed for two months, helped to support his family by taking odd jobs. Like Anthony, John was probably fated to a lifetime of coping with joblessness after a felony arrest and conviction. According to John, when the sister of a good friend was raped by another neighborhood resident, the police refused to take legal action. Taking matters into their own hands, John, his friend, and three others beat the alleged rapist severely, sending him to the hospital. For this assault, John served five and a half years. Because of his felony conviction, he was convinced that most employers would not consider him, even for jobs unrelated to his crime. And so, while he would not apologize for the assault ("whupping his butt, I still think it's worth it"), he did regret its effect on the probability of his gaining employment ("but me getting a prison number and stuff, no . . . I don't think that I have worked because of my background, because of my record").

Given this major obstacle to his employment, one would think that John would welcome assistance from kith and kin. He did not. When asked about the importance of using friends and family members to find work, John answered:

> If you tell me about they're hiring, that's fine. Don't refer me to nobody, because I don't want them to come back to you or look at you wrong because of something I've done. If I work there and they find out that we're related and whatnot, then it can go from there. I'd rather have it seem like something of mine and then I just won't let them know that a relative told me about it. I like to do things on my own since I have been on my own most of my life. So, I take their advice. I stick it in my ear. But I like to do it on my own. I can do it better on my own, because I know if I mess up then all the fallout is on me. I can say, "Okay."

Like Jeremy and Anthony, John was unwilling to rely on personal contacts at least in part because he was trying to protect the reputations of his job-holding relations. He did not want others to be held accountable for his inadequacies. John's fear was based in past experience—his actions on a job had led to the dismissal of a cousin who helped him secure the position. During one of his spells of unemployment, John had been approached by this cousin, a health spa employee, who offered to speak to his employer on John's behalf. Although his cousin held a supervisory role at the spa, he would not be John's superior; according to John, his cousin's responsibilities lay in another section of the spa. However, when John's work was deemed substandard by his supervisors, instead of managing him directly, they took their complaints to his cousin first, hoping that the cousin would mediate the conflict they presumed would result. In so doing, they established a precedent for how they would address problems relating to John's mediocre performance. This was to no avail. When their entreaties to his cousin failed to improve the quality of John's work, he was dismissed, and his cousin was too. At least in part because of this experience, John refused to rely on friends and relatives for job-finding assistance.

A desire to protect his contacts' reputations was not the only reason, however, that John was reluctant to employ personal contacts. By and large, he wanted to salvage his own reputation. In response to being fired and instigating the firing of his cousin, John expressed not compunction but anger and resentment, both toward his former supervisors *and* his cousin. Both parties, he reasoned, were complicit in tainting his reputation. Clearly, his supervisors should never have gone to his cousin to complain about his work; instead, he argued, they should have approached him first. By circumventing him, they deprived him of the opportunity to rectify the situation, thus disempowering and emasculating him. Furthermore, by taking their concerns to his cousin, they made public both his incompetence and their lack of confidence in him. His cousin only made matters worse by assuming responsibility for John's difficulties time and again. For this, John took great umbrage, chastising the very cousin who lost his own job for his complicity in John's tarnished reputation and job loss. Recounting the situation, he exclaimed:

> And he come to tell me and I'm like, "Hold up, cuz. Why didn't they come tell me? Why do they go to you when they got a problem with me about something when they should come to me and ask me about it, and I guess I could explain it to them. And you ain't got to explain it because they going to think you're covering for me, you know." He was like, "You're right, you're right, you're right, you're right." I said, "I know. If the person that having a problem is men, they can come to me. That's what you need to tell them, 'If they have a problem with my cousin, go talk to him, and he can tell you why, this, this, this, and that did not get done or why whatever happened.'"

By upbraiding his cousin in this way, John sought to salvage his reputation, and with his cousin's agreement regarding how everyone should have behaved, he succeeded in doing so.

Ironically, however, John's own reputational concerns might have actually contributed to the double firing. John hypothesized that his supervisors circumvented him out of fear. His stocky build and confident presence, he explained, often intimidated those around him. Indeed, he admitted that he cultivated this impression *in an effort* to intimidate; he told one supervisor he described as old, frail and timid, "You ain't got to worry about anybody doing anything to you as long as you don't put your hands on me." John associated this presentation of self with "a higher manner," an "upper-class-type" style, and he employed it as a source of empowerment. It became his buffer against the shame he felt in holding positions of subservience and being ineffectual in them. Recall that his supervisors approached his cousin several times with complaints about his performance. John was relatively ineffective, and he knew it, and constant attempts to correct him did little to change that. His frustration around this was probably exacerbated by the anger and resentment he felt because he had not been addressed directly with concerns about his performance. Indeed, his desire to intimidate employers could easily be interpreted as a response to his feelings of inadequacy and powerlessness on the job: when he used his commanding physical presence as a tool of submission, he was able to reaffirm his sense of worth when his skills and abilities were called into question. By doing so, however, he led his supervisors to feel uncomfortable about approaching him directly with their work-related concerns. And so when consultation with his cousin did little to address their concerns, both were terminated.

Like Jeremy and Anthony, John had a sullied labor market reputation, evidence of his limited efficacy in this arena. So, like them, he determined that he would eschew personal contact use altogether to protect would-be benefactors from any fallout that might result because of his incompetence. However, when he said, "Because I know if I mess up then all the fallout is on me," he was not only concerned with saving the reputations of others; he was mostly concerned with salvaging his own. By forsaking personal contact use, he gave employers no choice but to approach him, as a man, and thus he was responsible for his own affairs. Furthermore, he avoided the public disavowal that personal contact use made more likely.

Reputations Repaired, Hopeful Futures

Willing personal contact users did not share these fears. In contrast to the reluctant, willing contact users either had far less problematic public and private reputations or had managed to repair their reputations such that seeking or accepting assistance did not leave them feeling vulnerable. Take Karen Gordon, a thirty-two-year-old single mother of two daughters. Karen had been raised in a middle-class family in which most of her adult kin were professionals of one type or another. After divorcing her father, her mother went back to school to become a nurse and returned to school again to become a dentist; eventually she ran her own practice as well as a prison dental clinic. Among her mother's many siblings were a lawyer, two teachers, a librarian, an executive director of Ford, a president of a corporation, a doctor, and a nurse. In other words, Karen was not without positive role models.

The social and economic capital that one would assume Karen possessed did not provide her sufficient cover, however, from problems very similar to those described by some reluctant contact users. During her interview, she revealed that she was a recovering drug addict, having gone on and off drugs for many years. She also indicated that her employment history was likely to raise concerns for potential employers because of the sheer number of jobs she had held, many for only a few weeks or months. That she had received public assistance twice also seemed incongruous with her somewhat privileged background.

Nevertheless, Karen was trying to repair a reputation that she had sullied with addiction and labor market spottiness. First, although she had struggled with drugs in the past and their hold on her remained somewhat formidable, she felt she was winning this battle. Through drug rehabilitation and mental health therapy, she was addressing the demons that had led to her substance abuse and she had achieved sobriety. Furthermore, therapy gave Karen the tools to redefine her addiction and reclaim a positive self-image. Because of therapy, she came to understand that her retreat into drug use was the result of the emotional neglect she experienced as a child. While pursuing nursing and dental degrees, her mother had spent very little time with Karen—so little that for all intents and purposes her grandparents had raised her. In addition, after her parents' divorce, Karen had no relationship with her father. Consequently, she felt abandoned by the two most important figures in her life and ignored by the others. She explained:

> When I got out of treatment, I started to really focus on myself and start to love myself and to learn a lot of things that I had stuffed and didn't express. After I got out of treatment, I learned how to just conversate and be able to when we got around our family members, you know, and I shared it with them, on how I felt as a child, and then I also shared it with my cousins that are my age. . . . I think we were taught not to talk, you know, not to share things, and um, you know, just listen and don't speak.

Having identified this enforced silence as the central demon that led to her addiction, she could, in essence, absolve herself from blame while taking responsibility. She was not inadequate or unworthy. Instead, she was a victim of intense and prolonged neglect by an absent father and a busy and distracted mother. By reconstructing the history of her addiction, Karen reshaped her self-image and reclaimed the positive. But she also transformed the image that others had of her by sharing her story of neglect with family members and friends. Furthermore, her reputation was buoyed by the fact that she was a recovering addict. Although still tempted sometimes, she was no longer a slave to drugs. So, unlike Jeremy, for whom addiction was a source of shame and evidence of his profound inadequacy and unworthiness, for Karen addiction had come to represent an obstacle she had successfully overcome.

Second, although Karen had accumulated a less than stellar employment history, she did have labor market accomplishments of note. Foremost, in her estimation, was a management position she once held in which she learned how to manage a store and supervise others. She very much appreciated this position for the skills she had gained and the way the job had inspired her to do more. Having been bitten by the management bug, she was now setting her sights on an even higher-level position, that of district manager, which would allow her to explore in greater depth her newfound passion. Although this new opportunity had not yet materialized, her lasting impressions of her old management job were largely positive. These positive feelings were magnified by how she had gone about getting the position. As she explained with great wonder:

> I had no way in the world of thinking that I could get a management position. This guy had just actually told me about the position, and I had never had a management position. I had always done clerical work, worked as a dental assistant, and, man, I went in that office and I took . . . we had to take this test first to pass to see if you were on the level of even getting to the point of the interview, then they give you a second interview, and I just knew that I could do it, and I got it. I was like, wow, you know. I mean, if you just put your mind to it, and you have that . . . I just really believe you can get it. The society makes it hard for us really, as being blacks, but we can do it.

With experiences like these, Karen had come to believe in her own efficacy. Indeed, when asked which people have the best chance of getting a good job, Karen's response was that people who have "direction" and "confidence" and who "love themselves" had the best chance. In the past, these qualities had eluded her, but now, on her path to recovery, they were becoming hers. She explained, "That to me is very important and that's what I struggled with for years. That's, you know, where I'm at now. Just starting to get there again, so." Thus, although she had faced difficulties similar to those experienced by many of my reluctant personal contact users whose lives had come to be characterized by sullied reputations and fears of being exposed as unworthy and inadequate, Karen was eager to mobilize assistance or accept it when offered, because even after tarnishing her reputation with drugs and a spotty work history, she had managed to reclaim a positive image of herself. In the process, she reshaped her reputation with family members and friends such that she did not feel she would be unable to fulfill the obligations associated with assistance.

This was the case as well for Salima Joseph. Salima was a thirty-two-year-old single mother of three who lived with her boyfriend of four years, an unemployed social worker. Like Karen, she had grown up with some measure of privilege. Both her mother and stepfather worked on the assembly line at Chrysler, and they had raised her in a predominantly black, middle-class neighborhood. Her father, whom she visited frequently and then lived with from the age of eleven, was also a plant worker employed at General Motors. He and his wife, an employee of the county's school district, raised her in a predominantly white, upper-middle-class neighborhood. Most of her extended kin—aunts and uncles on both sides—were also plant workers.

Salima had a few other things in common with Karen. First, she had also been addicted to drugs, and like Karen, Salima had gotten clean. At the time of her interview, it had been a year since she last used. Second, although she had been employed for the past two years doing clerical work through Kelly Services, a temporary employment agency, she had gone through difficult periods that had led her to rely on public assistance. From the age of twenty-five, when her first child was born, she had drawn support on three separate occasions.

Also like Karen, Salima was not concerned that she would be unable to fulfill the obligations of exchange around job-finding assistance because, her prior drug addiction aside, she considered herself to be very efficacious. One year of going straight was evidence enough, but Salima had far more than that to support a positive self-evaluation. She considered herself to be an excellent worker with a good work ethic, someone instilled with drive and perseverance. As she put it:

> There's a lot of days I'm tired. You know, I don't want to go into work, but I don't miss time off my job. I go to work every day. I work Monday through Friday. I have Saturdays and Sundays off. That's a blessing. I work from eight to five, so I work nine hours a day. I think my work ethic's pretty good, though. I'm on time. I'm prompt. I'm doing what I'm supposed to do on the job. I don't, like, skip over stuff and leave work

for another person. I'm accurate. I'm positive. I think I have a good work ethic.

For Salima, these characteristics—persistence, motivation, and a positive attitude—were what distinguished those able to secure good jobs from their less successful counterparts.

Having established a great work reputation also protected Zelma Cabot from fears of seeking or accepting job-finding assistance. Zelma was twenty-seven years old, married, and unemployed. Like Salima, Zelma had been raised among plant workers. Her mother, who worked for a major insurance company, was one of the only adults in her community who didn't work for the plant. Her father, her extended kin, and most of her neighbors were all plant employees.

At the time of her interview, Zelma had been unemployed for some five months. Her last position was as a flight attendant for Northwest Airlines, where she worked roughly nineteen hours per week making almost $20 per hour. After eight months, she was dismissed for not meeting probationary requirements. Before her stint in the passenger comfort trade, Zelma balanced accounts at an insurance company for three years.

Having tried her hand with the airline industry, Zelma next wanted to pursue a modeling career. But in the meantime, she needed to find work. About this she had little insecurity. Her first job out of high school had set the stage for her positive self-assessments, and since then she had considered herself a wonderful asset on the job. As a cashier in food sales, she had become vital to daily operations. She was the go-to person when others failed to meet their obligations. She explained proudly, "I really got appreciated there for my hard work, and they always asked, will always look for me to, you know, if somebody didn't come in or call in, they know I'll do it. I even got an award on Employee Appreciation Day. I won a turkey because all the employees put in for me to win. It was around Thanksgiving." In this job, she was an agent of stability. Her presence made things happen, furthering the goals of the company. That she was able to tackle these challenges successfully, and that she received great praise from her coworkers for doing so, instilled in Zelma a strong sense of her own efficacy and communicated to her the great esteem in which she was held by her coworkers. She had few doubts that she was a hard worker, reliable and trustworthy, an asset to any firm.

Again, unlike reluctant contact users, who identified qualities and virtues they had difficulty achieving, willing contact users like Salima and Zelma saw these virtues within themselves. Thus, whereas many among the reluctant were filled with despair and hopelessness at hav-

Table 4.3   Orientation Toward Personal Contact Use, by History of
Responses to Past Requests

	Total	Willing Personal Contact Users	Reluctant Personal Contact Users
Was rebuffed in the past	31	22%	58%
Withheld unemployment status from relations	13	10	22

Source: Author's compilation.

ing established very questionable public and private reputations, willing contact users like Salima, even while frustrated by the hardships of
life, remained hopeful about the future because they had established a
great work reputation or had worked hard and succeeded at repairing
a sullied reputation.

The Job-Seeker's History of Responses

In addition to their own reputations, job-seekers determined whether
to assist by looking back at the history of responses to their past requests. Compared to willing personal contact users, the reluctant were
far more likely to report that their contacts had responded to their requests or offered assistance in a way that left them feeling ridiculed and
diminished. As shown in table 4.3, whereas 58 percent of reluctant personal contact users expressed this concern, only 22 percent of the willing did. Abigail Tyson fell into the former category.

Disparaged into Reluctance

When Abigail and I sat down to talk in the living room of her close
friend, she was a thirty-two-year-old single mother of two daughters
who for two months had been making $8.50 per hour working full-time
on the assembly line of a local manufacturing company. Abigail explained that in the past she had not had problems gaining employment
on her own; she could approach any employer, convince him or her of
her worth, and leave with a new job. Indeed, she had found both of her
prior steady jobs through a walk-in job search strategy. However, after
being convicted for retail fraud, a felony for which she received two
years' probation and a hefty fine—she had shoplifted two shirts and a
jacket from JCPenney three years before our meeting—Abigail had
found it exceedingly difficult to find work. Like Anthony and John, she
hypothesized that her conviction rendered her unattractive to employ-

ers, saying, "I used to go and fill out applications all the time and did not have trouble with an employer calling me, 'cause I didn't have a felony then. I could get a job like that." With the felony conviction, however, she believes that "people just throw [the application] away or something."

There were other reasons she doubted her marketability. From the time she had graduated from high school until I met her, she had held two steady jobs, each lasting less than two years. Indeed, together they totaled only forty months of steady employment over a nearly four-teen-year period, accounting for less than one-quarter of her adult life. But Abigail had not been completely jobless during this time. She had held several short-term jobs, none lasting much more than three months on average. This pattern, of course, is characteristic of work histories that would concern most employers, a point that Abigail raised and fretted about but felt unable to address effectively.

It seemed that Abigail could not overcome the persistent transportation problems to which she largely attributed her unreliability, a problem that posed a serious threat to her current job on the assembly line. Indeed, before she informed me of her felony conviction, she cited transportation issues as her most persistent problem. "Transportation," she said. "That's the only obstacle I ever had was transportation. It seemed like every car I got always broke down or something. I never could afford a new car, so I always had used cars, and they would always break down." As a result of her transportation troubles, she had to give up quite a few jobs and so accumulated a long list of short stints.[14] To conceal this job history, she often lied on applications about the number of jobs she had held, neglecting to list those that she thought would raise questions about her reliability and commitment to work. Of course, Abigail explained, these omissions presented other problems for her, most notably how to explain large gaps in her employment record. To solve this problem, Abigail confided, she would refer to pregnancies she had never had, hoping that employers would see these as more legitimate excuses for jobless spells.[15] However, this explanation probably only confirmed employers' other negative stereotypes about black women workers, specifically that child care responsibilities and other familial commitments are the source of black women's presumably greater unreliability.[16]

And yet, in the midst of these major and growing obstacles to employment, when asked about the importance of using friends and family members to find work, she responded, "I try not to use people to get a job mostly." Prompted to elaborate, she explained:

> I probably will use them for a reference or something, or call and be like, I used you for a reference. I'm going to apply for this job, or something

like that, but, you know, like sometimes [employers] say, do you know anybody that work here? Most of the time I say no. So, I try to . . . I feel if I can get in there by myself, then forget it. That's just the type of person that I am.

Abigail's steadfast commitment to finding work on her own, or at the very least without personal contacts, appears to make little intuitive sense. However, her general orientation to receiving job-finding assistance from friends and relatives does make sense when we consider her prior experiences in this realm—specifically, how she felt she was regarded by those she had approached in the past. Abigail explained that not long before our meeting she and a friend had approached her sister (and the friend's sister-in-law) for help securing jobs. Her sister was employed at a company that offered summer employment starting at $11 per hour—a very desirable wage in this community—with the possibility of permanent placement at summer's end. Abigail exclaimed,

Her job is easy. They got they own desk. All they do is get packages of information and put it into the computer. I mean, they lounge all day. Why wouldn't we want to work somewhere like that? It's wonderful. They got air conditioning. They all got they own computers, and then they got in new computers and the boss let 'em take the old computers home. So they got a computer in they house. Now why wouldn't we want to work somewhere like that? He give them like hundred-dollar bonuses on holidays and stuff.

However, when Abigail and her friend pressed her sister to provide assistance, pleading, "Won't you help us? Can you put our name in or something? We'd like to work here and get us some computer skills or whatever," Abigail recalled her sister replying, "No. I don't want you to work here. You ain't gonna mess up my name." Needless to say, both Abigail and the sister-in-law felt rejected, disappointed, and perplexed, feelings that only intensified when they discovered that, having refused to grant their request, Abigail's sister helped another woman get a job.

According to Abigail, her sister made no attempt to refuse their request in a way that would have preserved their dignity, reputations, and self-esteem and sustained a long-term relationship of expressive and instrumental exchange. On the contrary, her response was much more of an indictment against them—an indication that they were far from having earned the trust necessary to partake in such an exchange—and that response only served to sever ties. No doubt her sister was concerned about Abigail's spotty work history and felony conviction. Abigail was too high a risk to take. That history notwithstanding, however, Abigail interpreted her sister's rejection as an attempt to keep her down. Feeling deeply affronted, she vowed to reject any future requests her sister might make for assistance, especially, but not limited to, requests for job-finding assistance. But she was also disinclined to make requests for herself.[17]

Moments like these fed Abigail's disinclination to ask for assistance from others, including assistance to secure her dream job. Abigail's greatest wish was to gain employment at one of the "Big Three" auto manufacturers with the intention of earning wages and receiving benefits that would take her comfortably into retirement.[18] And although most other jobs she had gotten in the past did not require the assistance of family members or friends, she understood, as did many I interviewed, that the only way to secure employment at General Motors, Ford, or Chrysler was to have a personal contact who worked there speak to personnel on her behalf. According to Abigail, "Most of the people I know that's working at the plant, younger people like between the ages of twenty and thirty, a parent or a relative or a good friend got them in there. So yeah, a good job is hard to find, 'cause I've been trying to get in the plant for a long time."

Abigail's difficulty getting a plant job was probably not attributable to a lack of plant ties, however. Several of her older relatives and friends and family members of her own generation worked in these plants. She had not asked any of them for assistance, however, even when prodded by others to do so. Identifying different relations she could have approached, I asked her why she had not. About her aunts she said, "They're not trying to help me. They trying to help they daughters, so, you know, they don't care. They my mom's sisters. They kind of real private people, and I don't see them much. When I do see 'em, they be like, 'Oh, baby, how you doing [with great ostentation]. Blah, blah, blah.' They ain't going to talk about me on the phone to somebody. So I wouldn't deal with them that much." In reference to her mother's friend she said, "I was going to call her. I called her a couple of times, but she wasn't there. I left a message, and she hasn't returned my call, but I didn't tell her what I was calling her for"—as if to say this potential tie had not known enough about her motive for calling to reject her request. About her best friend's mother, who had been working at the plant for many years, she said she was "feeling kind of funny" and so had yet to call. These three sets of ties did not exhaust the list of people Abigail knew, either directly or indirectly, at the plants. After reviewing her list of contacts and her reasons for not making contact with them, she realized the extent to which she had been avoiding the issue.

Of course, requests for assistance do not guarantee that assistance will come. First, given massive corporate retrenchment over the last three decades (Kasarda 1995; Wilson 1987), which continued over the course of this project, it was unclear whether the Big Three were hiring on a noteworthy scale. So Abigail's friends and family members might not have had the opportunity to assist her. Second, as Abigail feared, her relations may very well have been unwilling to assist. She described relationships with aunts, for instance, that were characterized by a subtle but unmistakable social distance indicating their unavailability. Similarly, in Carol Stack's *All Our Kin* (1974) and Katherine Newman's *No Shame in My Game* (1999), the more advantaged members of extended families were observed distancing themselves from their less-well-off relations in an effort to avoid becoming overwhelmed by obligations of exchange that would deplete them of their growing resources and make even more tenuous their shaky grasp on upward mobility. However, even if both of these conditions would have reduced the likelihood of receiving assistance, Abigail's primary fear was of having her requests denied in a way that would leave her feeling inadequate and unworthy. It was this perceived threat—brought about, in part, by the subtle social distance, the unreturned calls, the indelicate rejections—that led Abigail to look for a job without assistance from family and friends, even though her felony conviction and spotty work history crippled her chances of securing a good job.

Chauncey Gibson was another example of a job-seeker whose pledge of self-sufficiency was largely motivated by a desire to avoid rejection after having suffered it at the hands of his parents. At the time of his interview, Chauncey was twenty-eight years old, married, and the father of two children. He and his wife were unemployed and drawing from public assistance to support their family. When asked about the importance of using kith and kin to find work, Chauncey replied:

> I know a lot of people, but I don't call on people. I just don't. I'm self-sufficient. Oh man, that's me. I don't get into that, man, because I've tried before, right? What I despise is the way people judge me when I'm in need, actually. They look at me almost as if I can't be serious.

Just moments into the interview, Chauncey began to lay the groundwork for understanding this statement. He had had a difficult childhood. Shortly after his parents divorced when he was six years old, his father, who was a recreation director at a community center, became a drug user, moved out of town, and thereafter maintained little contact with his son. Worse yet, with his father's departure, his relationship with his mother soured. Chauncey believed that his mother directed her anger toward her ex-husband on to him, his father's only son. Soon after her divorce, she remarried, and the gulf between mother and son grew. Chauncey despised his stepfather and was met with similar disdain. According to Chauncey, he grew up with a stepfather who tried to undermine his confidence by saying such things as "He's not going to be anything. He's not going to amount to anything."

The other male figures in Chauncey's life were no better. His mother's brothers were the leading drug dealers in the city until their violent overthrow. One uncle was murdered in his hospital bed. Another uncle was murdered in his car along with his wife. A third uncle, fearing for his life, fled to another state, where, Chauncey reported, he was doing well for himself. According to Chauncey, "that was the end of that legacy."

There is no question that these events had a negative effect on Chauncey's emotional and psychological well-being, motivating very delinquent behavior. By his count, he had been through twenty-three public schools, including all of the area's middle schools and seven of its high schools, and was expelled from every one, including several alternative schools. At age fourteen, he began dealing drugs, an occupation that culminated in his arrest and conviction for shooting six young men at a party over a conflict over drugs. He was sixteen.

Chauncey was determined to use the time in prison to turn his life around. He received his high school diploma, enrolled in college, and took several courses toward a degree. Two weeks after gaining his freedom at twenty-two, his sister got him a job. Then he joined his grandfather at UHaul, where he worked as a hitch mechanic. After working there for six months, he moved on to sales positions at various car dealerships, moving up to assistant manager within months. He also ran a barbershop in the basement of his home. In all, he estimated that he earned thousands of dollars monthly. It was with this employment history and confidence that he walked into one of the Big Three automakers and "got myself hired," making $14.80 per hour on the line. He held that job for nineteen months before an injury sidelined him.[19]

Most if not all of these undertakings were motivated by his desire to prove his stepfather wrong and, in the process, win back his mother's affection. After spending over four years rebuilding his life and reputation, he believed that he had redeemed himself enough to have earned his parents' acknowledgment and acceptance. He tested this hypothesis by requesting job assistance from his stepfather, a thirty-year veteran at General Motors, hoping that his parents' attitude toward him had changed in concert with his own personal growth and development. To receive assistance would have been something of a coup, especially since his stepfather had never once elected to provide him with a referral. However, it was not to be. According to Chauncey,

> I went to him. This was like about last year. And I said, "You know, what's up with a referral to GM? You know, I've already proven myself that I can get the job, work the job with the impeccable work record on

the job, in the factory. You know, at this particular time in my life, I could use a little help." Didn't get it. Like I said, I think that he really just wanted my mother to believe that she shouldn't put so much time and whatnot into me, because I would fail her anyway. But yet, he made sure that I failed. I felt like that would be there. I felt like it should have been there for me. That's why I asked, you know.

In effect, Chauncey's efforts to redeem himself had failed, because the people for whom his actions were intended had forsaken him once again. He had not gained his stepfather's respect or proven him wrong. Nor had his mother's disposition softened toward him. So, unemployed and contemplating his next move, he struggled with his stepfather's words from years before that he would not amount to anything. Chauncey's desire for self-sufficiency was rooted in this struggle between, on the one hand, the reputation he had spent years cultivating as a hardworking husband and father who had lifted himself from almost certain death and detention, and on the other, his parents' image of him as a thug who was good for nothing and would amount to nothing, just like his own father. By acting self-sufficiently, however, or at least by speaking in self-sufficient terms, he provided evidence disputing the claim that he was unworthy of acknowledgment, acceptance, or respect.

While Chauncey and Abigail avoided the disparaging remarks of others by not approaching personal contacts for assistance, others attempted to avoid such disparagement by refusing to tell their relations that they were unemployed at all. If job-seekers' friends and family members were not aware that they were unemployed and looking for work, the job-seekers could not be berated, whether subtly or not. Among the unemployed, fewer than 10 percent of willing personal contact users withheld their unemployment status, but 22 percent of reluctant personal contact users did. This was the case with Jessica Barnard, a twenty-eight-year-old unemployed mother of three sons. Jessica was on public assistance and anxious about her state of unemployment when I asked her how important it was to use friends, family members, and acquaintances to find work. She explained that while she would have liked very much to receive assistance from her employed friends, instead, she avoided approaching them at all:

I would like that, but it's like most of my friends that already work or already have jobs, they aren't supportive to me as saying, "Oh, I'll take you to go look for a job." They're more like, "Girl, you need to get a job. I know you tired of sitting here." Yeah, I mean, can you take me? But every now and then, I mean, I need the support for them just to talk to me instead of criticizing me, you know?

Perceiving herself as snubbed by those best positioned to aid her, Jessica decided that she would no longer share information about her employment situation with close associates, concluding, "I don't tell everybody my business, so they really don't know what be going on with me." She did this to avoid the negative stigma, the insinuation and not-so-subtle mockery that had come with her joblessness and welfare-dependence, which she felt was completely inconsistent with who she was, what she wished to achieve, and how she wished to be perceived. By not disclosing her jobless state, she was better able to manage others' image of her and obscure any evidence contradicting her presentation of self.

In so doing, however, she probably had made matters worse for herself. To avoid further stigmatization for being unemployed, she felt forced to undertake alternative methods of job search that were less effective than the use of personal contacts might have been. Furthermore, she inevitably isolated herself to a greater extent than might have already been the case.[20] Thus, while preserving a sense of themselves as worthy and self-sufficient, the consequence of avoiding personal contact use and embracing individualism defensively is that job-seekers become further disadvantaged in low-wage labor markets.

Supported into Openness

The reluctant personal contact users we have heard from so far in this section responded with ambivalence or cynicism to questions about the importance of help from friends, relatives, and acquaintances in finding work, responses that could be traced to a history of rebuffs to requests for job-finding assistance for over half of these reluctants. Among willing contact users, however, what stands out is the absence of narratives about prior rejections, subtle or otherwise. Instead, they listed numerous examples of having reached out without incident or of having their relations reach out to them in their time of need, and so there was an absence of fear that their job-holding ties might forsake them in a demeaning manner. Far from harboring concern about prior treatment, doubts about their competence and worth, and anxiety about how their requests for assistance would be met, willing personal contact users found that seeking or accepting job-finding assistance was as uneventful as looking in the want ads. Because of the nature of their prior interactions, they regarded this job search method as routine. Thus, whereas reluctant personal contact users voiced ambivalence and cynicism about relying on personal contacts to help them find work and avoided doing so altogether, preferring individualistic approaches to job finding, willing personal contact users expressed a commitment to all job search methods but embraced personal contact use as one of the most effective and efficient means of getting a job, especially a good job.

Monroe Laschley was one of many willing personal contact users for whom there was a conspicuous absence of narratives highlighting prior rejections, although the potential was certainly there. At the time of his interview, Monroe was a thirty-five-year-old, unemployed "professional maintenance man" who had been looking for work for two weeks. Two weeks prior he had completed a six-month residential treatment program for alcoholism, a program that precluded work, and so for at least six months he had been without a job. Before Monroe enrolled in the recovery program, however, he had found it increasingly difficult to hold down a job anyway.

According to Monroe, his problems with alcohol began five years before when he landed a job at United Garages working as a maintenance man. A garage supervisor told him about the position and helped him get the job. Soon after he began work there, their romantic relationship did too. She was much older than him—old enough to be his mother, he proclaimed—and he expressed a great deal of adoration for her because she had been so supportive of him. Indeed, he found her especially helpful with regard to finding work, explaining:

> She's very supportive. You know, she's constantly on me about, you know, what I'm saying, finding work or helping me out with résumés, putting out résumés. She's very helpful with that, you know what I'm saying? Or even friends of hers or whatever, she would like call friends of hers that I didn't know. She would always ask them, "Are they hiring where you at? Let me know, you know, if they doing any hiring, so we can try to get Monroe up in there or something." You know, always looking out for me as far as something that's going to benefit the both of us.

However, Monroe considered "his girl" to be something of a detriment to work as well. She had an addiction to alcohol and kept lots around the house. And as their bond grew, so too did Monroe's own dependency on booze. Both were relationships that negatively affected his ability to keep jobs:

> We had a real alcohol problem, man. That was pretty much the failure part, you know. We were really deep into the alcohol thing. She always had it around the house, you know what I'm saying? It affected me because it was always there, you know? I lost a couple of jobs by that. Because it was always there, it was like a temptation thing? It caused me to lose my job too. I'm not saying she's to blame for it. I'm just saying it was there, all the time, constantly. It was like a temptation thing.

Having undergone treatment, Monroe was back in the hunt for a new job. But he was having difficulty getting a job, citing transportation as his primary obstacle to employment. For instance, although he had been offered one job since completing the recovery program, he'd had to decline because the business was located far from any public transportation stop and he did not have a car. And so the hunt for work continued. But unlike reluctant personal contact users, who were disinclined to seek assistance from their job-holding ties and focused on individualistic approaches to finding jobs, Monroe combined job search strategies, including consulting with friends, relatives, and acquaintances. Since completing the program, he had visited the job center daily, walked into a number of establishments and submitted applications, and approached job-holders in his network to ask for information about job opportunities and possibly a good word on his behalf.

Given his spotty work history, one might wonder why Monroe was not disinclined to seek assistance and seemed not to fear that his reputation had been so badly tarnished by his alcoholism that no one would be willing to assist. What was different in Monroe's interview was that, whereas reluctant personal contact users were fairly quick to share stories of subtle and obvious rebuffs, he never shared such an experience. Instead, when asked if he had ever gone to anyone he knew to ask for help in finding work, he remarked, "Yeah, many times. I done went to people that's working somewhere and asked them, was they doing any hiring, and they'd tell me yes or no, whatever. I put in an application, and a couple of jobs I got hired like that, by a friend telling me." The last time this happened, Monroe recounted, "the person I asked was a good friend of mine, a longtime good friend. I asked him because I needed a job. I needed some work. I asked him was they hiring." In response, his friend, who did landscaping, talked to his boss on Monroe's behalf, explaining that Monroe was his cousin and needed some work. Monroe got the job, but just as important, he got the message that others were willing to go to bat for him in his time of need and despite his relationship with the bottle.

Monroe also got this message by observing his girlfriend's attempts to provide job-finding assistance. Recall that Monroe was impressed and encouraged by the fact that his girlfriend was willing to call her friends to ask about job opportunities on his behalf and that she was "always looking out for me." So, when asked about the positive aspects of helping others to find work, Monroe replied, "You know, just being helpful, man, trying to help somebody out. I know how hard it is, not working, not being able to find work right now with the situation that I am in, you know what I'm saying. If I can lend a helping hand, man, put a word in, help somebody get a job, I'm going to do it." And most importantly, Monroe continued, "*I would expect the same thing from my friends, so yeah."* Furthermore, in recounting situations in which his personal contacts had had no information for him, Monroe did not communicate about these interactions in such a way as to suggest that he had been rejected. Thus, because Monroe had largely met with positive responses to his requests for job-finding assistance, in spite of his drinking problem, he had not developed a disinclination toward personal contact use. Instead, he had developed an expectation that assistance would be forthcoming when needed.

Carol Ralph also expected that assistance would be forthcoming when she needed it. Carol was a thirty-four-year-old, recently divorced mother of two. Like Monroe, she was unemployed and receiving public assistance to support her children. But unlike Monroe, who had developed a spotty work history in large part because of his alcohol abuse, Carol had been a model of stability. For fourteen years—all of her adult life—Carol had worked at University Hospital, where she did housekeeping, worked in laundry service, and cleaned the operating room after procedures. Having hit some very bad times, however, she had only recently applied for a public aid grant, the first time she had ever done so. Carol was still finalizing her divorce, a process that had almost completely destabilized life for her and her two kids. Not only did it make keeping the job she already had more difficult, but breaking up with her husband also made finding work that much more difficult. After three months of job search, Carol was still unemployed, and she attributed this to her current instability. When asked why she had not been able to find work for three months, she explained:

> One, I haven't been able to apply myself the way I should because of all the different stuff that I've been going through. I've been going back and forth to court a lot because of the divorce, and other things. And I haven't, you know, I have to make sure my kids are stable, and we've been moving here and there, so I haven't really had the stability that was needed as far as looking for work the way you should be. Then, there was a clothing issue. My husband burned up all my clothes.

By receiving public assistance, Carol was able to gain some measure of stability while she tried to put her life back together by settling her divorce, finding a new job, and getting a new place.

Admittedly, finding work had not been Carol's top priority for a while, but as she worked through other major distractions, it quickly became that. She primarily drew from her network of relations to accomplish this goal. When asked how important it was to use family, friends, and acquaintances to find out about job opportunities, Carol explained, "I think that's very important, to network. I think that's basically the only way you get a good job is to know somebody or through networking. I don't know nobody that has walked into a place, as far as getting a good job with the Big Three, or even ever went and just applied for the job and got the job without knowing somebody. I don't know nobody that's ever done that." And when asked if she had ever gone to anyone for help finding work, she replied, "Yes, because they could be instrumental in helping to get the job." Indeed, Carol had submitted a number of applications to employers, and a good number she had found out about within one week of our interview by calling upon friends and associates she thought might be helpful to her. For instance, she had a friend who worked in the budgeting office at the hospital, she had another who worked at the local headquarters of the NAACP, and she was close to another who worked at Ford Motor Company. Through each of these contacts, she had submitted applications and was waiting to hear back. Because Carol had been employed in the same job all of her adult life, she had not had many opportunities to seek job-finding assistance from her network of relations, and so she did not have much of a history of responses to draw on to determine whether or not to do so. But what little history she did have instilled in her an expectation that assistance would be available when she needed it.

Such was also the case for Salima, the thirty-two-year-old single mother of three discussed earlier. The support her relatives had given her in the past helped her to stave off long-term spells of unemployment that would have made it difficult for her to support her children. When explaining who she would go to for job-finding assistance and why she relied on these people, she responded:

> Because it was like an easy way to get in. You know, like my cousin, she owns a beauty salon. So I asked her, you know, because she knew I needed a job. I asked if I could be a receptionist for her. And even though she didn't need one, she let me do it, you know, because she knew that I had . . . at that time, I had just had my son, but she knew that I had to feed and clothe him and pay rent and stuff. Like I said, I always ask my aunt and stuff are there, you know, openings, do they know any of their friends that have openings that own janitorial services and stuff like that that I could work a part-time job for or something. So I always use people that I know, you know, if they have a way to get in or whatever. They're the first ones I go to actually.

Because some of her family members owned businesses and were willing to use these resources on her behalf, she had access, despite a prior drug addiction and a somewhat spotty work history, to jobs that would allow her to support her family until, she explained, "I find something that I'm really interested in."

Zelma, the twenty-seven-year-old former flight attendant discussed earlier, also found kith and kin to be a great resource. As she put it, "They usually have the inside scoop." During her jobless spell, her friends and family members not only avoided treating her badly but had actually tried to help her find work. When asked how others treated her because of her jobless state, Zelma replied, "Everybody treats me the same, but they're, you know, more like trying to look for me, help me look for a job." Specifically, whenever relatives and friends heard about job openings, they let her know. And her plant contacts, mostly relatives, routinely provided her with applications just in case her disposition toward plant work changed. One aunt made it a point to provide Zelma with an application once every year. Thus, unlike reluctant personal contact users who had a history of being rebuffed, willing personal contact users, even those with troubled pasts, had a history of being embraced by their job-holding ties.

The Structural and Cultural Context of Social Resource Mobilization

The decisions that job-seekers made about whether or not to seek assistance or to accept it when offered were contingent not only on how risky they perceived themselves to be as workers and the history of rebuffs they had received to requests for assistance but also on the structural context within which these decisions were made. Specifically, job-seekers' orientation toward seeking or accepting assistance was affected by gender, access to social capital, and the state of the local economy.

Gender Matters

Although similar proportions of men and women (30 and 32 percent, respectively) expressed concerns about their ability to meet obligations and about their requests for assistance being met with scorn, 15 percent of women and 36 percent of men were reluctant personal contact users (see table 4.4). In other words, among men, fears were more highly correlated with reluctance than was the case among women. Whereas 29 percent of women who expressed these concerns expressed reluctance to use personal contacts, 67 percent of men who shared such fears expressed reluctance to seek assistance or to accept it when offered.

Why would a substantially higher percentage of men be reluctant to seek or accept assistance when faced with fears of failing to meet obligations and being maligned for requesting assistance? In part, we can attribute these gender differences in reluctance to men's more tarnished reputations. Not only were a higher percentage of men fired from their

Table 4.4   Orientation Toward Personal Contact Use, by Gender

	Total	Women	Men
Feared threats to face	31	32%	30%
Reluctant to use personal contacts	26	15	36
With fears, reluctant to use personal contacts	32	29	67
Past delinquency made finding work difficult	18	13	23
Fired from last job	26	16	35

Source: Author's compilation.

last job than were women (35 versus 16 percent), but a higher percentage also reported that their prior delinquency—drug and alcohol abuse and felony convictions—interfered with their ability to find work (23 versus 13 percent). Thus, because of their more disreputable pasts, men would have a far more difficult time protecting their face than would women. As a result, they were less inclined to seek assistance, because seeking assistance would make them vulnerable to disparagement. They would also be disinclined to accept help when offered because acceptance put the reputations of their sponsors at risk if their performance was found lacking for any reason. Receiving assistance also increased the likelihood that job-seekers' failings would become public.

We should not, however, locate reluctance solely in poor reputations. I contend as well that men's greater reluctance in seeking or accepting assistance has as much to do with having a narrower set of discourses available to them that legitimate their claims to assistance while also legitimating their claims to masculinity. Almost without exception, they cannot make claims to both. Indeed, how do men justify claims to assistance without also making themselves vulnerable to emasculation? To seek assistance when they sense great threat to their masculinity because normative paths to achieving masculinity (West and Zimmerman 1987) have been blocked and they have few tools, discursive or otherwise, with which to defend their masculinity effectively means that, for men in this context, the only appropriate response to a high risk of failure and to being rebuffed may very well be a declaration of individualism, an embrace of autonomy and self-sufficiency, even in a labor market context where this particular approach to job search yields relatively few fruit. Thus, the act of declaring itself can be interpreted as a "performance of masculinity," a way in which the disreputable and rebuffed, the low-income and lesser-skilled, can still be men.

John Richards is a prime example of someone who forsook assistance from personal contacts because that was the only way he felt he could experience himself as a real and worthy man, even if doing so severely limited his employment options. Recall that John was the thirty-six-year-old high school graduate whose poor performance on the job led not only to his own dismissal but also to the dismissal of the cousin who had helped get him the job. John felt that his masculinity was threatened in a number of ways in this situation. He was relatively ineffective in his position and he knew it, and while this may have been enough to frustrate his claims to masculine legitimacy, it was only the beginning. That his supervisors and cousin sought to address the situation without consulting him caused him to feel belittled and emasculated because he was not given the opportunity or the power to shape the circumstances of his employment. This is apparent in his recounting of his conversation with his cousin: "Why do they go to you when they got a problem with me about something when they should come to me and ask me about it, and I guess I could explain it to them? . . . If the person that having a problem is men, they can come to me. That's what you need to tell them."

In a context where he felt his claims to masculinity denied, John attempted to reclaim it through physical intimidation, using his stocky build and confident presence to assert his dominance over his supervisors and coworkers. But he also performed masculinity by declaring his autonomy and self-sufficiency with regard to job finding. It was a form of face-work, his way of accomplishing gender in a labor market context where he would have great difficulty legitimating claims in a normative fashion.[21] Thus, in this context, men may respond to concerns about their inability to fulfill their obligations and about being disparaged by their relatives and friends by forsaking assistance in future job searches because declaring themselves to be individualists, even if defensively so, allows them to assert claims to masculine legitimacy in the face of evidence suggesting otherwise.

When faced with fears of falling short of expectations and a history of being rebuffed, women generally responded very differently than men. Instead of declaring themselves to be individualists, they most often remained open. They were able to do so, I contend, because they had a much greater range of discourses from which to draw to defend themselves against threats to face (and thus establish their worth) *while also* legitimating their claims to assistance. Take, for example, Brenda Bowen, a separated mother of two. Her estranged husband, who provided no child support, had moved to Florida with his new girlfriend. During her most recent spell of joblessness—she had been looking for work for five weeks—she explained that her friends had become distant, saying, "They kind of talk down, or like look down on me. Some of my friends, you know, because most of my friends have good jobs, and they're still working and, you know, kind of pursuing what they started, they distance themselves because I'm not working right now." When asked why her friends might distance themselves, Brenda explained, "I think they feel like I probably would ask them for something, a handout or something. Yeah, it's just something there."

Among many reluctant personal contact users, such a perception would almost certainly have led to a strong ambivalence toward personal contact use. However, this did not occur with Brenda. Instead, she remained open to assistance, and she did so primarily by downplaying the significance of her friends' new aloofness.[22] Although she confessed to having been hurt by this decline in sociability, she admitted that she might respond similarly to a jobless friend. By responding in this way, Brenda depersonalized the condescension and the social distance such that the slight had very little to do with her. It was not that she was inadequate or unworthy. Aloofness was merely how some people responded when faced with others' hardship, and she would probably do the same. Through empathy and compassion, Brenda downplayed the significance of the slights she experienced, a coping mechanism that left her relationships relatively unharmed, at least on the surface, so that she could continue to benefit from them in other ways or leave open the possibility of benefiting from them in the future.

Unlike Brenda, Lindsey Gault did not downplay the significance of affronts she experienced or assume that they meant little about her own worth. Instead, she located her worth in her status as a wife. Lindsey was a thirty-one-year-old, recently married mother of three. Since leaving high school, she had held only one steady job. For one year, she worked part-time doing data entry with a courier service. Besides this job, she supported her family with income from public assistance. However, as Lindsey was quick to point out, she was the only member of her family who had not committed to the labor force—her father was a financial adviser at a state university, her aunt was an executive at Coca-Cola, her grandmother was a retired schoolteacher, and numerous other relatives held positions at various plants. And they frequently reminded her of her status vis-à-vis their own in an attempt to encourage her to do more. She explained, "It's my family. They be on me, because all my family have careers. I'm the only one. I kid you not. They don't like that."

Her joblessness also inspired disapproval in others. When asked how others treated her because of her joblessness, she said:

You know what? It be the females that are the ones that, they be playa' hatin' because they got to work. That's all it is. And they always want to sit up and talk about what they done did. "Yeah, I went to work today," you know. Females are real sheisty, real sheisty. I'm serious. That's why I do not have any [female friends]. I really don't hang around anybody, just my sister-in-law I'm with.

In both cases, Lindsey responded to the comments she received by deflecting attention away from her almost perpetual state of joblessness and pointing to her status as a wife. For instance, in response to her family's concerns, she responded, "I'm married, though. I told them, 'I'm married. My rent paid. What else?'" Given that relatively few black women get married, Lindsey was suggesting that her recent marriage was an impressive achievement that not only was the equivalent of having a career but should buffer her from disparagement for being unemployed. To the women who subtly indicted her for her jobless state by talking about their own employment experiences, Lindsey turned the tables, indicting them for jealousy because they *had* to work. Because she was married, she did not. Here again, she made claims to her own worth by pointing to her status as a wife, which she believed should buffer her from criticism related to joblessness.

Shirley Wyatt did not locate her worth in her status as a wife. She wasn't one. Instead, Shirley was a twenty-seven-year-old single mother of four children, and she legitimated her claims to worth and assistance by pointing to this very important role that she played, one that she played without assistance. Although she had held a number of steady jobs in the past, the recent birth of her fourth child, a son, led her to public assistance. After three months, however, she was ready to return to work. The day she was interviewed, she had been looking for work for slightly less than two weeks. Her experiences with personal contacts were very similar to those of more than a few reluctant personal contact users. Family members often chided her about finding work, but few seemed willing to offer assistance that would facilitate her finding and keeping a job. Indeed, she pointed to this reluctance as a way to deemphasize the significance of her jobless state and to make claims to worth and assistance. She complained, "Everybody like, 'You need to go on back to work.' I'm like, 'Okay, but ain't nobody volunteering to watch my kids, you know. Don't nobody tell me what I need to do if you're not going to lend out a hand, or at least, you know, saying I'll pay you. Don't tell me that.'" By pointing to the struggles of single-motherhood, Shirley turned her detractors' criticisms back on them, implicating them in her joblessness while also legitimating claims to worth and assistance.

John and men like him did not have such flexibility in responding to threats to face that called into question their masculinity and worth. Unlike Brenda, they could not downplay the significance of interactions that left them feeling belittled. Such responses were themselves considered acts of emasculation and would only have worsened matters. Nor could they locate their worth as men in their status as husbands or fathers in the same way that Lindsay and Shirley legitimated their claims to worth in their status as wives and mothers. Without steady, well-paying jobs that allowed them to support their partners and children, such claims would have been highly contested, highlighting even more their inefficacy and threatening them, once again, with emasculation.

It is in large part because men lack access to a set of discourses from which to draw to justify their circumstances and make claims to worth and masculinity that they get boxed into proving their worth and performing masculinity through individualistic approaches to finding work. Even though similar percentages of women and men raised concerns about losing face, because women do have a set of discourses from which to draw to justify their circumstances and legitimate their claims to worth, they have the resources to defend themselves effectively against face threats, and thus they can remain open to assistance from personal contacts during the job search process.

Access to Social Capital

Orientation toward personal contact use was also associated with access to social capital. When comparing the number of positions to which job-seekers reported access, willing and reluctant personal contact users differed little if at all. As shown in table 4.5, whereas willing personal contact users reported access to 8.2 positions on average, reluctants reported access to 8.1.[23] But there were differences in types of access that might help to elucidate further differences between willing and reluctant personal contact users. If we examine access not to individuals occupying specific occupations but to individuals in occupations of specific skill levels—lesser-skilled, skilled or semi-professional, and professional—and examine differences by the nature of these relationships and the frequency of contact, noteworthy differences between them. Although reluctant and willing personal contact users differed little from each other with regard to the *number of ties* in each skill category to which they had access, the two groups did differ substantially in terms of the *share of their working connections* who were unskilled.[24] Among willing personal contact users, a greater share of working connections were unskilled (41 versus 34 percent), and that was especially so when these relations were personal (37 versus 28 percent) and frequently in contact (33 versus 23 percent). Differences between willing and reluctant personal contact users in the share of working relations who were skilled or semi-professional and professional were minor. Thus, reluctants not only had less access to those in occupations for which they were best suited—lesser-skilled positions—but their con-

Table 4.5   Orientation Toward Personal Contact Use, by Access to Social Capital

	Total	Willing Personal Contact Users	Reluctant Personal Contact Users
Number of positions known	8.2	8.2	8.1
Zero positions known	1%	0%	3.8%
One to five positions known	25	24	27
Six to nine positions known	34	35	31
Ten or more positions known	40	41	39
Access to positions by skill level (number of positions)			
Unskilled	3.1	3.2	2.8
Personal	2.7	2.8	2.4
Frequent	2.4	2.5	2
Skilled and semi-professional	2.9	2.8	3.1
Personal	2.1	2.1	2.1
Frequent	1.7	1.7	1.9
Professional	2.3	2.2	2.5
Personal	1.6	1.6	1.7
Frequent	1.2	1.1	1.4
Shares by skill level			
Unskilled	39%	41%	34%
Personal	35	37	28
Frequent	31	33	24
Skilled and semi-professional	35	34	38
Personal	25	25	25
Frequent	22	21	23
Professional	25	24	27
Personal	18	17	19
Frequent	13	12	16
Number of discussion partners	2.3	2.4	1.7
Zero discussion partners	18%	13%	35%
One to two discussion partners	41	43	35
Three or more discussion partners	41	44	31

Source: Author's compilation.

nections to lesser-skilled workers were less likely to be personal and characterized by frequent contact—the types of relationships that best facilitate assistance in time of need.

As further evidence of this relative lack of access, reluctants reported significantly fewer people with whom they spoke on important matters. Whereas willing personal contact users reported 2.4 such people on average, reluctants reported just 1.7. Categorically, whereas 13 percent of willing personal contact users reported having no discussion partners, 35 percent of reluctants reported that they did not discuss important matters with anyone.[25] So, while the reluctants and the willing had similar access to working relations, a significantly lower share of reluctants' working relations held jobs that were the ones best suited for their skill set (lesser-skilled), and a lower percentage of these lesser-skilled working connections were personal and frequent in contact— the type who were best positioned and most willing to provide assistance in time of need. This finding is important, because it indicates that although willing and reluctant personal contact users differ little with regard to their embeddedness in networks that provide opportunities for vertical, or upward, mobility, reluctants are disadvantaged relative to the willing in terms of their embeddedness in networks that would provide access to opportunities for horizontal mobility and allow them to move between jobs of similar status. This is important because Katherine Newman reports in *No Shame in My Game* (1999) that although the subjects of her study generally lacked access to relations who could provide them with opportunities to get better positions, the fact that they could rely on these networks for similar-status jobs allowed them to stave off long-term spells of unemployment.

These findings suggest that decisions about whether or not to seek assistance are affected by the extent and nature of job-seekers' connections to working relations, and specifically to unskilled workers—that is, fewer connections to the unskilled (rather than to skilled and semi-professional or professional workers) seem to reduce job-seekers' willingness to seek assistance. How might we understand this relationship? I contend that with fewer job-holders to call on for assistance, each job-holder in this context has to deal with a greater number of requests for a limited number of positions. To determine whom to assist, they construct relatively strict criteria that are probably based a great deal on those used by employers to distinguish potentially good workers from bad ones. Furthermore, they justify their decisions to assist or not by deploying discourses of joblessness that problematize the behavior of the jobless to explain their joblessness, a deployment that seems rational because the jobless often behave in ways deemed problematic. Thus, in somewhat smaller networks of unskilled working relations, job-seekers' requests for assistance are more likely to be met with scorn and derision, which leads job-seekers embedded in such networks to take a more individualistic approach to job finding to avoid being treated badly.

Neighborhood Poverty and Local Labor Market Conditions

Upon first glance, there does not appear to be much of a relationship between reluctance to use personal contacts and neighborhood pov-

Table 4.6   Reluctance to Use Personal Contacts, by Neighborhood Poverty and Employment Status

	Low-Poverty	High-Poverty
Reluctant	25%	25%
Employed	27	30
Unemployed	27	11

Source: Author's compilation.

erty status. One-quarter of residents from both low- and high-poverty neighborhoods described themselves as reluctant. However, as with job-holders, employment status mediates this relationship. Among the employed, there is little difference in reluctance between those who lived in low-poverty neighborhoods (27 percent) and those who lived in high-poverty neighborhoods (30 percent). But noteworthy differences emerge among the unemployed. Among this group, 27 percent of unemployed job-seekers from low-poverty neighborhoods expressed reluctance compared to just 11 percent of the unemployed from high-poverty neighborhoods (see table 4.6). No doubt a dearth of institutional and social resources prevents the unemployed in high-poverty neighborhoods from forsaking whatever assistance they can get.

Local labor market conditions mattered as well, if only a little. The first two years of data collection coincided with the tail end of the period of economic expansion. As stated in the previous chapter, in 1999 and 2000 the average monthly unemployment rates in Michigan were 3.9 and 3.7 percent, respectively. By 2001 the period of great prosperity had clearly ended. That year Michigan's average monthly unemployment rate had risen to 5.2 percent, and it increased again in 2002 to 6.2 percent.[26]

Job-seekers' reluctance to use personal contacts also seemed to decline, if only slightly, as the economy soured. Among those interviewed in 1999 and 2000, one-quarter expressed an unwillingness to rely on personal contacts to find work. However, a slightly lower proportion of job-seekers interviewed in the two years that followed—one-fifth—expressed the same unwillingness to seek assistance or accept it when offered. A good economy appears to embolden otherwise extremely vulnerable job-seekers to seek work on their own. But it appears that as labor market conditions worsen and work becomes that much more difficult to find, job-seekers become slightly more open to receiving help from friends, relatives, and acquaintances in finding work. Unfortunately, their resistance declines somewhat during a period when job-holders' distrust and reluctance grows.

Conclusion

In the previous chapter, I showed that even in the context of job information and influence, job-finding assistance was not necessarily forthcoming from job-holders because they perceived that high risks were
associated with providing aid. Job-holders in this context had to deal
with job-seeking ties who were beset and beleaguered by multiple barriers to employment that made finding and keeping work difficult, and
they themselves were doing so in fairly tenuous employment positions
that might be jeopardized to varying degrees by job-seekers' presumed
problematic behavior. To protect themselves, their jobs, and their reputations, they often had to forsake job-seekers; they would do so by
pointing to job-seekers' behaviors as evidence of the risk they would be
taking, then espouse tenets of individualism as the primary solution to
job-seekers' persistent and chronic joblessness.

In this chapter, I add to this picture by showing that job-finding assistance was not always sought. Indeed, one-quarter of job-seekers were
reluctant to seek assistance from friends, relatives, and acquaintances or
to accept assistance when offered for fear that they would not be able to
fulfill their obligations or that they might be maligned by their job-holding ties. Job-seekers' willingness to seek or accept assistance was contingent on three key factors. First, they took their own reputations into consideration to assess their ability to fulfill obligations toward job-holders
who were willing and able to assist. To the extent that they deemed
themselves risky prospects, they were unwilling to mobilize their social
resources on their own behalf. Second, they considered the history of responses to their requests for assistance. If they perceived themselves to
have been rebuffed in the past, especially by those close to them, job-
seekers were disinclined to reach out for help. Third, structural context,
in the form of gender, access to social capital, neighborhood poverty,
and local labor market conditions, mattered. Men were far more likely
than women to express great reluctance to seek assistance or accept
help, in part because they were more vulnerable to threats to face, but it
also appeared that with fears of falling short and being maligned, they
were more likely to express reluctance. Just as job-holders' decisionmaking process was contingent on his or her access to social capital, access was also associated with job-seekers' decisionmaking. Reluctant
personal contact users were embedded in networks with fewer connections to *unskilled* workers, and so the extent and nature of their access
was associated with the nature of the interpersonal dynamics between
them and their job-holding relations. Local labor market conditions
were also somewhat associated with their decisions.

As understandable as their reluctance might be, however, withdrawing from personal contact use during job search probably only

worsened job-seekers' chances of finding employment. In low-wage labor markets, employers rely heavily on their employees to screen and recruit job candidates because this represents the cheapest, most efficient way to find "qualified" workers.[27] And while some employers also use this method to bypass pools of workers they find undesirable—poor blacks most often top this list (see Kirschenman and Neckerman 1991; Neckerman and Kirschenman 1991; Kasinitz and Rosenberg 1996)—for those who do not completely exclude blacks from consideration, having a personal contact vouch for a job-seeker's adequacy and worth can overcome whatever reservations the employer might harbor (Newman 1999). Without this backing, employers would probably look elsewhere to fill vacancies, and the time that job-seekers spend in their jobless state would lengthen, leading to greater economic strain and frustration and deeper feelings of inefficacy.

In *Facing Up to the American Dream: Race, Class, and the Soul of the Nation* (1995), Jennifer Hochschild reports that the black poor are far more likely than their middle-class counterparts to express a strong affinity with the major American tenet of individualism. In the land of opportunity, where it is widely held that, regardless of their origins, everyone can participate equally in the American dream and that success is all but guaranteed if one wants it badly enough, the black poor strongly believe that if blacks do not achieve, they have only themselves to blame. Furthermore, it is believed that the structure of opportunities is such that status and rewards are available to anyone who tries hard enough, regardless of race. In this view, self-sufficiency is the key to achieving the American dream.

We expect self-sufficiency and self-reliance among those who have the financial and cultural capital to achieve their desired goals without having to rely too heavily on social resources. Indeed, suburbia is teeming with upwardly mobile families fleeing the constraints of familial obligations because they can afford to pay for all of the services that family and close friends have traditionally provided (Sennett and Cobb 1972). And while some might interpret the black poor's strong sense of individualism as a desire to adhere to mainstream values in spite of structural constraints, the evidence presented in this chapter suggests that the strong sense of individualism among the black urban poor is less a function of a desire to adhere to mainstream values (although this exists) *in spite of structural constraints* than a function of *the context of structural constraints*—specifically, it is the result of widespread avoidance for those ill equipped to protect themselves from the threats that joblessness poses to their already depressed social status and reputations. In other words, declarations of self-sufficiency and the concomitant avoidance of personal contact use emerge among black poor job-seekers only after they perceive that help is not forthcoming and, in some cases, should not be forthcoming, not primarily because their ties are unable to provide assistance, but because they are unwilling to do so. Instead of mobilizing or accepting job information and influence, job-seekers perceive imminent threats to their reputation or feel that they have already tarnished their reputation on a fairly regular basis. By embracing individualism, then, they attempt to protect the reputations of their job-holding ties, to protect or rebuild their own reputations, and to demonstrate their strength and self-sufficiency in the face of evidence that suggests otherwise. "I like doing things on my own," then, becomes a mantra of defensive individualism among those for whom dignity, self-worth, and mastery have been difficult to achieve.

As suggested earlier, "I like doing things on my own" included seeking assistance from formal institutions that provide links to employers. In the next chapter, I show that even within the context of institutional social capital, the job center and its staff often forsook black, poor job-seekers, just as job-holders did, deeming them too unmotivated, too needy, and too delinquent to assist without heavy costs. As a result, from these labor market intermediaries, too, black job-seekers often failed to receive the institutional resources they needed to find work.

Chapter 5

The Job Center: Barriers to Employment and the (Im)Mobilization of Institutional Social Capital

Southeast County's job center is housed in what appears at first glance to be a strip mall, a fairly narrow building the length of one city block. The building, which stands one story high, is constructed of light tan cement blocks that occupy the lower two-thirds of the building's facade. The top third has wood siding and is slightly lighter in color than the cement blocks. Though simple, the building is well kept. The back of the building faces a main thoroughfare, Central Avenue, which runs east and west. Although windows extend the length of the building, they are sun-screened to protect occupants from the heat and glare of the southern exposure. The front of the building faces north and is abutted by the center's parking lot, which is equal in length but somewhat wider than the center building. It can accommodate roughly fifty cars. On Mondays, the busiest day of the week, it is not uncommon for all the spaces to be filled.

Visitors can access the parking lot from Anderson Street, a two-way street located on the east side of the center, and Mitchell Street, a one-way street located on the west side and running south toward Central Avenue. Most visitors enter from the east, and it is from the eastern wall of the building that its occupants are most clearly identified. As you approach Anderson from Central Avenue, you see a three-by-six-foot sign on the upper part of the building informing you:

MICHIGAN WORKS!

SERVICE CENTER

SOUTHEAST COUNTY

The background of the sign is white, and except for one word, the text is black. The word "WORKS!" is highlighted in magnified, bold, bright red, all-capital letters in the biggest font size. This word—this declaration really—is meant to stand above all else. On the left side of the text, and occupying the middle three-fifths of the sign, is a drawing of two hands bordered in blue. One hand is outstretched, as if asking for a handout. The other is reaching from above for the first, as if providing assistance. The seal of Southeast County is inscribed on the hand providing assistance. To the right of the text is an image of a flag, constructed of six stripes of alternating white and blue and attached to a soaring half-star. The message here is not difficult to decode. The red, white, and blue colors are meant to evoke the imagery of work and America, of being American, and the agency housed in this building is there to provide assistance to those in need, but an assistance centered on work, the most American of enterprises. This agency is charged with the task of assisting individuals in the process of their own uplift.

The messages continue inside. Framed posters decorate the center's self-service resource room and classrooms. I counted twenty-one in all, each strategically placed in an area where clients are most likely to view them. Fourteen are placed in the main resource room—by the job leads board and the copier, adjacent to the computers—and in the waiting area. Seven are hung in two of the three classrooms. No posters are displayed in the areas where staff have their cubicles.

Produced by Corporate Impressions, the posters have a consistent pattern to their design.[1] Each is mounted and framed in black. In the upper two-thirds of each poster is a spectacular, awe-inspiring photograph, usually an image of some magnificent part of nature, a machine executing a simple task while conveying a profound meaning, or a person attempting a remarkable feat that challenges assumptions about what is possible. Most of these messages are obvious, some painfully so. This is especially true of the posters featuring men and women undertaking extraordinary acts and those displaying nature's wonders, as with the posters of a kayaker descending a waterfall, an American eagle soaring high, and a long-distance runner alone on a seemingly never-ending desolate road. In other posters, especially those depicting machines, which are far more abstract in quality and content, the meaning of the message takes more time and imagination to decode.

Whether visually subtle or not, however, the values or ideals being propagated are explained clearly. In the lower third of the poster, one word or term is spelled out in bold and colorful letters that can be seen from several feet away. Underneath this in a relatively small font is an "inspirational" quotation that can only be viewed up close. Examples include:

"Dare to Soar": The message accompanying an image of an American eagle flying high and confidently is: "Your attitude almost always determines your altitude in life."

"Attitude": Pictured simply and elegantly is one drop of water making ripples in a pool. The caption reads, "Attitude is a little thing that makes a BIG difference." "Big" is in all capital letters and highlighted in blue, in contrast to the other words, which are highlighted in white. "Attitude" is also highlighted in blue, making the connection, through color, between the two.

"Persistence": Here we have an image of a woman running in full stride. In the background the sun is setting behind a series of jagged mountain ranges. The message reads, "The race goes not always to the swift . . . but to those who keep on running."

Other inspirational posters focus on achievement, teamwork, risk, integrity, and perseverance.

Apparently the center hopes to endorse some values more than others. Three posters focus on individuals' attitude—seven (or one-third of all posters) if we include others that also focus on attitude without actually using the word ("Dare to Soar," "Power of One," "Believe and Succeed," and "Never Give Up"). Each has a unique quotation, but each sends the same message that your outcomes are largely a result of your own thinking. Change your thinking, change your attitude, and you will change your life. Other messages are repeated twice, including those having to do with innovation, goals, success, and teamwork. The exhortation about teamwork is most perplexing because its message that success results less from individual initiative than from working together with others is so infrequently communicated in the center.

By hanging these posters, the center seems to communicate that regardless of external circumstances, about which you may have little or no control, you have the power to determine your own employment path, and with heavy doses of the right attitude, innovative thinking, and persistence, you will achieve whatever career goals you can imagine for yourself.[2] If you fail to find employment and to keep a job that excites, challenges, and sustains you financially, you need look no further than your own attitudes, your initiative (or lack thereof), and the actions you have taken to this point. Win or lose, good or bad, prosperous or impoverished, you yourself, the prints tell you, have largely created the circumstances of your own life.

The messages conveyed through these posters reveal more about the center itself, however, than about its embrace of the ideology of the American dream. They hint at the role the center plays in helping individuals to achieve that dream. Through three principal programs and services, the one-stop employment service center attempts to address the needs of all job-seekers by providing what appears at first glance to be a wealth of resources to aid them in their job search activities.

Through core employment services, job-seekers gain access to information about job opportunities, information about how to undertake a successful job search, and some resources to facilitate the application process. The overwhelming majority of resources provided in core employment services require that job-seekers be self-directed, but staff assistance is available. The Workforce Investment Act (WIA) is designed primarily to assist dislocated workers and unemployed adults by funding training, whether on-the-job or in the classroom, and by cultivating relationships with employers in an effort to facilitate job matches. Work First is a four-week jobs program designed to strengthen welfare recipients' attachment to the labor market by providing resources to aid their efforts to find work as quickly as possible, as mandated by the state, typically without formal education or job skills training. Thus, this one-stop employment service center represents an institutional form of social capital that provides information and, in some cases, influence to facilitate job matches between job-seekers and employers.

Through in-depth interviews with center staff and observations of staff-client interactions, I found that for many black, poor job-seekers mobilizing this institutional form of social capital for job finding was much easier said than done. Job-seekers with multiple barriers to employment were often forsaken, denied assistance because they were deemed too untrustworthy, too unmotivated, too needy, too delinquent, and thus too risky to deserve access to the center's finite resources. And because job-seekers with multiple barriers to employment are disproportionately black and poor in this context, they have come to symbolize these problematic job-seekers.

In what follows, I first highlight the extent and nature of job-seekers' multiple barriers to employment and explain how and why these "difficult-to-employ" or "hard-to-serve" job-seekers have great difficulty mobilizing the institutional forms of social capital in the center's programs. I show that it is not only black poor job-holders who are reluctant to assist their job-seeking relations in job finding. Institutions like the job center, which are specifically charged with the task of aiding job-seekers, are also reluctant to assist them. Here again I demonstrate that the problem of social capital deficiencies is not solely one of access; mobilization is at issue as well.

Barriers to Employment

ATTITUDE:
THE PEOPLE WHO GET ON IN THIS WORLD ARE THE PEOPLE WHO
GET UP AND LOOK FOR THE CIRCUMSTANCES THEY WANT, AND, IF THEY
CAN'T FIND THEM, MAKE THEM.
—GEORGE BERNARD SHAW

In anticipation of the 1996 welfare reforms, which would require most recipients to work for the cash assistance and benefits they received, a number of researchers began to examine the extent and nature of the barriers to employment that recipients might face and that would make it very difficult if not impossible for a significant minority, if not a majority, to find and keep work (Kalil et al. 1998; Kramer 1998; Loprest and Zedlewski 1999; Olson and Pavetti 1996). These investigations revealed that upwards of 90 percent of AFDC recipients would face at least one obstacle to employment, including low basic skills (Nightingale et al. 1991; Pavetti 1993; Zill et al. 1991), physical disabilities or health limitations (Loprest and Acs 1996), mental health problems (Bassuk et al. 1996; Belle 1990; Kessler et al. 1995; Moore et al. 1995; Nichols-Casebolt 1986; Zill et al. 1991), health or behavioral problems with their children (Heymann, Earle, and Egleston 1995; Meyers, Lukemeyer, and Smeeding 1996), substance abuse (Olson and Pavetti 1996; U.S. Department of Health and Human Services 1994), domestic violence (Bassuk et al. 1996; Colten, Cosenza, and Allard 1996; Curcio 1996; Lloyd 1996; Raphael 1995), involvement with the child welfare system (Shook 1999), and housing stability (Browne 1993; Pavetti 1995; Quint, Fink, and Rowser 1991).[3] Furthermore, having barriers to employment affected the likelihood that AFDC recipients would be employed (Olson and Pavetti 1996).[4] These early studies anticipated accurately the challenges that a majority of TANF welfare recipients would face under the 1996 welfare reforms.

Researchers at the University of Michigan's National Poverty Center (Danziger et al. 2000) have found that major barriers to employment are indeed quite pervasive among TANF recipients. Just 15 percent of their respondents reported no major barriers. One-fifth reported one, another fifth reported two, 17 percent reported three, and more than one-quarter reported four or more major barriers to employment.[5] Thirty-one percent of respondents had low levels of education, 15 percent had low levels of work experience, 21 percent had few skills, 9 percent had poor knowledge of work norms, 14 percent perceived employer discrimination, 47 percent lacked transportation, 25 percent were clinically depressed, 15 percent had post-traumatic stress disorder, 7 percent suffered general anxiety disorder, 3 percent were alcohol- or drug-dependent, respectively, 19 percent of mothers and 22 percent of children had health problems, and 15 percent had experienced domestic violence. Others have reported an even greater prevalence in obstacles to employment.[6]

Not surprisingly, having major barriers negatively affected women's employment. Specifically, those with barriers related to human capital deficiencies and who experienced discrimination, depression, or health problems were less likely to work twenty hours or more each week. Furthermore, as the number of their barriers to employment increased,

Table 5.1   Barriers to Employment

	Welfare Recipients	Entire Sample
Number of barriers		
No barriers to employment	7%	10%
One barrier	40	52
Two barriers	33	24
Three barriers or more	20	15
Types of barriers		
Human capital	48	36
Lack of transportation	39	32
Familial obligations	25	15
Lack of jobs	16	15
Employer discrimination	13	15
Substance abuse	12	18

Source: Author's compilation.

the likelihood of their working declined significantly. While 82 percent of women with no major barriers worked, 62 percent of women with two to three barriers worked, and 40 percent of women with four to six barriers worked, an astonishingly low 5 percent of women with seven or more major barriers to employment worked (Danziger et al. 2000).[7]

The welfare recipients in my sample reported 1.6 barriers to employment on average. Four in ten reported one barrier to employment, one-third reported two, and one-fifth reported three. Just 7 percent reported no major obstacles to finding a job. When asked what obstacles they faced finding work, 48 percent referred to human capital deficiencies, 39 percent pointed to lack of transportation, 25 percent mentioned familial responsibilities like child care, 16 percent referred to a lack of jobs, 13 percent identified employer discrimination, and 12 percent listed substance abuse (see table 5.1).

Welfare recipients are not the only group for whom multiple barriers to employment are pervasive and inhibiting. Among my full sample, respondents reported 1.5 barriers to employment on average. Roughly 10 percent reported no major barriers. However, 52 percent reported one, 24 percent reported two, 13 percent reported three, and 2 percent reported four major barriers to employment. When reporting the obstacles they faced during the process of finding work, 36 percent referred to human capital deficiencies, 32 percent pointed to lack of transportation, 15 percent mentioned familial responsibilities like child care, 15 percent referred to a lack of jobs, 15 percent identified employer discrimination, and 18 percent listed substance abuse as major hurdles to employment. Individuals with these obstacles had an even greater need for job-finding and job-keeping assistance, institutional or otherwise. Ironically, however, having these barriers made the mobilization of these resources much more difficult to achieve.

"Help Yourself"

NEVER GIVE UP:
GO OVER, GO UNDER, GO AROUND, OR GO THROUGH. BUT NEVER GIVE UP.

Southeast County's one-stop employment service center, in existence since 1999, is one of more than one hundred such centers in the state of Michigan charged with the task of assisting all job-seekers, regardless of their circumstances of unemployment, by offering the necessary resources and tools to find work. Michigan first introduced the one-stop career center model, called Michigan Works Service Centers (MWSCs) in 1993. Two years later, these centers became the primary means by which the state delivered these services.

Centers are a part of a relatively complicated, ever-changing, interorganizational structure initiated by the state of Michigan to address the employment problems faced by a significant minority of the state's population. Upon receipt of federal monies for TANF, the Family Independence Agency transfers funds to the Michigan Department of Career Development (MDCD), which administers at the state level jobs-related programs and services. MDCD then distributes funds for employment and training services to local workforce development boards and their staff, called Michigan Works! agencies (MWAs) (see Seefeldt, Danziger, and Danziger 2003).[8] MWAs also receive funds from the federal government for WIA programs. There are twenty-five local MWAs in the state, each serving one to ten counties. However, they do not provide services directly. Instead, they contract these out to service delivery providers that are selected through a competitive bidding process. Delivery service providers are responsible for managing a wide variety of programs designed to match employers and job-seekers. At Southeast County's one-stop employment service center, the primary programs are core employment services, WIA, and Work First. However, for job-seekers with serious barriers to employment, mobilizing these resources is much easier said than done.

Core Employment Services

GROWTH:
SMALL OPPORTUNITIES ARE OFTEN THE BEGINNING OF GREAT ACHIEVEMENTS.

Core employment services are situated in the center's self-service resource room for job-seekers and employers. Any job-seeker can take advantage of the services offered, but in order to do so he or she must first sit through an informational session about the center's offerings. The session is conducted by one of the resource room attendants, who first invites visitors to sit with him or her at a small, round table, offers each a packet of information, and then proceeds to conduct what I can only describe as an information blitz: listing the contents of the thick packet by offering detailed information about almost every aspect of the center's offerings—much of it random or superfluous—in about three minutes. The experience is dizzying. During this brief tidal wave of information, few of the clients' questions are answered, and many are left dazed, confused, and angry.[9] Once the blitz is over, the resource room attendant encourages job-seekers to become registered with the Michigan Talent Bank, a web-based job-matching service to which employers also post information about job vacancies and search for job candidates throughout the state. Resource room attendants cannot assist job-seekers who fail to register with the Michigan Talent Bank.[10]

Once registered, job-seekers gain access to numerous center resources. They can search the Internet from any of the eighteen computers available with Internet access; attend face-to-face job fairs that occur biweekly; peruse job binders that post details about area job openings; get and complete job applications for local, low-level service industry employers; check recent job postings at the "Hot Off the Presses!" job leads board, listings not posted on the Internet; read employment-related books, magazines, and videos on how to write a résumé or a cover letter and how to prepare for a successful interview; make employment-related local calls at the phone stations; use the copier and fax machine, with the assistance of center staff; use the Michigan Occupational Information System to ascertain the requirements related to occupations of interest; and attend weekly workshops for tips on interviewing, conducting a successful job search, doing an Internet job search, creating a successful résumé, writing cover letters and thank-you notes, and more. Those interested in furthering their education can also search catalogs and obtain applications from dozens of colleges, universities, and training centers in Michigan.

Although the overwhelming majority of the resources provided in core employment services require job-seekers to be self-directed, resource room attendants are available to assist in a number of capacities. However, the extent and nature of the assistance provided by attendants depend in great part on their subjective assessments of job-seekers' motivation to find work and level of self-sufficiency. Indeed, as previous research has shown, when frontline welfare workers have flexibility in making decisions about the services they can offer, what they offer depends on how they perceive the clients before them. Jodi Sandfort, Ariel Kalil, and Julie Gottschalk's (1999) qualitative study of frontline workers is an example. Their study revealed that frontline workers typically categorized clients in three ways. "Abusers" were those who tried to manipulate the system, largely through deception, in order to get benefits. "Hostile" clients were those who knew their rights and frequently asserted them, challenging workers' competence and authority. "Deserving" clients were seen as honest and helpful individuals who were truly committed to their own betterment. Although workers' categorizations of clients were not always consistent with each other, Sandfort and her colleagues discovered that how workers categorized clients affected the tone they set for the interview, the information they provided to clients, and the way in which they processed clients' case materials (Sandfort et al. 1999, 80). The extent and nature of resource mobilization, then, depended in great part on the staff's assessments of the clients with whom they came into contact.

At the job center, this was never clearer than in attendants' dealings with young, black, male job-seekers. Their perceptions of these young men were far more negative than the perceptions they held of any other type of job-seeker. In an environment where the ability to be self-directed is highly valued and persistence is prized, attendants deeply distrusted the commitment of young black men to conventional employment and to undertaking the series of tasks required to find work because they interpreted these job-seekers' inability to navigate the center's system without intensive aid as a sure sign that they lacked motivation and were uninterested in achieving self-sufficiency. Adopting Sandfort, Kalil, and Gottschalk's parlance, attendants saw them as "abusers" of the system and, as such, undeserving of center resources. This perception not only guided all of the attendants' interactions with young black men but often led them to withhold even the most basic assistance in an effort to push these job-seekers toward self-sufficiency.

When I approached Debra Anderson, a dynamic black woman in her early forties, to discuss her experiences working at the center, she immediately and without my coaxing launched into a passionate discussion about her concerns about young, black, male job-seekers, who, she explained, seemed wholly ill equipped to undertake successful job searches and, more importantly, seemed unwilling to do so. Debra, who was a resource room attendant and also ran the interview techniques workshop, began by explaining that if two young men were to walk through the door, one black and one white, she could predict with almost 100 percent certainty that the black job-seeker would require far more energy, input, and patience from her than his white counterpart. Resource room attendants were available to assist clients with registering, writing and revising résumés, and uploading and activating their résumés on the Michigan Talent Bank website. Although job-seekers often asked attendants one or two questions during this process, Debra said that most of them figured it out by themselves. However, young black men did not. Instead, they required intensive assistance throughout and asked for so much help that Debra came to believe that they wanted her to do the work for them. She attributed some small part of their "neediness" to their low proficiency in basic skills, since many seemed never to have written a résumé and few had a working knowledge of computers. However, Debra mostly interpreted their neediness in terms of their attitude. As far as she could tell, the values and ideals displayed on the center walls were alien to them. These young men appeared unwilling to be proactive, to create their own futures. They looked uninterested in working hard to achieve their goals. They took no initiative. Instead, they seemed to be waiting for someone to come along and do it for them. What convinced Debra of this was that some called on female relations—friends, girlfriends, or wives—to assist them, or, more accurately, Debra thought, to do the work for them: to write their résumés, to register them with the Michigan Talent Bank, and to submit their résumés to employers while they sat idly by, seemingly disinterested in and disengaged from the whole process. Debra had observed young white men also recruiting female companions to assist them, but she estimated that young black men were far more likely to do so.

This pattern of dependence and codependence infuriated Debra. She interpreted it as an effort by these young men to game the system, to get more out of it than they were willing to put in. Furthermore, she felt that such an approach would only disadvantage them in the long run, reinforcing the notion that they did not have to work hard to achieve their goals while at the same time inhibiting their personal and professional growth. This interpretation led Debra to withhold assistance from them. If anyone from this class of job-seeker asked her a question about writing a résumé, for instance, she responded of course, but she responded with only enough information to get them started, and then she walked away, hoping that they might find the motivation they needed to work through their difficulties and complete the necessary job search tasks on their own. In her mind, this was the only way to force them to be men. She pushed them toward self-sufficiency by providing them with opportunities to help themselves, and she counseled other attendants to do the same.

Joann Crawford, a thirty-four-year-old black woman, did not need advice or encouragement to withhold more than the most basic assistance from these job-seekers. Thinking much as Debra did, if not more vehemently, she did so willingly. Like Debra, Joann interpreted young black men's behavior as neediness stemming partly from low levels of proficiency in the most basic skills but mostly from their unwillingness to do for themselves. They were unmotivated and lacked initiative; they seemed to expect assistance, or they sought it at every step in the process, and they would not do anything unless they were told to do so, a point that Joann punctuated when she exclaimed with a great deal of exasperation, "Inhale, exhale, inhale, exhale, inhale. . . ." The message was clear—they even needed instructions on how to breathe. Joann was angered by this behavior in young black men and by their apparent unwillingness to do for themselves, to challenge themselves, and to take the initiative on their own behalf.

Joann was also fearful, however. A single mother of two sons, twelve and three years old, she was concerned that her oldest was not living up to his potential. He seemed content to do just enough to get by, and she worried about what this would mean for his future. In ten years' time, would he resemble one of the many young black men who visited the center and were not only unable but, even more troubling to Joann, unwilling to help themselves? Not coincidentally, to address her fears she had hung miniature versions of the "Challenge" and "Success" posters on the walls of her sons' bedroom in the hopes of inspiring them to challenge themselves and to become self-sufficient in an environment where she perceived these values as non-normative. And although this was hardly the only action Joann had taken to try to build her oldest son's character—he played basketball, ran track, and took clarinet lessons—in her mind each positive reinforcement counted. Thus, while at home with her sons, she engaged with them completely and vigilantly, hoping to build their characters such that they would learn to challenge themselves and become self-sufficient, unlike a disproportionate share of the young black men with whom she had contact at the center. At work, however, she withdrew from these young men, withholding the kind of assistance that she typically gave to other clients.

Unlike Debra and Joann, Donavon Stinson did not interpret young black men's behaviors as an effort to game the system. Instead, Donavon, a twenty-four-year-old black man himself, located the patterns described in low levels of high school completion, high rates of early imprisonment, and weak labor force attachment. However, when Debra advised him to distance himself and to limit the assistance he ordinarily provided as a resource room attendant, he complied, reasoning that it would not hurt to have these young men take greater responsibility for themselves during the job search process. And so, like Debra, he would answer their questions, but he would do so in the most minimal way and then walk away, allowing them to "peck away," he explained, as he mimicked them typing with one finger.

Interestingly, none of the attendants I spoke with distrusted young black women in the way they seemed to distrust young black men. Unlike their male counterparts, whom attendants perceived as "needy abusers" resistant to performing the tasks necessary to find work in ways prescribed by the center, black women tended to be categorized as "deserving" because they were perceived as far more motivated, far more likely to take the initiative, and far more likely to try to problem-solve on their own, attributes that staff members located in their desire to care for their children. Although attendants perceived black women to have greater proficiency in basic skills like reading, writing, and typing, they understood the gender differences they saw solely in terms of attitude. They seemed not to consider that the neediness they experienced in young black men resulted from their low levels of basic skills relative to their female counterparts. Consequently, staff were more willing to trust that black women wanted to be self-sufficient and were willing to do what was necessary to achieve that goal, and so they engaged with them far more within the context of core employment services.

The Workforce Investment Act and Divestment from the Economically Disadvantaged

INNOVATION:
THE BEST WAY TO PREDICT THE FUTURE . . . IS TO CREATE IT.

The Workforce Investment Act (WIA) program is designed to assist two categories of job-seekers at Southeast County's job center—dislocated workers and a general category of adults.[11] The former are workers who have been laid off or whose jobs ended in a declining industry. The latter are individuals who are eighteen or older and in need of employment assistance.[12] WIA provides assistance in part by funding training, whether on-the-job or in the classroom, and by cultivating relationships with employers in an effort to facilitate job matches.

WIA is the most recent federally funded workforce development program, the successor to the Manpower Development and Training Act (MDTA) of 1962, the Comprehensive Employment and Training Act (CETA) of 1973, and the Jobs Training Partnership Act (JTPA) of 1982.[13] However, WIA has evolved from its predecessors in at least three distinct and important ways—what I call the three "Ds." First, WIA marks a continued progression toward the *devolution* of power and decisionmaking authority from the federal government to state and local governments (Guttman 1983).[14] Second, compared to its predecessors, WIA is far more focused on the economic *development* of the business community and has authorized that the business community have decisionmaking power equal to that of local government officials in determining the form and content of local employment programs (Guttman 1983; O'Shea and King 2004).[15]

Third, and most importantly, WIA has *divested* from programs specifically designed to address the special needs of the economically disadvantaged, the focal population of many of its predecessors. Instead, it has adopted a more "universal" focus. MDTA, for instance, retrained dislocated workers and trained economically disadvantaged workers. CETA provided block grants to states and local governments to fund job-training programs, including classroom instruction, on-the-job training, and work experience, for the economically disadvantaged, the unemployed, and the underemployed (U.S. Congressional Budget Office 1982). Services also included job search and job placement assistance, but these were secondary to human capital development. Roughly half of CETA participants had classroom instruction, which focused primarily on developing occupational skills, such as typing and keypunching. To a lesser extent classroom instruction also taught general skills—the equivalent of what is needed to pass the general educational development test for the General Equivalency Diploma (GED). One-tenth of participants received on-the-job training in which they learned specific occupational skills, such as auto repair, while in job settings. Finally, four in ten gained work experience. Unlike the classroom instruction and on-the-job training, which sought to provide training for specific skills, the objective of work experience programs was to generate in low-income workers basic work habits and positive work attitudes. These relatively short-term programs lasted approximately twenty weeks, cost an average of $2,400 per participant, and achieved modest results.[16]

Upon CETA's expiration in 1982, JTPA was enacted. JTPA was similar to CETA in many ways. Here again the federal government provided block grants to states and local governments to create programs that would increase employment and earnings and reduce welfare dependence among economically disadvantaged youths, unskilled adults, and dislocated workers.[17] However, unlike CETA, JTPA did not allow public-service employment—which had been the engine of Franklin Delano Roosevelt's Depression-era WPA—and thus highlighted a shift toward divestment from public-service employment and a move away from addressing the needs of economically disadvantaged workers. WIA took this a step further. Resources were redistributed and moved away from the most disadvantaged in an effort to serve everyone with a "universal" approach that would include all unemployed individuals, incumbent workers, in-school and out-of-school youth, adults with little or no work experience, dislocated workers, individuals with disabilities, welfare recipients and former welfare recipients, and low-wage workers. It would do so by providing funds for training and developing relationships with employers in an effort to promote job matches between employers and WIA participants.

At Southeast County's job center, however, job-seekers must pass through two important steps of the program before WIA supervisors will agree to pay for education or training on their behalf. In the first step, participants are expected to undertake an intensive job search through the center's core employment services—for example, posting résumés on the Michigan Talent Bank, searching on the many Internet job search websites, and using the available reference materials. If they fail to find work using self-directed and staff-assisted core employment services, then job-seekers can move to step two, described as intensive services. In intensive services, staff conduct a comprehensive and specialized assessment of the job-seeker's employment strengths and weaknesses, develop an individualized employment plan, undertake career planning, encourage attendance in center workshops, and identify appropriate support services. If these do not lead to employment, the participant can make a pitch about the type of work he or she would like to do, propose a training program that would develop the necessary skills and certification, and indicate the type of job most likely to follow from that training. If this proposal meets with program criteria, the WIA program is very likely to fund the training, either by paying for the job-seeker to enroll in a training program or by paying an employer to hire and train the participant on the job. WIA employment and training specialists, the frontline workers of the WIA program, determine subjectively participants' progression from one step in the process to another.

WIA is not, however, an entitlement program. Hopefuls must apply, and WIA supervisors determine whom they will approve for participation. Applicants are told that the primary consideration for approval is something called the target wage. The target wage is 90 percent or greater of the average weekly gross dollar amount the job-seeker earned in the prior year. These data are collected and reported by the state's department of wages. To have their training paid for by the state, job-seekers must show that after training they will be able to earn their target wage in a position for which the WIA program has paid for training. If post-training wages are predicted to be lower than the target wage, WIA supervisors will decline the application.

Other criteria drive the decisionmaking process as well. First, training duration matters. Shorter periods of training are better than longer periods, with most participants receiving between three and six months. Supervisors do not seriously consider programs that approach or last longer than one year. Second, and related, the cheaper the cost of training, the greater the likelihood of having one's application accepted. Supervisors can pay employers up to $3,000 to hire and provide on-the-job training to program participants, and they can allot the same for coursework leading to certification. Not surprisingly, they prefer to pay much less.

Third, and most importantly, applicants with multiple barriers to employment are avoided at almost all cost. Indeed, according to Gary Marshall, a WIA employment and training specialist, every morning WIA program staff meetings end with supervisors reminding specialists to avoid job-seekers with multiple barriers, including those with low levels of educational attainment and spotty work histories and, most especially, those with felony convictions. This message is reinforced daily primarily because of WIA performance standards and incentives. Contractors who manage the WIA program must show that they have achieved positive results as defined by the federal government: every quarter they have enrolled a certain number of participants in the program; participants have received training or taken part in job search; and, most importantly, after a relatively short training period participants are employed at or above their target wage and have stayed on that job for eighteen months or more. For every step achieved—enrollment, productive activity, employment—the program receives some credit, but it is only when participants have worked for eighteen months that the federal government deems the investment cost-effective and gives the program full credit. Furthermore, contractors' ability to continue managing the program is contingent at least in part on whether they meet these performance standards.

Thus, even though the WIA program lists job-seekers with multiple barriers to employment, there are actually disincentives structured into the program that make it unlikely that specialists will engage productively with such job-seekers, and these disincentives most negatively affect black, poor job-seekers, both men and women, who represent a disproportionate share of job-seekers with multiple barriers. These job-seekers have come to symbolize excessive risk in the minds of WIA specialists, who not only distrust their desire to do the work necessary to find work but question whether they will be able to remain on the job long enough for the program to receive credit for placement. Fearing for their own job security, WIA specialists avoid this type of job-seeker. After all, there is no certainty that the time and energy devoted to a difficult-to-place job-seeker will lead to employment at all, much less employment that lasts eighteen months or more. And in the time it takes to train and place one job-seeker with multiple barriers to employment, staff can do the same for at least two job-seekers without any barriers, increasing the likelihood that they will meet performance goals.

Even with the informal mandate to avoid expending limited resources on job-seekers with multiple barriers, Gary did do so on occasion, driven by his concern that black men who visited the center were systematically alienated from its programs and services. This concern arose from his conversations with black male job-seekers who shared that they felt ignored by center staff (consistent with staff's own reports) and dissatisfied with its programs and services. As a black man himself, Gary had felt obliged to do whatever he could, within reason, to assist some of these difficult-to-place job-seekers. However, Gary did not help everyone who approached him. Clearly, he could not. He had to be discriminating, to sort the "good" from the "bad." To do otherwise would have garnered more negative attention than he felt comfortable with from supervisors wary of the overall impact that his assistance to multiple barrier cases would have on the bottom line.

To achieve this fine balance, Gary had developed an informal but very elaborate testing process to determine who among the difficult-to-place he could trust enough as a client in whom to invest center resources. Gary largely assumed that most of the men he came into contact with could not be trusted to do the work necessary to find and keep a job. In his eyes, they lacked self-sufficiency. Indeed, he estimated that 70 percent needed every aspect of the job search process explained to them in great detail in order to make any headway. In addition, he found that they often lacked the motivation to take advantage of opportunities when they did arise.

To identify the few who had some measure of self-sufficiency and motivation, Gary began his "test" with a gaze from across the room. While tending to other clients in the self-service resource room, Gary, who received the special attention of a growing number of men with multiple barriers to employment who had learned of his willingness to assist from prior beneficiaries of his aid, could feel eyes watching him, following his every move. With eye contact, such a job-seeker would approach him, introduce himself, and ask for a moment to explain his circumstances. At this point, Gary would escort the man to his cubicle and listen, encouraging him to share any major barriers to employment he had, especially felony convictions. This was the first test: if Gary sensed that the person was not forthcoming with this vital information, he would decide against helping, explaining that he was not in a position to offer the kind of assistance the job-seeker needed. After all, his ability to place job-seekers, especially those tainted by a disreputable past, was highly contingent on his own reputation with employers, which had been built on successful prior matches. If he vouched for a client who was only later revealed to have major shortcomings, his reputation would be soiled and employers would begin to distrust him as an intermediary who took their concerns seriously. It would then become that much more difficult for him to call on that employer in the future. This is not to say that employers are categorically against training and hiring job-seekers with multiple barriers. But those who do, like the employers with whom Gary had established good relationships, want to know with whom they are dealing so that they can assess their own risk and decide whether the risk is worth the funding they will receive from the WIA program. Thus, if for any reason Gary suspected that the man before him was not being forthcoming, his interactions with that person ended immediately. However, if he sensed that the job-seeker was honestly revealing the extent and nature of his past employment-related problems, Gary would continue on to the next stage of the process—task completion.

In stage two, Gary had to determine the extent to which the difficult-to-place job-seeker was self-sufficient and motivated, and so he would request that he complete a series of tasks assigned one at a time, most but not all related to self-directed and staff-assisted core employment services, such as résumé writing and interview techniques. He did this until he was convinced that the individual's motivation and self-sufficiency were not in question. If the job-seeker failed to complete any task that Gary had assigned in a timely manner, he dismissed that person. But if the job-seeker showed a willingness and ability to complete the task punctually, Gary would do his part. This was step three. He would contact employers with whom he had established relationships and vouch for the client, who, through this series of tests, had proven that he could be trusted with the center's resources, including Gary's reputation with employers.

If one of Gary's employers agreed to train the participant, Gary took the fourth step: approaching his supervisor for approval of the job-seeker's application for participation in the WIA program. Even through all of this, employment would not be assured, but Gary's efforts would have significantly increased the likelihood that the job-seeker would find employment, and job-seekers who received his assistance were thankful because they knew that he had tried. Given their experiences with other staff members at the center, they knew that Gary had given them far more assistance than most staff members were willing to provide. A consequence of this, however, was that Gary's multiple barrier cases often came back to him with one or two friends in tow who had experienced similar difficulties. Gary would try to explain that while he wanted to be able to help more, he could assist only one multiple barrier case at a time, and he would ask that they not spread the word until he had completed their specific case. Not only was he incapable of dealing with so many cases, but assisting multiple barrier cases, especially those with felony convictions, was strongly discouraged, and he feared that doing too many of them would endanger his own job.

Gary was not alone. According to O'Shea and King (2004), performance standards and incentives often affect WIA specialists' behaviors in ways that negatively affect the clients they are charged to serve. For instance, it is not uncommon for specialists to withhold WIA registration from potential participants who appear unlikely to get and keep a job for the required employment period. It is also not uncommon for specialists to discourage unemployed or dislocated workers from applying for participation in WIA if the specialists estimate that their prior wages are too high to meet their target wage, even if the worker is willing to experience a drop in salary. Ironically, some specialists even encourage workers who had a high-paying job to remain unemployed for several months in order to reduce their average weekly gross the prior year so that they might meet their target wage. O'Shea and King find that more tenured WIA staff, like Gary, often ignore performance standards and incentives in an effort to better serve their clients. But efforts such as these are constrained by the larger forces at work at the center. These efforts are anomalies, not the norm. That norm makes the mobilization of social capital for black men through WIA very difficult.

And how do WIA program staff deal with poor black women? Hardly at all. Although the WIA program was designed to assist both dislocated workers and adults eighteen and older who have had difficulty finding work, many WIA specialists believe that more than enough resources are already being spent (and wasted) on the undeserving through programs like Work First. Of the three programs administered through the center, Work First had the largest budget, expending some 40 percent of all the funds brought into the center. The WIA program consumed 34 percent.[18] Knowing this, staff members complained to me that it would be the height of injustice to expend WIA resources on clients whose needs were already being served by another program that was much better funded, especially when recipients who were worthy of assistance by virtue of their strong attachment to the labor market—dislocated workers—were also in need. Besides, they reasoned, because of their multiple barriers to employment, Work First participants were not likely to find and keep jobs for the eighteen months required to meet performance goals. As a result, these WIA-eligible job-seekers were also discouraged from participation in the WIA program. Thus, whereas poor black men were avoided because of the risks they posed as former felons to the program's bottom line, poor black women were avoided both because they were deemed undeserving of the WIA funds by virtue of their eligibility for welfare and the Work First program and because, as a population beleaguered by multiple barriers to employment, they too threatened the program's bottom line. However, for women with multiple barriers, mobilizing resources through Work First was also a major challenge.

Work First

BELIEVE AND SUCCEED:
COURAGE DOES NOT ALWAYS ROAR. SOMETIMES, IT IS THE QUIET VOICE AT THE
END OF THE DAY SAYING, "I WILL TRY AGAIN TOMORROW."

In August 1996, President Bill Clinton signed into the law the Personal Responsibility and Work Opportunity Reconciliation Act (PRWORA), which dismantled Aid to Families with Dependent Children (AFDC) and replaced it with Temporary Assistance for Needy Families (TANF), a time-limited, block grant program designed to do what AFDC did not: promote work and discourage nonwork among welfare recipients.[19] Under TANF, the following conditions apply. First, states can no longer use federal funds to provide never-ending assistance to families. After a period of sixty cumulative months, either states have to support recipients with state funds or single parents have to find alternative means of support, such as through employment or private charity. Second, single parents must participate in some sort of work activity, and each year states are required to provide evidence to the federal government that the percentage of recipients who work has increased; when no such increase can be shown, states suffer penalties. Third, states must sanction recipients who fail to comply with program requirements (Gallagher et al. 1998). Recipients can forever lose their right to receive public assistance for noncompliance, in which case they must find alternative sources of financial support. However, states have a great deal of flexibility in deciding what form their specific reforms will take to encourage "personal responsibility" and "self-sufficiency" among their welfare recipients. The state of Michigan took advantage of this flexibility.[20]

Without question, Michigan has been one of the most groundbreaking welfare reform states in the country. In the 1980s, well before Bill Clinton came to office, Michigan was one of only a few states to begin experimenting with different approaches to job creation for welfare recipients. During the 1990s, Michigan's lawmakers often led the charge toward reforms geared at putting recipients to work (Seefeldt, Danziger, and Danziger 2003). For instance, in 1991, under Republican governor John Engler, Michigan became the first state to terminate general assistance to able-bodied and childless adults, a move that left some 83,000 recipients without support.

The termination of general assistance, however, was only the beginning. Engler launched a series of experiments that arguably would lead to the most comprehensive welfare reform program in the country. In 1992 the governor initiated To Strengthen Michigan Families (TSMF), a welfare demonstration project operated under welfare waivers by the Michigan Family Independence Agency (MFIA) from October 1992 to September 1996. TSMF eventually became Michigan's Family Independence Program (FIP), the state's version of TANF. The main objective of TSMF and FIP was to shrink welfare caseloads significantly and improve employment and earnings among Michigan's low-income population. To achieve these objectives, Michigan targeted key elements of federal and state welfare policy that politicians felt discouraged work and encouraged nonwork. For instance, under AFDC recipients were under no obligation to take part in "productive activities" in return for the public assistance they received. Many observers, such as the political scientist Lawrence Mead (1985, 1992), have argued that such a system only fostered a learned helplessness that made it unlikely that recipients would ever come to value work and self-sufficiency over the leisure and dependence that they assumed welfare receipt promoted. In an effort to shift the supposed cultural orientation, under TSMF, and now FIP, recipients are required to sign a "Social Contract" whereby they agree to engage in some type of productive activity—school, work, volunteering. At the beginning of reforms, recipients were expected to put in at least twenty hours per week in such activities, but since April 2002 they have had to agree to do so for at least thirty-five hours per week. These activities are largely supervised under Michigan's Work First program.

Work First is a four-week jobs program designed to strengthen recipients' attachment to the labor market by mandating that they undertake intensive job search activities in an effort to find work as quickly as possible, typically without any formal education or job skills training. Although program models vary considerably across the state, Southeast County's Work First program can be most accurately characterized as a job search model.[21] It provides eligible participants with the skills— résumé writing, interviewing techniques, and application preparation—and the tools—a job posting board, Internet access, phone banks, and newspapers—to look for work in a self-directed manner.[22] However, consistent with the job-seeking support model, which attempts to match job-seekers with employers (Anderson and Seefeldt 2000), Southeast County's Work First program also organizes biweekly job fairs.

Interestingly, when I began recruiting respondents for participation in this study at the job center, Southeast County's Work First program could more accurately be characterized as a job-seeking support model. Not only did it hold biweekly job fairs, but it also engaged employers in the area to learn about job vacancies, brought employers in for onsite interviews, and attempted to match appropriate job-seekers with employers. Similar to what WIA employment and training specialists do, Work First staff would contact employers in the area to generate interest in the welfare population, assuring them that recipients would be motivated, self-sufficient, and responsible workers. Work First staff generally felt comfortable making these assurances because they would have put recipients through a series of their own "tests." Whether or not recipients were placed in jobs and how good these jobs were depended just as much on how well they performed during these tests as it did on how much human capital they had accumulated. However, as the economy continued to sour after 2001 and it became increasingly difficult to interest employers in hiring welfare recipients when they had few vacancies to fill, the structure of the program changed, such that job finding became the primary responsibility of the job-seeker.

In the job search model, the first week of Work First participation is devoted to workshops on résumé writing, interviewing skills, job search techniques, and the very basics of computers (aptly called "Computers Don't Byte"). These are conducted through core employment services. Participants are also taken on field trips designed to acquaint them with the local public transportation system.

In the remaining three weeks, participants' focus shifts from workshops to job search. In the mornings, they are mandated to apply for jobs based on lists they generated in previous days of employers with vacancies to fill. In the afternoons, if participants have not found employment, they meet at the center with Work First case managers to review and evaluate their morning's activities, to network with other participants, and to discuss interviewing and job search techniques as well as other strategies for future searches. These meetings take about an hour. Participants commit the rest of their afternoon to identifying employment opportunities and contacting employers to generate additional lists of hiring employers for the next morning's job search. If after four weeks participants still have not found jobs, they receive face-to-face intensive services in the hope of identifying and resolving their barriers to employment.

With the implementation of Work First, then, politicians have placed a priority on quickly transitioning individuals into positions in which they will gain "valuable" work skills through experience while also having their cultural orientation to work transformed, and they have done so with what has been characterized as a carrot-and-stick approach. The metaphorical carrot, the reward for doing the right thing and taking personal responsibility, includes greater earned income disregards, which allow recipients to keep a greater percentage of earned income than they were allowed to keep under AFDC, and "supportive services," such as child care referral services and transportation vouchers.

Sanctions, of course, are the stick. Through TSMF and now FIP, Michigan has sought to discourage nonwork by implementing heavier financial penalties for noncompliance with Work First requirements, which are many. Recipients are compelled to spend a certain number of hours each week looking for work and applying for positions with hiring employers. Furthermore, they must comply with reporting requirements by providing evidence that they have looked for work and applied to hiring employers. The state also requires that recipients accept whatever job offers they receive, and they cannot quit their jobs or be fired from them without "good cause."[23] Recipients are also required to attend scheduled meetings with caseworkers and to attend all of the classes and workshops in which they were enrolled.

For any misstep, recipients can be sanctioned for noncompliance.[24] If they fail to meet "reporting requirements," they can be sanctioned. If they quit their jobs or are fired without good cause, they can be sanctioned. If they are tardy or fail to attend scheduled meetings with caseworkers, classes, and workshops, they can be sanctioned. Michigan is a graduated sanction policy state, which means that families lose some but not all of their cash and noncash assistance for the first infraction.[25] Thereafter, they lose 100 percent of their benefits. Michigan reduces a family's monthly cash assistance and food stamp allotment by 25 percent upon the first instance of noncompliance, a penalty that lasts for one month. For repeated or prolonged noncompliance, the maximum penalty in Michigan is closure of the family's case for at least a year without the possibility of reinstatement until the sanction period has ended. As is the case nationally, 5 percent of Michigan's caseload experiences sanctions each month.

This carrot-and-stick approach has worked, reducing caseloads dramatically while at the same time contributing to an impressive increase in single mothers' employment over the 1990s.[26] For recipients with multiple barriers to employment, however, attempting to find and keep a job under Work First's rigid bureaucracy has been close to impossible. Ironically, Work First programs, in their many forms and across different states, have yet to address adequately the multiple barriers that participants face, barriers that make them vulnerable to noncompliance and the resulting sanctions. As Sandra Danziger and Kristin Seefeldt (2002, 157) argue, "The failure to identify problems puts the 'hard to serve' at higher risk of sanctions if their problems make them less likely to comply with welfare program requirements."

Previous research has shown that some recipients are at higher risk of sanctions for noncompliance owing specifically to the barriers that they face. Kalil, Seefeldt, and Wang (2002), for instance, compared sanctioned and nonsanctioned recipients and found that the sanctioned were significantly more disadvantaged. They were younger, less likely to live with another adult, more likely to be African American, and less likely to have completed high school. Sanctioned participants also had significantly less work experience and longer welfare spells, and they were more likely to struggle with transportation, child care, and health issues (U.S. General Accounting Office 2000). Furthermore, being sanctioned created material hardship above and beyond the hardship that had led to being sanctioned in the first place. Participants who had been sanctioned were more likely to report that their utilities had been shut off, more likely to engage in hardship-mediating behaviors, and more likely to perceive future material hardship (Kalil, Seefeldt, and Wang 2002).

The reader might recall Jackie York from chapter 3. Her experiences highlight the many difficulties that recipients with multiple barriers to employment face when trying to navigate a bureaucratic system that not only fails to take into consideration their special needs but actually penalizes them for noncompliance resulting from their special needs. Jackie was a twenty-seven-year-old, never-married mother of five children, ages one through thirteen. Since graduating from high school, Jackie had held over five steady jobs, but she had also received three public aid grants. When she and I sat down to talk, she was not an aid recipient. Although Jackie struggled mightily to make ends meet—she was two months behind in the rent and even while being interviewed seemed to expect at any moment that her utilities would be turned off—Jackie refused to apply for another grant. When I asked why, she cataloged a list of complaints:

> I've done that, but I'm still in the same situation, 'cause once again, reality sets in. Aid is, the system is a lot different now. Engler, he cuttin' up. No, he's just, he ain't right, you know. He got you doing the flips and turns and, and that was the reason why I'm in the situation that I'm in right now. I had to go to Work First and work till you get the Work First. They want you to work to find a job. Who's putting gas in my car? Now, if I didn't have a car, they would be giving me tokens, but I got a car and I got to have gas, oil, tires. . . . [Interviewer: So they help if you don't have a car, but if you have a car, then they assume you can make it on your own?] Right. Or then they will pay for mileage. Girl, I'm not trying to write down no meter every time I get out the car. You can't give me just a flat allowance and say, here's twenty dollars a week or forty dollars a week, depending on how many places I go or whatever, and this is what I have to work with. But there's not guidelines, or, I mean, it's so far out of reach. It's like you're going awry and you ain't got enough string to reel it in.

Furthermore, unlike a job, which allows workers time off when familial issues develop, Work First makes no such allowances. If single parents need to take time off to handle emergencies, for instance, under Work First's rules they cannot without being sanctioned for doing so. Unfortunately for Jackie, she was a single mother of five children. Emergencies relating to her children arose frequently and required her immediate attention. If she chose to ignore them, her children would suffer. If she attempted to address the situation by taking time off from job search, Work First would penalize her and her children would suffer. When I asked what Work First's expectations of her were in situations like those she described, she exclaimed, "You tell me. Two or three times of that and you're kicked out of Work First. Kicked out of Work First. Your case goes back to social services and they taking you off, you know."

But Jackie's problems with Work First did not end there. Other obligations associated with welfare receipt further complicated her life. Even for the most organized mother, it would have been difficult to manage the multiple and overwhelming challenges faced in attempting to abide by Work First rules. Because of this, Jackie was convinced that the program was designed to entrap recipients, force them into a corner, and then terminate their participation in the program.[27] She explained:

> If you at Work First, then they want you to sit there and be called and read the newspaper and make phone calls for three or four hours. You got to get that signed and blah, blah, blah [referring to reporting requirements]. So we come out [after] an eight-hour day. I got kids, leaving to and from school. I got two in day care, and somebody got to be in and out to put the one boy on the bus 'cause he only go a half a day. Other boy getting off earlier than half a day. I got one that might get kicked out of school that day, and I'm just flipping and flopping and that four hours I've been looking for a job might not get done. Oh, you didn't bring that paper in so that means you got to do a whole 'nother eight hours to make up for the four you didn't do plus still go out and do four more for that day. So, it, it was just unreal. I couldn't. Then by the time I looked . . . trying to get everybody in the house . . . I still got them two kids over at the day care. It's six-thirty. Day care closed at six. You're dealing with a twenty-five-dollar late fee with them, plus the attitude, you know.

As structured, Work First arguably did little to aid in Jackie's own quest for self-sufficiency, but it did a great deal to create unnecessary chaos. In essence, it ignored Jackie's multiple barriers to finding and keeping a job. Although she did own a car—which needed over $1,500 worth of repairs when I met Jackie—she did not have the money to buy gas so that she could drive around looking for work. This is hardly surprising—Jackie was poor, and as Kathryn Edin and Laura Lein (1997) point out in *Making Ends Meet*, the cost of working itself can be a major hurdle to keeping work. Jackie's experience highlights the need as well to have enough resources to find work. And because she had five kids with five very different schedules and very different needs, she understandably did not have the time or inclination to keep detailed accounts of her mileage so as to receive reimbursement. Given her hectic life, a flat allowance would have been preferable. However, it was not something that the state would allow, because it had to be certain that recipients were not "abusing" the system.

Furthermore, Work First's requirement that recipients spend almost the equivalent of a full-time job searching for work—three to four hours each day looking in newspapers and then another three to four hours each day going out to employers to apply for work—could not be rectified given that Jackie had five children, each one needed to be dropped off at day care or school and picked up at different times, and failure to do so was met with its own penalty (the $25 late fee). In other words, Southeast County's Work First program essentially ignored the multiple barriers to work that recipients like Jackie faced and then faulted and sanctioned them at every turn for not taking "personal responsibility." Thus, it is no surprise that Jackie felt that her efforts to take responsibility and seek self-sufficiency were being thwarted by the very program that was established to promote just that.

This is why Jackie decided to end her participation in FIA and Work First and to begin caring for children in her own home. She was also looking for flexible part-time work. It was all she could do to maintain her sanity and try to create a positive environment for her children. Jackie explained:

> I didn't want to miss anything, and I was just running around like a chicken with my head cut off. I was so exhausted I couldn't even think for myself, let alone give [the kids] anything, you know. And that bothered me a lot. You know, I'm rushing and running around like I'm crazy, and for what? At the end of the day I'm still tired. At the end of the day the kids got to be picked up and I still, or they ain't got no clothes to wear tomorrow 'cause I've been gone all day. And I just felt lost. I felt compelled. I felt angry. I felt bitter and all of these things. I was still struggling, still bills wasn't getting paid. Lights would get cut off. I'm at school and they coming to cut the water off. And I just couldn't win for losing, and I just had to believe in my heart there was a better way even though I was sacrificing.

Jackie's decision highlights how disillusioned she became after trying to meet the requirements of an unforgiving welfare-to-work program while also trying to be present for her children, two seemingly contradictory goals in an era of "Work First." And Jackie is not alone. According to Hays (2003), despite their appreciation for what they perceived as the moral underpinnings of welfare reform, both welfare recipients and caseworkers became increasingly disillusioned as it became clear that these reforms were not designed to address the multiple obstacles that many recipients face in trying to manage work and family.

That welfare recipients tend to have a higher prevalence of characteristics that make finding and keeping work difficult has not gone unnoticed by the federal and state governments.[28] State governments in particular have begun to take steps to better address the needs of their truly disadvantaged populations. However, these measures vary considerably by state, in terms of both the actions that states take to identify their hard-to-place or difficult-to-employ populations and the strategies they use to assist these recipients in finding and keeping employment (Hays 2003; U.S. General Accounting Office 2001). Some states proactively take steps when recipients are enrolled to identify those with characteristics indicative of the difficult-to-employ and to direct them to programs and services that might better address their needs. Other states, like Michigan, do little to identify recipients who have multiple barriers to employment. Instead, these states have adopted a "test the job market" approach in which all recipients are required to look for work and the market determines who among them is difficult to employ. Only recipients who fail to find employment after a specified period—four weeks in Michigan's Work First program—are assessed for multiple barriers and considered for more targeted services. The rationale for taking this approach is that it avoids labeling some recipients as difficult-to-employ before giving them an opportunity to find jobs on their own. Furthermore, states adopting this approach want to make it very clear to their recipients that "TANF is temporary and that employment is the immediate goal" (U.S. General Accounting Office 2001, 20). This argument is understandable, but it fails to consider that recipients with multiple barriers to employment are also those with multiple barriers to compliance. By failing to identify multiple barrier cases early, these states increase the likelihood that such cases will experience sanctions that will only decrease their access to institutional social capital and make finding and keeping work that much more difficult.

States and localities also take varied approaches to addressing the needs of the hard-to-serve. Some have adopted intensive case management approaches, while others have developed programs designed specifically for the difficult-to-employ, including on-the-job training and classes on soft-skill development, which tend to focus on teaching recipients how to cope with the obstacles they face rather than addressing the obstacles specifically. It is unclear how well these more targeted programs fare.

So much focus on the multiple barriers cases, however, takes attention away from the fact that many recipients without multiple barriers also find their way back to the welfare office. Most recipients find work, even those with a barrier or two. The problem is that their jobs do not last long. Relatively few stay employed for a full year (Olson and Pavetti 1996). Hays (2003, 100) discovered this pattern while studying two welfare offices:

> Then, welfare mothers who had left earlier started coming back. Eighteen months into reform, the majority of clients walking into the Arbordale welfare office were repeat customers. People who had left with jobs had

lost them and were seeking help once again. In fact, there were so many repeaters in this relatively small city that the life skills classes were temporarily discontinued, since it seemed that nearly the entire population of poor single mothers had been through them by now.

Thus, these single mothers who helped to make welfare reform a "success" by finding work relatively quickly, either through Work First or by some other method, have also highlighted welfare reform's failures. While promoting self-sufficiency and personal responsibility, welfare reform and its crowning jewel, Work First, have almost guaranteed the long-term dependency of its participants and made them a captive, cheap workforce, because the services Work First offers do relatively little to address the multiple barriers to employment that often make welfare a struggling parent's most reasonable option.[29]

Conclusion

I began this chapter by describing the posters that adorn the Southeast County job center's walls. Although some of the images in them are truly striking, they are hardly intended solely as decoration. Instead, by hanging the posters, the center hoped to communicate two things: first, regardless of their circumstances, anyone has the power to determine his or her own employment path; and second, the center hinted in these posters, its own role in helping individuals to achieve their dream would be limited. Unlike the federally funded work development programs of past decades that attempted to address the specific needs of economically disadvantaged job-seekers through programs and services offering general and remedial education, occupational skill development, and work experience, the programs and services at Southeast County's job center, including core employment services, WIA, and Work First, focus primarily on self-directed job search activities with the intention of helping job-seekers to find work, any work, as quickly as possible.

For poor black job-seekers, who were disproportionately beset by multiple barriers to employment, mobilizing this institutional form of social capital was much easier said than done. By their own accounts, resource room attendants, the heart of the center's core employment services, systematically withheld assistance from young, black, male job-seekers, whose "neediness" they interpreted as a disinterest in helping themselves and doing the work required to find work. WIA employment and training specialists were actively and regularly discouraged from assisting multiple barrier cases, especially ex-felons and welfare recipients, by supervisors concerned with how such assistance might affect the bottom line. And under the Work First program, recipients with multiple barriers to employment were systematically sanctioned at higher rates for noncompliance, since the barriers that made finding and keeping work difficult also made staying in compliance with welfare rules and regulations close to impossible.

Together with chapters 3 and 4, this chapter illuminates the irony that during the job search process, access to personal and institutional social capital is at best only part of the problem. Instead, hindered by a set of discourses and structural constraints that inspire distrust and noncooperation among those who are well positioned to assist, not only do poor black job-seekers have difficulty mobilizing job-finding assistance from their job-holding friends, relatives, and acquaintances, but they also have a tremendous amount of difficulty mobilizing institutional social capital toward this end. The job of finding work is thus made that much more difficult for a population already beleaguered by multiple barriers to employment.

Chapter 6

Conclusion

Engage most urban poverty scholars about the persistent joblessness of the black poor, and depending on who you talk to, you are likely to hear one or more of the following explanations: because of the changing structure of urban economies, there has been a dramatic loss of good-paying jobs for lesser-skilled workers, and this loss has had a disproportionately negative effect on black, inner-city workers; despite claims to the contrary, race is still one of the most important factors affecting blacks' life chances, as evidence from audit studies on employer discrimination has shown, and this effect is most profound for black ex-offenders; embedded in subcultures of defeatism and resistance, the black poor do not value work as a productive enterprise in and of itself and so have endless excuses for why they cannot engage in it; and the black poor, especially residents of neighborhoods characterized by concentrated disadvantage (a disproportionate share of the black poor), are socially isolated from mainstream ties who could inform them about job opportunities, and so they do not find out about job opportunities even when they arise. While these theses do not exhaust the list of possible explanations, they represent the intellectual discourses that are most often deployed regarding persistent black joblessness.

In this book, I have contended that although each of these theoretical frames is compelling and each has wide appeal, we cannot draw from them singly or in combination to come to a complete understanding of persistent black joblessness because, with very few exceptions (see Newman 1999), none of these perspectives examines the process of finding work in ethnographic detail, engaging the black poor in in-depth interviews about the job-finding process. Two negative consequences for understanding persistent joblessness result from neglecting this approach and the assumptions that underlie it. The first has to do with meaning-making. Structural accounts of black joblessness, although profoundly insightful, often fail to consider the extent to which the black poor actually understand their circumstances as such. To the extent that researchers do consider this, they largely assume that the black poor understand that their employment problems are largely rooted in structural constraints. Proponents of the cultural deficiency perspective do not ignore the meanings that the black poor attribute to their labor market circumstances. Instead, they critically misstate them, arguing that the black poor do not work either because they do not believe that they can handle the difficulties associated with finding and keeping work or because they find the opportunities to which they have access morally repulsive.

However, the black poor do not see structural factors as the ones that are most pressing, nor are they motivated by subcultures of defeatism or resistance. Instead, they largely explain persistent joblessness as a failure on the part of individuals to uplift themselves. Although employer discrimination and the changing structure of the urban economy have had the most profound effects on the employment of the black poor, prior survey research suggests that among the black poor, structural factors such as discrimination and job loss do not register as major impediments to achieving their goals. Deficient motivation and individual effort do. Thus, even while acknowledging the prevalence of discrimination and other structural constraints, most poor blacks nonetheless conclude that hard work and individual resolve are most essential for blacks' achievement.

My own respondents were no different in this regard. The majority indicated that finding a job was not difficult at all, because jobs were readily available. To the extent that they were not, *those with perseverance would nevertheless prevail; any job-seeker with motivation and drive could find one.* Those who could not were simply not looking, and their joblessness indicated a weakness of character, a failure on their part to fight for what they wanted. Furthermore, with an abundance of programs and services available to aid the poor's transition to employment, they argued, the jobless had no credible defense for their joblessness. By failing to examine closely the process of finding work, proponents of these perspectives have neglected or misstated the meanings that the black poor attribute to their employment circumstances; these meanings affect both their actions in the economic realm and their employment outcomes above and beyond the structural factors that also constrain them.

These views have consequences for how black poor job-seekers and job-holders engage each other during the process of finding work, but in failing to examine the process of finding work in ethnographic detail, researchers have failed to recognize the interactional nature of that process. Instead, they imagine job search as a process undertaken by and affecting individuals—specifically job-seekers, who make decisions about what steps to take during job search as free-standing actors in isolation, essentially determining the costs and benefits of each action and taking constraints and opportunities into consideration based on their own individual mental calculus (Pescosolido 1992). But individuals are not free-standing actors, and the decisionmaking process is not undertaken in isolation, because the dynamics of the decisionmaking process are at least in part a function of social interactions with others that provide a framework for interpreting and acting within the economic realm (Pescosolido 1992). Because the dominant perspectives on joblessness neglect the interactional nature of the job search process, they ignore the significance of these patterned social relations, most especially between job-seekers and job-holders, the two fundamental nodes in the job-matching process. These perspectives also fail to take into account that, given the explanations for joblessness that the black poor most often deploy, tensions and conflicts pervade the interpersonal relations between these two sets of actors, fueling distrust and provoking uncooperativeness.

Specifically, when in possession of job information or influence, the overwhelming majority of job-holders expressed concern that job-seekers in their networks were too unmotivated to accept assistance, required great expenditures of time and emotional energy, or acted too irresponsibly on the job, thereby jeopardizing job-holders' own reputations in the eyes of employers and harming their already tenuous labor market prospects. Consequently, they were generally reluctant to assist. To justify their unwillingness, these job-holders literally ranted about the importance of self-reliance, espousing the importance of bringing individualistic values to the job-finding process.

Job-holders did assist, but assistance was highly contingent on job-seekers' reputations, the job-holders' own reputation and status, the strength of the relationship between the job-holders and job-seekers, and the job-holders' structural embeddedness. Overwhelmingly they made determinations about whether to assist based on their job-seeking relations' reputations, both at work and at home, as these gave them some indication of how these job-seekers might behave on the job, and so their decisions were at least in part based on their cognitive assessments of job-seekers' trustworthiness. Job-holders were displeased by job-seekers who transitioned in and out of jobs frequently, who were habitually absent or tardy, and who had poor work attitudes. They were also concerned about whether their job-seeking ties would "bring the street to the job," behavior that included showing the effects of alcohol and drug abuse, acting raucously and boisterously, stealing, and intimidating authority figures and coworkers. Job-seekers' reputations were important because of the potential damage they might do to job-holders' own reputations. Indeed, it was the interaction between the two—job-holders' and job-seekers' reputations—that seemed to matter most in the former's determinations. Both job-seekers' and job-holders' reputations dominated job-holders' concerns about whether to assist.

There was a contingency, however, to reputational concerns. Even for job-seekers of ill repute, job-holders could be mobilized if their levels of social and economic stability were very low and they felt they had nothing to lose. Those who perceived their situations to be dire were willing to provide assistance to almost anyone who came along, regardless of reputation, in the hope that the beneficiary of their assistance would quickly become a source of social and material support. Job-holders who were less overwhelmed by their social and economic circumstances because they had greater personal, social, or material sources to draw upon were less likely to come to the aid of others without regard to reputation.

Whether or not job-holders could be mobilized for job-finding assistance was also affected by job-holders' history of prior attempts to assist. Specifically, those whose attempts to assist had been met with disengagement were far less open to providing assistance than those whose history of assistance included successful matches of motivated job-seekers. With the former, a psychology of distrust developed such that they eventually stopped trying to assist; they perceived assistance as a waste of time because they deemed job-seekers to be too unmotivated to take advantage of the information they had to offer or the influence they could wield.

But psychologies of distrust prevailed in certain contexts more than in others. Access to social capital and neighborhood poverty status interacted to affect job-holders' willingness to assist. Among the employed of low-poverty neighborhoods, greater social capital was associated with a willingness to assist. However, among the employed of high-poverty neighborhoods, greater social capital was associated with reluctance. This relationship is unfortunate, even if understandable, given that the latter job-holders reside in neighborhoods where access to social capital among the unemployed appears inferior. Furthermore, all job-holders are making decisions in a larger labor market context, one in which the growing significance of soft skills is negatively affecting employers' perceptions of low-income black workers, and one in which cyclical changes in the economy affect job-holders' recruitment and screening decisions as they relate to their employers' hiring practices.

Not surprisingly, job-holders' distrust and reluctance had consequences for job-seekers' search behavior. Indeed, one-quarter of job-seekers were reluctant to seek assistance from friends, relatives, and acquaintances or to accept assistance when offered for fear that they would not be able to fulfill their obligations or might be maligned by their job-holding ties. Job-seekers' willingness to seek or accept assistance was contingent on three key factors. First, they took their own reputations into consideration to assess their ability to fulfill obligations toward job-holders who were willing and able to assist. To the extent that they deemed themselves risky prospects, they were unwilling to mobilize their social resources on their own behalf. Second, like job-holders, they also considered the history of responses to their requests for assistance. If they perceived themselves to have been rebuffed in the past, especially by those close to them, they were disinclined to reach out for help. The third factor was structural context: gender, access to social capital, neighborhood poverty, and local labor market conditions all mattered. When faced with fears of falling short or being maligned, men were far more likely than women to express great reluctance to seek assistance or to accept help when offered, in part because men had much greater difficulty protecting themselves and their sense of masculinity from suggestions that they were undeserving failures. Reluctance was also associated with embeddedness in a network of relations with fewer connections to unskilled workers, those best positioned to offer assistance or access to the jobs for which job-seekers were most qualified. However, as local labor market conditions worsened, reluctance to use personal contacts to find work seemed to ease a bit. Thus, within the context of poverty, friends, relatives, acquaintances, and institutions in their social milieu blamed the black poor and the jobless for their condition of persistent joblessness and deployed discourses of joblessness that highlighted individuals' moral shortcomings and stressed personal responsibility and self-sufficiency as the panacea. Cognizant of how they were viewed and how their joblessness was understood, job-seekers were pushed into defensive individualism, but they also embraced individualism and self-reliant approaches to job search as their own distrust toward themselves and their intermediaries grew.

Unfortunately, pervasive distrust and noncooperation were not unique to relationships between job-seekers and job-holders. They also characterized relationships between job-seekers and job center staff who were charged with facilitating their clients' labor force participation. These interpersonal dynamics also had consequences for the black poor's ability to mobilize institutional social capital. For black, poor job-seekers, who were disproportionately beset by multiple barriers to employment, mobilizing institutional social capital was much easier said than done. By their own accounts, resource room attendants, the heart of the center's core employment services, systematically withheld assistance from young, black, male job-seekers, whose "neediness" they interpreted as a disinterest in helping themselves and completing the tasks required to find work. WIA employment and training specialists were actively and regularly discouraged from assisting multiple barrier cases, especially ex-felons and welfare recipients, by supervisors concerned with how this assistance might affect the bottom line. And under the Work First program, recipients with multiple barriers to employment were systematically sanctioned at higher rates for non-compliance since the barriers that made finding and keeping work difficult also made staying in compliance with welfare rules and regulations close to impossible. Thus, even within the context of institutional social capital, job-finding assistance was not necessarily forthcoming but instead was part of an elaborate decisionmaking process framed and affected by job-seekers' multiple barriers to employment, the discourses of joblessness that gave primacy to individuals' shortcomings and cultural deficiencies, and, most importantly, institutional pressures to avoid assisting the hard-to-serve.

Not surprisingly, there are a number of similarities in the experiences of the labor market intermediaries discussed here—job-holders and center staff. By cataloging these, we might come to a better understanding of the emergence of pervasive distrust and noncooperation—a psychology that, I contend, further disadvantages the black poor in labor market competition. The first and most obvious similarity that these two sets of labor market intermediaries share is the population they are charged with assisting, formally or informally: a black poor population disproportionately beset by major barriers to employment, including low levels of basic skills, limited access to safe, affordable, and reliable child care and transportation, addiction to drugs and alcohol, prison records, and negative stereotyping by employers, leading to employer discrimination. These barriers to employment also significantly decrease the likelihood that job-seekers will act in trustworthy ways because their barriers will negatively affect their ability to do so.

Second, these labor market intermediaries have few resources, personal or institutional, at their disposal with which to effectively help job-seekers address their barriers. Reluctant job-holders tend to reside in communities of concentrated disadvantage that offer little access to quality education and training, safe, affordable, and reliable child care and transportation, drug and alcohol treatment programs, and programs to help integrate ex-offenders back into the larger society. Similarly, center staff are employed by an institution that promotes self-sufficiency and personal responsibility as the panacea for chronic joblessness while actively dissuading the black poor from taking part in the jobs programs that might best address their needs.

Third, for both sets of intermediaries, third-party concerns help to create and intensify pervasive distrust and noncooperation. Assisting black, poor job-seekers is a risk because the institutions in which they are embedded create disincentives toward facilitating their hire. While job-holders fear the effect that making a bad match will have on their own reputations and status on the job, center staff also worry about how their relationship with their employer might be affected if they facilitate hires for job-seekers with multiple barriers. Not only do they fear that doing so will ruin their reputation with their employer, but they fear that facilitating these hires will also reduce the likelihood that they will achieve the state's performance goals, which help to determine whether they will continue to manage the programs in years to come. Thus, because of third-party concerns, both job-holders and center staff worry a great deal about the effect that their brokering will have on their own standing, which both sets of actors perceive as very tenuous. Combined, these three factors have a profound effect on both sets of labor market intermediaries, feeding pervasive distrust and noncooperation toward black, poor job-seekers.

How do we address this issue? I would suggest a series of targeted approaches embedded within a larger systemic approach to significantly reduce the multiple barriers to employment of the black poor while also building bonds of trust and cooperation. Specifically, I propose that states reinvest in the development of institutional resources within low-income black communities. They should do so in ways that (1) help residents gain much-needed, market-relevant skills, (2) provide jobs, (3) facilitate residents' ability to find and keep work, and (4) provide opportunities to build relationships of trust and cooperation. As an example, finding safe, affordable, reliable, and flexible child care is a significant problem for low-income workers, and this one problem represents a major barrier to finding and keeping work. Instead of providing child care referral services, which is what most states currently do to assist single mothers with child care needs, states could remedy this problem by subsidizing neighborhood-based child care centers. Under this plan, states would open child care centers within poor communities. The number and location of centers would depend on the number of children located in the neighborhood as well as on where they tend to reside, but no center could care for more than fifty children. States would either train workers or subsidize their training for certification through programs like WIA. These workers, residents of the poor communities themselves, would then use these skills to operate the child care centers located in their communities.

This approach has a number of benefits. First, it provides a muchneeded institutional resource to poor black communities. According to prior research, poor black women are far more likely than their white counterparts to rely on free child care from friends and relatives (Brewster and Padavic 2002; Hogan, Hao, and Parish 1990), and one reason is that safe, affordable, reliable, and flexible child care options are in such short supply (but see Small 2006; Small and Stark 2005). However, black women are also more likely to report that the kin care they receive is inadequate given their needs. State-subsidized, neighborhood-based child care centers could meet this need, reducing by one the multiple barriers to employment faced by black poor job-seekers while also having a profound effect on low-income black communities. This brings us to my second point: these state-subsidized facilities would also provide employment opportunities for residents of the neighborhood. Third, by facilitating the training of poor black residents to operate child care centers in their communities and to care for their children within that context, states would assist these residents in the acquisition of valuable human capital, and they could use these skills and their experience working in child care centers to find employment in the private sector as well. Fourth, as work by Mario Small and his colleagues (Small 2006; Small and Stark 2005) suggests, by opening neighborhood-based child care centers, states would also facilitate the development of community-level social capital. As residents dropped off and picked up their children at their neighborhood child care center each day, they would come into regular and frequent contact with other parents. They would also get to know employees of the center, residents like themselves, with whom they could develop relationships of trust and cooperation.

Similar steps could be taken to address concerns about public safety and about the paucity of safe, affordable, reliable, and flexible public transportation systems that serve poor communities. Through innovative approaches such as these, we could facilitate the development of community-based institutions that serve multiple purposes, bring people together, and aid in the development of valuable social capital from which the whole community can benefit.

Appendix A:
Sample, Data, and Data Collection Strategies

Between 1999 and 2002, I collaborated with Alford Young Jr., associate professor of sociology at the University of Michigan, and a small team of graduate students to interview 105 low-income, young, black men and women from "Southeast County," Michigan. Relative to the state and the nation as a whole, Southeast County's population of 323,000 (according to the 2000 census) is highly educated, occupationally well placed, and financially stable. Some 92 percent of residents age twenty-five or older had graduated from high school, and almost half (48 percent) had a bachelor's degree or higher. Ninety-six percent of labor force participants were employed, and among the employed, almost half worked in just two major industrial categories—one-third worked in educational, health, and social services while another 15 percent worked in the manufacturing sector.

Furthermore, almost half of the employed had managerial or professional positions. Given their relatively high levels of educational and occupational attainment, it should come as no surprise that median household income in 1999 was $52,000 (compared to Michigan's $45,000). Just 5 percent of the county's families fell below the poverty line, and only 2 percent of all households received public assistance income. On its face, then, Southeast County appears to be one of the last places anyone would turn to as a site for examinations of persistent joblessness among the black poor. Within this sea of relative affluence, however, are a few islands of socioeconomic despair, with blacks disproportionately represented among their inhabitants.

Estimated at 40,000, Southeast's black population is 12.3 percent of the county's residents. Although on the whole they are not as affluent as the white residents of the county, they are not doing badly either. In 2000 the overwhelming majority, some 84 percent, were high school graduates, and one-quarter had a bachelor's degree or higher. Ninety-three percent of black labor force participants were employed, primarily in the educational and health industrial sectors, where most worked as administrative support staff, professionals, or service workers. However, at $35,000, median household income for blacks was substantially less than the county average of $52,000.

Southeast County's black residents disproportionately experienced the county's problems of joblessness and poverty. Although the unemployment rate in Southeast County was less than 3.8 percent in 2000, among black residents it was almost twice that, at 7 percent. Furthermore, personal poverty was twice as high as the county average, family poverty was three times as high, and public assistance use was six and a half times higher than the county average—13 percent of black families in the county received public assistance compared to only 2 percent countywide. What this means is that although blacks were only 12 percent of the county's residents, they were one-fifth of the unemployed, one-fifth of the *individuals* in poverty, one-third of the *families* in poverty, almost half of the families on public assistance, and slightly under one-third of the female-headed families in the county.

Although many of Southeast County's black poor resided in just a few census tracts and thus were not terribly difficult to find, they were not necessarily an easy population to recruit for participation in this study. As is often the case when studying low-income populations, we found it difficult to recruit participants through random sampling techniques (Edin and Lein 1997), even though we made great efforts to do so. In the summer of 1999, we contacted GENESYS Sampling Systems, a service that provided us with the publicly listed names, addresses, and telephone numbers of 350 randomly selected residents from Southeast County's poorest census tract. Although we had initially thought to restrict the sampling to those age twenty-five to thirty-four (the 1990 census indicated that there were 379 residents in this census tract in this age group), because there were so few listings for residents this age (only forty-eight records), we broadened our criteria. From GENESYS, we received the names, addresses, and telephone numbers of 350 residents. We attempted to contact residents with the phone numbers we had been given but found ourselves facing three major obstacles: lines were no longer in service, residents had moved, or households did not have a resident matching our criteria. Thus, from August to December 1999, we had a yield of only nine interviews.

Our next approach was to canvass the community and record every address for every housing structure. We then mailed recruitment letters asking respondents to participate and promised to provide a $25 incentive for participation. This method generated only two additional interviews.

Our third strategy was to canvass the community by going door to door and requesting participation. We began canvassing the area's housing projects with the intent of working our way through all of the projects in the community. We usually canvassed between 10:00 A.M. and 5:00 P.M. Although few people who fit the criteria refused to participate when asked, we were presented with some challenges. The projects that housed the most disadvantaged residents were relatively unsafe. Gang activity, including drug dealing, occurred conspicuously. Violent crime was so prevalent that few residents we spoke with would allow their children to play outside or ventured outside themselves except to leave the neighborhood. Furthermore, residents would often refuse to answer their doors. Many had eviction notices posted outside their apartments, and they may have thought that we were bill collectors. We also believed that some did not want interviewers to see their homes. Self-conscious about her dwelling, one respondent requested that we conduct the interview in her barely functioning car.

Because we perceived ourselves to be in some danger, and because many residents clearly had issues of trust where interviewers were concerned, we then decided to recruit residents from social service agencies; conducting interviews in this semi-public arena would reassure interviewers who feared for their safety, as well as reassure residents who feared for their own well-being. To resolve this issue, contacts in the area suggested that we would find all of the participants we needed if we were to go to either of two social service agencies. He was only half right. One of the agencies to which he referred us catered to residents experiencing various housing issues and provided some employment assistance as well; however, because this agency was not overwhelmed with clients, there were relatively few participants to be found there. The other agency, the job center, was far more fruitful, yielding the bulk of our 105 interviews (71) between August 2000 and June 2002. Our contact's statement and the truth behind it indicate the reach that this one institution has in the lives of Southeast County's black poor population. In all, 72 percent of respondents were recruited at both social service agencies, two-thirds at the job center alone. During this time interviewers took up residence at the job center's office during regular business hours. With the assistance of center staff, subjects who fit the study criteria were recruited. We were seeking black men and women between the ages of twenty and forty who resided in Southeast County and who had no more than a high school diploma or GED.

Respondents were surveyed about their family background, networks, employment history, and job-finding methods. They were also questioned in depth about their childhood (including childhood impressions of work); marriage, relationships, and children; employment history, experiences, and impressions of work; job referral networks; philosophy of employment; and attitudes and opinions about the extent and nature of job opportunities for low-skilled workers like themselves. Interviews averaged between two and three hours and were conducted by African Americans.

Table A.1 displays mean sample characteristics by data collection strategy.

Also, in an effort to speak to concerns raised in the urban poverty literature about the effect of neighborhood poverty concentration, respondents' addresses were matched with corresponding census tracts to de-

Table A.1   Mean Sample Characteristics by Data Collection Strategy

	Full Sample (N = 103)	Random Sample (N = 27)	Center-Recruited Sample (N = 76)
Age	28.4	30.1	27.8
	(5.9)	(5.5)	(6.0)
Gender (female)	.52	.67	.46
Never married	.78	.67	.83
Have children	.75	.74	.75
Number of children (if parent)	2.5	2.6	2.5
	(1.4)	(1.1)	(1.5)
High school graduate or GED	.84	1.0	.78
Employed	.50	.89	.36
Hourly wages	$9.30	$8.57	$9.57
Public assistance			
Currently receiving	.31	.19	.36
Ever received	.46	.58	.40
Neighborhood poverty rate			
Low to moderate poverty	.67	.37	.78
High to extreme poverty	.33	.63	.22

Source: Author's compilation.

termine the family-level poverty status of their neighborhoods. Employing a variation of the categories of neighborhood poverty concentration typically used in urban poverty studies, I found that 69 percent of respondents lived in census tracts in which rates of family poverty were low to moderate (0 percent to 29.9 percent), and 31 percent resided in the type of neighborhoods characterized by much of the urban underclass literature, with rates of family poverty that were high to extreme (30 percent or higher). Not surprisingly, in terms of social and demographic indicators, low- to moderate-poverty neighborhoods differed substantially from the neighborhoods in which poverty rates were high to extreme. In the low- to moderate-poverty neighborhoods, in which two-thirds of respondents lived, 31 percent of residents were black (compared to 78 percent of the residents in the high- to extreme-poverty neighborhoods), 11 percent had not completed high school (compared to 26 percent), 30 percent were not in the labor force (compared to 43 percent), 13 percent lived in poverty (compared to 43 percent), and just 5 percent received public assistance (compared to 23 percent). Literally located just a stone's throw away from the southwest border of the neighborhood with the highest rates of poverty, unemployment, public assistance receipt, and female headship and, not coincidentally, the highest concentration of black residents is Southeast County's job center.

Appendix B:
In-Depth Interview Protocol

Background Information

I'd like to begin this part of the interview by asking you a few questions about how life was for you as a child.

1. Describe your relationship with your parents and/or guardians.
2. Describe the neighborhood(s) in which you were raised.
   a. What kind of relationship did you and your family have with your neighbors?
3. Did you have any role models?
   a. Who were they?
   b. Why/how did they become role models?
   c. Why types of discussions/activities did you do with this person/these persons?
   d. What sort of work did this person/these persons do?
   e. Did you discuss jobs with your role model?

Childhood Impressions of Work

Parents' Employment

4. Describe the types of jobs your parents/guardians held.
5. Do you think they were satisfied with their job situations?
6. When you were growing up …
   a. How did you feel about your parents' jobs?
   b. Why did you feel this way?
   c. Did you ever visit your parents' work site? Describe the experience.
7. If your parents/guardians ever received welfare …
   a. How long did they receive welfare?
   b. Why did they receive welfare?
   c. As a child, what did you think about your parents receiving welfare?

d. How do you feel now about your parents/guardians receiving welfare?

Extended Kin, Neighbors, and Work

Now I'd like to discuss your extended family members with regard to work. This includes your aunts, uncles, cousins, grandparents, etc.

8. Thinking back, how would you describe the employment situation of your extended family members?
   a. Would you say that they were mostly employed, unemployed, or maybe on welfare?
   b. What type of work did most of your extended family members do?
   c. Do you think they were satisfied with the work that they did?
9. To the best of your knowledge, what type of jobs did your neighbors have?

General Questions

10. During your childhood, can you remember any major positive events involving your parents/guardians' work situation that had a major impact on your home life? When I say "major events," I mean getting a promotion or big pay raise. If so, please describe the situation as completely as possible, as best as you can remember.
11. During your childhood, can you remember any major negative events involving your parents/guardians' work situation that had a major impact on your home life? When I say "major events," I mean losing a job, for instance. If so, please describe the situation as completely as possible, as best as you can remember.

Family Situation, Marriage, and Children

Marriage and Relationships

Now I'd like to ask you a few questions about your current family situation.

12. Describe your current or most recent long-term or steady relationship.
    a. Was this person a spouse, partner, girl/boyfriend?
    b. How long did/has your relationship last/lasted?
    c. Do/did you live together?
    d. Do you have children together?

13. In general, how would you characterize the level of support that your current or most recent spouse, partner, or steady girl/boyfriend gave you with regard to work?
14. Describe situations in which your spouse, partner, or steady girl/boyfriend made it easier for you to achieve your work or career goals.
15. Describe situations in which your spouse, partner, or steady girl/boyfriend made it more difficult for you to achieve your work or career goals.
16. In general, would you say that your experiences with this spouse, partner, or steady girl/boyfriend are consistent with the level of support that other partners have shown you?
17. How important is it to you that your spouse, partner, or girl/boyfriend work or bring home a paycheck? Explain.

Children

Now I'd like to ask you a few questions about children.

18. How many children do you have, if any? [If none, go to question 21]

For Those with Children
19. How has having children affected your work life?
20. Because of your children, what are some of the obstacles you must overcome to find and keep jobs?

For Those Without Children
21. Why haven't you had children?

Employment History, Experiences, and Impressions of Work

22. How would you rate your work experiences from the time you left school until now? In other words, do you have a positive overall opinion of the jobs you've held or a negative overall opinion?
23. Discuss which job(s) made for a positive experience, and why.
24. Which job(s) made for a negative experience, and why?
25. What would you say that you've learned about yourself from working at each of these jobs?
26. What are the skills and talents you bring to the workplace and where did you learn these skills?
27. What are your future career goals, and how do you plan to achieve them?

If Unemployed

28. Are you looking for work now? [If no, go to question 34]

If Looking
29. How long have you been looking for work?
30. What are some of the steps you've taken to find work?
31. What kind of jobs are you looking for?
32. Why do you think that you've been unable to find a job so far?
33. How do others treat you because you don't work or have never held a job? [Go to question 35]

If Not Looking
34. Why are you not looking for work?

Job Referral Networks

Now I'd like to ask a few questions about finding work.

35. In general, how difficult would you say it is to find a job, any job?
    a. How difficult would you say it is not to find a good job?
36. What obstacles have you had finding work?
37. How important is it to use friends, relatives, and acquaintances to find out about job opportunities?
38. When you hear about job openings at your workplace or elsewhere, what do you do? In other words, do you tell the people you know about them? Explain.
39. Have you ever gone to anyone you know to ask about job opportunities for yourself or anyone else you know? [If no, go to question 40]
    a. Who did you ask and why did you ask this person?
    b. What does this person do for a living and what types of jobs could s/he help you find?
    c. Would you say that this person has influence or power on the job?
    d. Has this person helped you on more than one occasion?
    e. How did this person help?
    f. Did you get the job?
    g. Would you have been able to get this job without the help of this person?
40. Has anyone ever come to you for help in finding or getting a job?
    a. Who has come to you for help and why?
    b. What types of jobs did this person/these persons ask about?
    c. How did you help, if at all?

    d. Would you help again?

    e. Did this job-seeker/these job-seekers get the job?

41. Now I want you to think about situations in which you have helped someone to find a job. Once the job-seeker has been hired for the job, to what extent have you helped that person get accustomed to the job?

42. When people you know approach you for help in finding work, how do you determine whether you will help or not?

43. What do you think are the positive aspects of helping others to find work?

44. What do you think are the negative aspects of trying to help others to find work?

45. I want you to think about all of your family members, friends, and acquaintances. Is there a specific person you know who is helpful in finding work for others?

    a. Who is this person?

    b. What types of jobs does this person find for others?

    c. What does this person do for a living?

Philosophy of Employment

The Good Job

46. What is your idea of a good job?

47. Is it more important to have a job that pays well or to have a job that you enjoy? Explain.

    a. What job would give you complete satisfaction right now? Explain.

48. Are the following important: health care benefits, hours/flexibility, location, relationships with bosses and coworkers, salary, opportunity for promotion, and/or union membership?

49. Which people have the best chance for getting a good job and why?

50. Do you know anyone personally who you feel has a good job right now?

    a. What does this person/these persons do?

    b. Why do you think it's a good job?

    c. What is it about this person/these people that allows them to have good jobs?

51. What does it take to get a good job?

The Bad Job

52. What makes a job a bad job?

    a. Give examples of specific occupations or jobs.

    b. List qualities of those jobs that make them bad, such as lack of

health care benefits, bad hours/no flexibility, faraway location, poor relationships with bosses and coworkers, low salary, few or no opportunities for advancement, and/or no union membership.
53. What do you think the minimum wage is and would you ever work for minimum wage?
54. What is the minimum amount of money that you would work for (per hour, week, bi-week, month, or year)?
55. Would your decision depend on the type of job you held? For instance, would it make a difference if the job was an office job, a factory job, a job in a fast-food restaurant, or a job on a construction site?

Attitudes and Opinions

56. What type of jobs would you say exist today for blacks with a similar level of education and work experience as yourself?
    a. Do opportunities differ for black men and black women?
57. How secure do you feel in today's job market?
58. Do you think there is more or less opportunity for people to find a good job than in the past ten years? Why do you feel this way?
59. Where do you see yourself in terms of work and employment in the next year, five years, and ten years?
    a. What steps do you plan to take to achieve these goals?
60. What do you think about the following statement: "The hardest-working people have the best jobs."
61. What do you think about the following statement: "People who can't keep a steady job or who are unemployed are lazy."
62. How would you describe your work ethic to people?
    a. Do you think you need any improvement regarding your attitude toward work? Why or why not?
    b. Has anyone ever challenged your work ethic?
63. Finally, for young adults moving from school to work, what advice would you give about jobs?
    a. What advice would you give about the job situation today?
    b. What advice would you give about how to deal with coworkers?
    c. What advice would you give about how to deal with bosses and/or supervisors?
    d. What advice would you give about how to find jobs?

Conclusion

64. Do you have any questions or issues about the interview that you would like to raise with me?
65. Is there anything that you left out of our discussion that you would like to discuss now?

Appendix C:
Survey Instrument

Section A: Demographics and Household Composition

The first set of questions is about your own background.

A1. Are you currently married, separated, divorced, widowed, or have you never been married?
   1. Married
   2. Separated
   3. Divorced
   4. Widowed
   5. Never been married
A2. How many times have you been married (including your present marriage)?
A3. When you got married for the first time, how old were you?
A4. Do you have any children?
   1. Yes
   2. No (Go to A9)
A5. How many children do you have?
A6. How old were you when your first child was born?
A7. Do all of your children live with you?
   1. Yes
   2. No
A8. What is the total number of people who usually live in your household?

To help us understand your living situation, I would like to make a list of persons who usually live here and get some basic information about each person. Please include the adults as well as the children. Let's start with you, then continue with the other adults, then the children (up to eleven household members total). It will help if we identify them by name, but that is not necessary. For each . . .

A9. Is this person male or female?
  1. Male
  2. Female
A10. How is this person related to you?
  1. Spouse/partner
  2. Own child
  3. Parent
  4. Extended kin
  5. Unrelated
A11. How old was this person on his/her last birthday?
A12. What is the highest grade of school or college he/she has completed?
A13. Is this person currently working for pay?
  1. Yes
  2. No
A14. Does this person contribute financially to the household?
  1. Yes
  2. No

Section B: Family Background

B1. Primarily, when you were growing up, did you live in a two-parent home, single-parent home, foster care or group home, or another type of home?
  1. Two-parent home
  2. Single-parent home
  3. Foster care or group home
  4. Other (please specify)
B2. I'm going to read a list of women who may have helped raise you when you were growing up. After hearing this list, please tell me which of these women, if any, you lived with the most before the age of eighteen.
  1. Biological mother
  2. Stepmother
  3. Father's girlfriend/partner
  4. Adoptive mother
  5. Grandmother
  6. Aunt
  7. Other female relative
  8. No mother figure
B3. How old was she on her last birthday?
B4. As far as you know, what is the highest grade of school or college she completed?
  1. Eighth grade or less

2. Some high school
3. High school/GED
4. Some college
5. College or higher

B5. During the time you were growing up, would you say she worked for pay all of the time, most of the time, about half of the time, some of the time, or none of the time?
1. All of the time
2. Most of the time
3. About half of the time
4. Some of the time
5. None of the time (Go to B8)

B6. Thinking about her current or last job, what are/were her most important activities or duties?

B7. Thinking about her current or last job, in what kind of industry does/did she work?

B8. To the best of your knowledge, has she ever received any form of government assistance such as SSI, AFDC, or food stamps?
1. Yes
2. No

B9. Is she still living?
1. Yes
2. No (Go to B11)

B10. Is she currently working for pay?
1. Yes
2. No

B11. Now I'm going to read a list of men who may have helped raise you when you were growing up. After hearing this list, please tell me which of these men, if any, you lived with the most before the age of eighteen.
1. Biological father
2. Stepfather
3. Mother's boyfriend/partner
4. Adoptive father
5. Grandfather
6. Uncle
7. Other male relative
8. No father figure (Skip to B19)

B12. How old was he on his last birthday?

B13. As far as you know, what is the highest grade of school or college he completed?
1. Eighth grade or less
2. Some high school
3. High school/GED

     4. Some college
     5. College or higher

B14. During the time you were growing up, would you say he worked for pay all of the time, most of the time, about half of the time, some of the time, or none of the time?
     1. All of the time
     2. Most of the time
     3. About half of the time
     4. Some of the time
     5. None of the time (Go to B17)

B15. Thinking about his current or last job, what are/were his most important activities or duties?

B16. Thinking about his current or last job, in what kind of industry does/did he work?

B17. Is he still living?
     1. Yes
     2. No (Go to B19)

B18. Is he currently working for pay?
     1. Yes
     2. No

B19. Including those who have passed away, how many sisters and brothers do you have in all?

Let's talk more about your sisters and brothers, including those no longer living. Starting from the oldest and going to the youngest, please tell me the names of all your sisters and brothers. For each . . .

B20. Is this person your sister or brother?
     1. Sister
     2. Brother

B21. How old was this person on his/her last birthday?

B22. What is the highest grade of school or college he/she has completed?
     1. Eighth grade
     2. Some high school
     3. High school diploma
     4. Some college
     5. College plus

B23. How frequently are you in contact with this person?
     1. Almost daily
     2. Once a week
     3. Few times a month
     4. Few times a year
     5. Less than once a year

B24. Is your sister or brother currently working for pay?
    1. Yes
    2. No
B25. What are her/his important activities or duties?
B26. In what kind of business or industry does she/he work?
B27. Has your sister or brother ever received any form of government assistance such as SSI, AFDC, or food stamps?
    1. Yes
    2. No
B28. If you needed a job, would you ask this person for job info or help finding a job?
    1. Yes
    2. No
B29. If this person needed a job, would you help him/her obtain a job at your place of employment?
B30. Do you have any other siblings?
    1. Yes
    2. No

Section C: Employment History

Now let's talk about your current and past work experience.

C1. Since leaving full-time schooling, how much of the time would you say that you have worked—almost all of the time, most of the time, about half the time, or almost none of the time?
    1. Almost all of the time
    2. Most of the time
    3. About half the time
    4. Almost none of the time
C2. Since leaving full-time school, how many steady jobs have you had, that is, jobs that lasted for six months or more?
C3. Are you currently receiving a public aid grant in your own name? By public aid grant I mean ADC or AFDC or SSI (Social Security Insurance).
    1. Yes
    2. No (Go to C5)
C4. What kind of aid do you receive—AFDC/ADC, SSI, or some other kind of assistance?
    1. AFDC/ADC (Go to C7)
    2. SSI (Go to C7)
    3. Other (Go to C7)

C5. Have you ever received a public aid grant in your own name?
1. Yes
2. No (Go to C9)

C6. What kind of aid did you receive—AFDC/ADC, SSI, or some other kind of assistance?
1. AFDC/ADC
2. SSI
3. Other

C7. How old were you when you received public aid for the first time?

C8. To the best of your recollection, how many times have you received public aid grants?

Now let's talk about the times you've had steady work, that is, when you were working for six months or more doing the same thing. Except for military service, this includes any kind of work for money. Let's start first by discussing your current or most recent job and then going backwards. For each . . .

C9. Who is your current or most recent employer?

C10. Do you still work with this employer?
1. Yes
2. No

C11. When did you start working at this job? (month/year)

C12. How long have you worked/did you work at this job? (years/months)

C13. How many hours per week do/did you usually work at this job?

C14. What are/were your most important activities or duties?

C15. In what kind of business or industry do/did you work?

C16. How much do you currently earn or did you earn at this job before leaving?

C17. Is/was this hourly, weekly, biweekly, monthly, or annually?
1. Hourly
2. Weekly
3. Biweekly
4. Monthly
5. Annually
6. Other

C18. Are/were you a member of a union at this job?
1. Yes
2. No

C19. How did you find out about this job?
1. Friend/relative
2. Other persons

3. Newspaper ads
4. Other means

C20. What was the main way this person helped you?
1. Told me
2. Hired me
3. Talked to employer
4. Gave reference
5. Other

C21. If no longer employed there, what was the main reason this work ended?
1. Fired
2. Quit
3. Promoted
4. Job over
5. Other

C22. Did you have any jobs before this job?
1. Yes (Go to next job)
2. No (Go to section D)

Section D: Discussion Partners

Now I have some questions about the people with whom you discuss important matters. Since we've already discussed your parents, siblings, and household members, we won't discuss them again. May I have a list of up to six people with whom you discuss important matters? For each . . .

D1. Is this person a male or female?
1. Male
2. Female

D2. How is this person related to you?
1. Friend
2. Relative
3. Coworker
4. Neighbor
5. Other

D3. What is the highest grade of school or college he/she has completed?
1. Eighth grade
2. Some high school
3. High school diploma
4. Some college
5. College plus

D4. How long have you known this person?

D5. How frequently are you in contact with this person?
   1. Almost daily
   2. Once a week
   3. Few times a month
   4. Few times a year
   5. Less than once a year
D6. Is this person currently working for pay?
   1. Yes
   2. No
D7. What are her/his important activities or duties?
D8. In what kind of business or industry does she/he work?
D9. Has this person ever received any form of government assistance such as SSI, AFDC, or food stamps?
   1. Yes
   2. No
D10. If you needed a job, would you ask this person for job information or help finding a job?
   1. Yes
   2. No
D11. If this person needed a job, would you help him/her obtain a job at your place of employment?
   1. Yes
   2. No
D12. Do you have any other discussion partners?
   1. Yes (Go to next discussion partner)
   2. No (Go to section E)

Section E: Position Generator

Finally, I'm going to ask you a few questions about your connection to people of different occupations. For cases in which you know more than one, pick the person closest to you and discuss him or her.

E1. Among your relatives, friends, and acquaintances, are there people who have the following occupations: accountant, cashier, child care worker, computer programmer, electrician, high school teacher, lawyer, machine operator, nursing aide, police, physician, registered nurse, secretary, social worker, taxicab driver/chauffeur?
   1. Yes (Go to E3)
   2. No (Go to E2)
E2. If you don't know anyone with this job, is there someone you could go through to find such a person?
   1. Yes (Go to E3)
   2. No (Go to E1)

E3. What is the nature of your relationship with this person?
   1. Professional
   2. Personal
   3. Both

E4. What is his/her relationship to you?
   1. Friend
   2. Relative
   3. Coworker
   4. Neighbor
   5. Other

E5. Have you already discussed this person in this interview?
   1. Yes
   2. No

E6. How frequently do you have contact with this person?
   1. Daily
   2. Weekly
   3. Monthly
   4. Yearly

E7. Would you be able to call on this person for help finding work?
   1. Yes
   2. No

Notes

Chapter 1

1. Higher from the start, employment among white and Latino men fell far less steeply, and so gaps in employment over this period grew even wider—employment was twenty-four percentage points higher among white men and fourteen percentage points higher among Latinos. Just three years prior, gaps, while still substantial, were considerably less at fourteen and nine percentage points, respectively.
2. Browne and Kennelly (1999) also contrasted employers' images of black women with the characteristics of Atlanta's actual labor force. They found that employers' images were nothing more than stereotypes. Although a higher percentage of black women workers than white women workers were single mothers, fewer than one-fifth were. Furthermore, Browne and Kennelly found that although a high percentage of both black and white women reported tardiness, absences, and changes in work schedules due to familial obligations, a higher percentage of white women (54 percent) than black women (43 percent) did so, contradicting employers' stereotypic notions.
3. Recent evidence suggests, however, that we should take employers' responses with a grain of salt. In "Walking the Talk? What Employers Say Versus What They Do," Devah Pager and Lincoln Quillian (2005) examine the relationship between employers' attitudes toward hiring ex-offenders and their actual hiring behavior. They also use employers' self-reports and actual hiring data to determine employers' willingness to hire black and white ex-offenders. They find that employers who said that they would hire ex-offenders were no more likely to do so than employers who said they would not hire ex-offenders. In addition, although surveys of employers revealed that hiring decisions would not be affected by the race of the job candidate, analysis of actual hiring behavior revealed quite the contrary. Hiring decisions were strongly associated with the race of the job candidate, to black men's noteworthy disadvantage.
4. Employers have many concerns, and they are difficult to resolve (Holzer et al. 2002a). First, the law prohibits employers in certain occupations or industries from employing ex-offenders, especially those with felony convictions (Hahn 1991). Second, under the theory of negligent hiring (Glynn 1998), some states hold employers liable for the criminal actions that their employees commit. Employers may fear that if they hire ex-offenders who

then harm their coworkers or customers, they will be held liable and forced to pay excessive damages and court fees. Third, depending on applicants' prior offenses, employers may not trust that their merchandise and lives are safe with ex-offenders (Kasinitz and Rosenberg 1996).

5. Given the incredibly high rates of incarceration among young black males, the consequences of employers' discriminatory behavior cannot be overstated. In 2002, while only 1 percent of white men of working age were incarcerated, almost 8 percent of black men were. In other words, black men's rates of incarceration were 7.4 times higher than rates for whites. In twelve states and the District of Columbia, black men's rates of incarceration were at least ten times higher than for whites. Furthermore, while only 12 percent of the male population nationally, black men represent well over 40 percent of the male prison population. In thirteen states and the District of Columbia, they represent well over half. Among young black men, especially those with low levels of educational attainment, these figures are far bleaker. According to the sociologists Becky Pettit and Bruce Western (2004, 164), "In 1999, about 30 percent of such men had gone to prison by their mid-thirties. Among black male high school dropouts, the risk of imprisonment had increased to 60 percent." Indeed, they contend that incarceration among young black men has become so commonplace that it has overtaken college graduation and military service as an important stage in the life course and fundamentally reshaped adulthood among less-educated black men by reducing the likelihood that they will achieve the "positive" milestones that the mainstream takes for granted, such as marriage and employment. Harry Holzer and his colleagues argue that these high rates of incarceration explain, in great part, black men's continued high rates of joblessness throughout the 1990s, a period when the labor market expanded a great deal and young black women experienced tremendous employment growth (Holzer et al. 2004, 2005; Holzer and Offner 2004).

6. The likelihood of their hire increases, however, if employers conduct criminal background checks. Harry Holzer, Steven Raphael, and Michael Stoll (2002b) investigated the extent to which the race of the most recently hired employee was affected by whether or not employers conducted criminal background checks on applicants. They found that employers who were unwilling to hire ex-offenders were more likely to do so if they conducted criminal background checks than were employers who did not. This is hopeful news. The only problem is that most employers—two-thirds—do not conduct criminal background checks.

7. In *Still the Promised City?* (1996), Roger Waldinger disputes this thesis. Focusing on New York City, Waldinger argues that blacks were actually underrepresented in manufacturing. For immigrant Latinos and Chinese, however, manufacturing represented something of an ethnic niche. Furthermore, because blacks had higher levels of educational attainment on average, they were better positioned than other groups to take advantage of growing opportunities in fields that required higher levels of education and training. Paradoxically, however, blacks' employment eroded while the employment of other groups improved. Thus, Waldinger (1996, 18) ar-

gues, at least in New York City, skills mismatches cannot explain blacks' employment decline. He points instead to an ethnic queue in which "entire groups of people are *ordered* in terms of desirability for preferred jobs, with skill-relevant characteristics serving as additional weights" (emphasis in original). Blacks lost out because employers did not value them highly as workers, and when some industries sought their labor, prior discrimination in those industries had caused blacks to seek opportunities elsewhere.

8. Research by John Bound and Harry Holzer (1993) provides at least partial support for Wilson's and Kasarda's claims that throughout the 1970s and 1980s deindustrialization negatively affected the employment of young, less-educated black men. Indeed, they report that although the effects of deindustrialization were relatively small for most groups, they accounted for between 40 and 50 percent of the decline in young, less-educated black men's employment. Among black women, however, deindustrialization has had a less profound effect on employment.

9. Although deindustrialization goes a long way toward explaining the employment crisis among young black men during the 1970s and 1980s, it fails to account adequately for their continued high rates of joblessness during the 1990s, a period when the economy expanded tremendously and the employment of most other groups either stabilized (as with young white and Latino men) or grew impressively (as with young black women, especially single mothers). As Holzer, Offner, and Sorensen (2004, 6) state, "Though blue-collar and manufacturing jobs continued to decline as a share of the economy, these factors seem to account for little of the declining employment of young black men." Instead, they point to the dramatically rising rates of incarceration among black men during the 1990s as a key factor feeding their continued relative labor market detachment during the same period (Holzer et al. 2004, 2005; Holzer and Offner 2004). To a lesser extent, they also point to a rise in child support enforcement efforts, which, they argue, tax low-income, noncustodial fathers so harshly that they create disincentives for them to work.

10. More collectivist versions of this thesis include Oscar Lewis's (1968, 193) notion of the culture of poverty, which "refers to one way of life shared by poor people in given historical and social contexts." Lewis observed a number of distinct social, economic, and psychological traits among those living in a culture of poverty, including but not limited to critical attitudes toward the basic institutions of the dominant society; community disorganization; early initiation into sex; male desertion and female-headed families; a predisposition toward authoritarianism; feelings of marginality, helplessness, fatalism, dependence, and inferiority; and a superficial embrace of middle-class values. Lewis argues that these characteristics were most likely to emerge among the lower classes that hold a marginal position in a "class-stratified, highly individuated, capitalistic society" (188) and a rapidly changing society coping with deteriorating social and economic systems. As such, the culture of poverty is a response—and a positive response at that—to the feelings of marginality, helplessness, fatalism, and inferiority the poor feel. The culture of poverty, then, is indica-

tive of the poor's resilience and resourcefulness in the face of multiple and overwhelming barriers to social and economic achievement. Unfortunately, this culture differs significantly from the mainstream, is self-replicating, and interferes with the poor's ability to achieve social and economic mobility even when economic opportunities become available. However, Lewis (1968, 198) assures us, the culture of poverty can be overcome (although it will take generations) "by creating basic structural changes in society, by redistributing wealth, by organizing the power and giving them a sense of belonging, of power, and of leadership, revolutions frequently succeed in abolishing some of the basic characteristics of the culture of poverty even when they do not succeed in abolishing poverty itself." Thus, Lewis firmly locates the causes and solutions to the culture of poverty in larger societal forces and not with the poor themselves.

11.   To some extent, Elliot Liebow provides evidence to support Mead's claim. In *Tally's Corner* (1967), Liebow argues that in the face of opportunities to do better, the men he studied often shied away. Fearing that they were too incompetent and "too dumb" to undertake their responsibilities successfully, even when evidence to the contrary existed, they turned down positions that could have improved their chances for upward mobility. "Convinced of their own inadequacies," Liebow (1967, 54) observes, "not only do they not seek out those few better-paying jobs which test their resources, but they actively avoid them, gravitating in a mass to the menial, routine jobs which offer no challenge—and therefore pose no threat—to the already diminished images they have of themselves." Thus, Liebow continues, "Richard refuses such a job, Leroy leaves one, and another man, given more responsibility and more pay, knows he will fail and proceeds to do so, proving he was right about himself all along. The self-fulfilling prophecy is everywhere at work" (55–56).

12.   Ronald Burt (1992, 9) defines social capital as the "friends, colleagues, and more general contacts through whom you receive opportunities to use your financial and human capital." Unlike Bourdieu, Burt's conceptualization seems fixed in the economic sphere, with the primary emphasis on returns to investments. Burt argues that under conditions of perfect competition, social capital is constant, but because perfect competition does not exist in such arenas as the marketplace, social capital makes the difference. In the marketplace, where individuals with similar financial and human capital endowments compete for finite opportunities, the extra edge is given to those who can mobilize contacts with the right resources. These resources are often in the form of information, whether in terms of access, timing, or referrals. Because information does not flow equally to everyone, individuals in a position to capitalize on opportunities are those with access to personal contacts who can provide valuable information before the average person receives it. Such access allows connected individuals to exploit opportunities before they become widely known, thereby reducing the pool of likely competitors. Personal contacts may also act as referees, disseminating information about connected individuals in such a way that opportunities become available without any real effort by the connected individual. Similar to Bourdieu, Burt (1992) explains that trust, obligation, and exchange are necessary for social capital's reproduction.

James Coleman (1988, S98) defines social capital by its function as "a variety of entities with two elements in common: they all consist of some aspect of social structures, and they facilitate certain actions of actors—whether persons or corporate actors—within the structure." Although Coleman's definition of social capital is so vague and all-inclusive as to be somewhat meaningless, both theoretically and empirically (Lin 2001; Portes 1998), of particular value is his position that social capital is transmitted through its three forms: the structure of obligations, expectations, and trustworthiness; norms and effective sanctions of behavior; and information channels.

13. Based on her ethnographic study of Harlem's working poor, Newman (1999) provides evidence that they are not as disconnected from mainstream ties as previous research has suggested. Instead, she describes the working poor as essentially having two different types of social circles. One consists of people like themselves who work in jobs very similar to the ones that they have. The other circle consists of older relatives and friends of relatives who have—or once had—good, stable jobs that support a middle-class life in neighborhoods beyond the ghetto. According to Newman, many in the latter social circle can no longer assist the younger generation, either because they no longer have these jobs or because the industry in which they held these jobs—primarily public-sector—contracted and so no longer provides the opportunities that they themselves were able to take advantage of. As a result, these networks do not provide many opportunities for vertical mobility. Similarly situated friends and relatives in the former social circle are positioned to assist, but they can only do so in jobs that provide opportunities for horizontal mobility.

14. To protect the identities of the study's participants, I have chosen not to reveal the real name of the area in which they lived.

15. My notion of defensive individualism shares key components with Martin Sanchez Jankowski's (1991) concept of defiant individualism, which he developed to describe the character of gang members and gang organizations he observed in Los Angeles, New York, and Boston. Like defensive individualism, Sanchez Jankowski's defiant individualism incorporates feelings of mistrust, a desire to be self-reliant, and concomitant social isolation that emerge within the context of poverty. For Sanchez Jankowski, however, competitiveness, born from struggles for resources in environments of scarcity, was at the root of gang members' defiance and fed other key elements of defiant individualism, including a survival instinct, a social Darwinist worldview, and a defiant air. These traits were not characteristic of the defensive individualism I observed. The roots of that individualism could be found not in competitiveness but in feelings of rejection and abandonment.

Chapter 2

1. As Stack (1974, 41) explains, "Since an object swapped is offered with the intent of obligating the receiver over a period of time, two individuals rarely simultaneously exchange things. Little or no premium is placed

upon immediate compensation; time has to pass before a counter-gift or a series of gifts can be repaid. While waiting for repayments, participants in exchange are compelled to trust one another. As the need arises, reciprocity occurs." What Stack describes is known as generalized exchange, which should be distinguished from "restricted" exchange, in which the conditions are clearly defined—I will give you this for that, and the exchange will be complete by this time. Restricted exchanges also differ from generalized exchanges to the extent that they are not based in trust; nor do they build trust.

2. Even those who initially find a black advantage report that this advantage becomes a distinct black disadvantage when marital status and living arrangements are taken into consideration (Hogan, Hao, and Parish 1990).

3. Even though black women are more likely than white women to report that they receive free child care from their relatives, they are also more likely to report that the child care they receive is inadequate (Hogan et al. 1990).

4. Rates of personal contact use also vary somewhat by city (Falcon and Melendez 2001).

5. James Elliot and Mario Sims (2001, 341) report that Latinos "are generally more likely than blacks to acquire jobs through personal contacts, but this racial difference shrinks considerably in very poor, co-ethnic neighborhoods. However, results also indicate that within these respective neighborhood contexts, Latinos are significantly more likely than blacks to use neighbors and eventual workers to acquire jobs; whereas blacks are more likely to use residential and organizational 'outsiders.'"

6. Even after taking into consideration important controls, such as whether or not the job contact worked for the firm, Latinos' advantage persists (Smith 2007).

7. Similarly, in his study of competition between blacks and immigrants, Roger Waldinger (1997) notes that one of his respondents, a hotel manager in Los Angeles, stated that blacks don't produce referrals to explain why there were so few blacks in his workforce despite his desire to employ more.

8. Stack (1974) also suggests that distrust was more characteristic of the friendships than of the kin relations she observed.

9. Although Coleman (1988, 1990) has argued that social closure enhances the flow of information such that accurate assessments of others' behavior exist for all, others point to the ways in which structural embeddedness characterized by network closure actually constrains information flow, making social judgments at best only rough estimates of actual quality. For instance, to explain the loose linkage between a producer's status and the actual quality of the goods he produces, Joel Podolny (1993) points to the actor's network of relations as a mediating factor and argues that embeddedness can inhibit access to others who are able to provide the latest information about the quality of products, creating a lag between the time when the quality of the product has changed and the time when actors have perceptions of the product. Similarly, embeddedness in a network of relations can constrain access to up-to-date information about one's repu-

tation such that it may no longer correspond with one's most recent behaviors and actions.

Roger Gould (2002) also cautions against assuming that an individual's status is an accurate reflection of his or her qualities. Instead, because actors use others' judgments as a general guide for their own assessments of individuals of interest, socially influenced judgments are often amplified such that, as Gould (2002, 1146) explains, "actors who objectively rank above the mean on some abstract quality dimension are overvalued while those ranking below the mean are undervalued—relative to the baseline scenario, in which social influence does not operate." Although Gould's objective is to theorize about the persistence of status hierarchies, the analogue to reputation, another socially influenced judgment, is evident.

Ronald Burt's (2001) bandwidth and echo discussion is also of note here, as he also takes to task the notion that embeddedness marked by closure enhances information flow, an argument consistent with a bandwidth hypothesis. Instead, he argues that closure constrains access to new and different information by encouraging only the echoing of others' social judgments such that these judgments become amplifications of original dispositions, whether positive or negative. Because of etiquette, information contrary to others' observations becomes difficult to share, and thus the accuracy of social judgments is questionable.

10. See Kollock (1994) for evidence of reputation's role in the formation of stable exchange relationships under conditions of uncertainty.

11. See Coleman (1990) for the distinction he makes between intermediaries as advisers, guarantors, and entrepreneurs.

12. Drawing from Amato (1993), Karen Cook, Russell Hardin, and Margaret Levi (2005) contend that there are regional differences in how trust and cooperation are achieved. In rural areas or small communities, trustworthiness is assured by communal norms of cooperativeness and community-backed assurances and sanctions; trustworthiness and trust are properties of the community. However, in cities or larger areas, trust and trustworthiness tend to be properties of dyadic relations. Cooperation, then, results from reciprocity.

Burt (2001) argues that although social closure may indicate when it is safe to trust, it does not necessarily produce conditions that make trust advantageous, because closure does not place individuals in the optimal space for taking advantage of new opportunities in the way made possible by embeddedness in a network rich with structural holes.

13. Like Suttles (1968), Frank Furstenberg and his colleagues (1999) also make note of the loose network structures that characterize low-income parents' distant and uncooperative relations toward each other.

14. To the extent that residents do cooperate or assist others, it is solely within the context of close friendship ties, for, as Peter Kollock (1994, 318) makes clear, "Faced with a situation in which one can be taken advantage of, a natural response is to restrict one's transactions to those who have shown themselves to be trustworthy."

15. According to W. E. B. Du Bois (1899/1996), the first black church in the United States emerged in the mid-1790s from the Free African Society, an

organization created by two men who determined that they were no longer willing to sit in the gallery of the white Methodist church.

16. According to Drake and Cayton (1945/1993, 419), "The major criticisms ran somewhat as follows: (1) Church is a 'racket,' (2) Too many churches, (3) Churches are too emotional, (4) There's no real religion among the members, (5) Churches are a waste of time and money, (6) Ministers don't practice what they preach, (7) Ministers don't preach against 'sin,' (8) Church places too much emphasis upon money, (9) Negroes are too religious."

17. About black churches, Wacquant (1996, 10) notes, "Most of the churches that used to form the organizational back-bone of Chicago's 'Bronzeville' in its heyday have also closed down. Those that remain are small and fragile organizations with only a handful of members and cramped facilities, if not 'store-front' operations whose existence hinges on the tireless activity of their individual founders. They still attempt to make up for the glaring lack of governmental services by organizing pantries to feed the hungry, shelters for the growing ranks of homeless, and drug counseling programs, job banks, literacy campaigns, and community clean-ups or social gatherings. But their most pressing problem today is survival in the face of dwindling attendance and sagging resources."

18. Karin Brewster and Irene Padavic (2002) find that between 1977 and 1994 relative-provided child care declined significantly among all subgroups of employed black mothers with preschool-age children owing to women's increasing employment, a related decline in the number of relatives available to provide care, and an increase in alternative sources of child care. However, the most disadvantaged mothers, those who were younger, single, and less educated, were more likely to receive child care assistance from relatives. As Brewster and Padavic (2002, 546) put it, "Thus, by 1994, employed Black mothers who most needed relatives' child care support received it, while those who could manage without such help did so." Thus, their research supports the notion that poor black women are more likely to be embedded in networks of extensive exchange in order to survive, although receipt of this form of assistance has declined over time.

Chapter 3

1. After graduating from high school, Diana held three steady jobs before becoming pregnant at the age of twenty-one. For ten months she earned $4.25 per hour working part-time as a cashier and customer greeter at Kmart. In her second job, which she held for one year, she earned $5.35 per hour doing data entry full-time. "To get more work experience," Diana moved on to her third position. For two and a half years, she worked full-time as an order entry and billing clerk at a sporting goods supply center, making $6.75 per hour. After giving birth to her son, however, she decided that she wanted to be a full-time mother and so she quit her job and signed up for public assistance. Although there are a number of costs to welfare receipt, including the stigma associated with dependency—which results in a lack of self-respect (Ellwood 1988; Moffitt 1983)—for single mothers

like Diana the benefits of receipt must be considered as well. With public assistance, single mothers do not have to struggle with finding safe, affordable, reliable, and proximate child care; they have access to health care, which is not often provided with low-wage work; they struggle less with competing work-family obligations; and they have more opportunities to spend time with their children (Garfinkel and McLanahan 1986; Ellwood 1988; Harris 1993).

As happens with most recipients, however, welfare receipt did not last long for Diana. According to the sociologist Kathleen Mullan Harris (1993), the majority of women who entered the rolls pre-TANF exited within three years. Within just a few months of welfare receipt, Diana was back in the labor market working weekends and earning $8 per hour as a data entry clerk at a bank. Wanting more hours, however, she quit this job and, through a temporary employment agency, secured a full-time position as a clerical secretary at General Motors making $9.75 per hour. Her position at GM ended two years later, and she found herself out of work. Almost one month passed before the temp agency finally called with her next assignment. It was as a meter reader for the water company. Four years later, Diana was still employed at the water company, earning $19 per hour and enjoying great benefits and union membership.

2. In *Getting a Job* (1974/1995, 59), Mark Granovetter argues that information dissemination is just like formal means, "because the process is less likely to involve *influence*. Just as reading about a job in the newspaper affords me no recommendation in applying for it, neither does it to have heard about it fifth-hand" (emphasis added). Thus, although job information from personal contacts can be helpful, without a good word—without influence—job-seekers lose the real benefits of personal contact use.

3. When asked how important it is to use friends, relatives, and acquaintances to find out about jobs, 86 percent reported that it is important or very important.

4. These are not mutually exclusive categories. While 19 percent of respondents did not express any type of distrust of job-seekers, 63 percent expressed distrust around one of these three issues, and 19 percent expressed concern around two of the issues raised.

5. This is what Newman (1999, 82) observed among some of her respondents as well; for instance, "Larry trains a critical eye on the people in his own family and realized that though he loves them, they are not always good bets as referrals. He thinks his sister is lazy and doesn't want to work. His mother doesn't work either and hasn't for as long as Larry can remember. The nose-to-the-grindstone types are rarer than they should be." Thus, while closeness may facilitate instrumental aid, because it is also associated with greater knowledge about relations' behavior, closeness has its costs as well.

6. I chose this approach over the more conventional "name generator" approach because name generators are inadequate to the task of identifying one's connection to mainstream others because they are relational in character. Not only are they biased toward the reporting of strong ties, but the information gleaned about ties' social structural location is biased as well.

Noting the limitations of name generators, Nan Lin, Yang-chih Fu, and Ray-May Hsung (2001) conceived of the position generator as an instrument to elicit information about respondents' direct connections to labor market participants. Because the position generator is not content-bound or biased toward strong ties, respondents are able to identify their weak ties as well as their strong ones, providing a more comprehensive sketch of their network of ties. More importantly, however, by asking respondents about the extent and nature of their relations to ties within the labor market context, this instrument permits a direct assessment of the black urban poor's connection to mainstream contacts, thereby allowing us to determine the extent and nature of their linkages to mainstream ties.

7. This finding is inconsistent with findings from some prior work (Fernandez and Harris 1992; Rankin and Quane 2000; Wacquant and Wilson 1989), but consistent with others (Sosin 1991). For instance, using the Urban Poverty and Family Life Survey (UPFLS), Loic Wacquant and William Wilson (1989) and Roberto Fernandez and David Harris (1992) report that neighborhood poverty is positively associated with social isolation (the inverse of social capital). And while Bruce Rankin and James Quane (2000) also find that access to employed relations is negatively associated with neighborhood status, they link much of residents' variation in social isolation to individual-level characteristics rather than to neighborhood poverty itself. However, using the UPFLS, Michael Sosin (1991) finds that neighborhood poverty is not associated with the number of workers to whom the poor have access. Some of these differences can be attributed to differences in measures of social capital.

8. However, drawing from Fernandez and Harris (1992) and Newman (1999), a higher percentage of employed residents' social networks are probably composed of unemployed friends, relatives, and acquaintances, such that even if they have similar numbers of employed relations, a greater share of their relations are unemployed and disadvantaged.

9. Indeed, this is what Frank Furstenberg and his colleagues (1999) suggest in *Managing to Make It*. They show that the parents in low-resource communities who best facilitated their children's successful development were those who undertook *promotive strategies*, that is, strategies that provided opportunities for their children to develop talents and skills, usually in structured learning environments. These strategies often involved making connections with other people and institutions (that is, developing social capital) *outside of the community* to get the resources they needed since their own communities could not provide them. Parents who undertook promotive strategies were compared to those who engaged in *preventive strategies*—strategies intended to shield children from the negative influences in their social milieu. In contrast to promotive strategies, preventive strategies often *isolated* children, usually in the home, in ways that did little to develop their cognitive skills or promote their psychological development. Furthermore, this strategy made social capital accumulation less likely.

10. Some will argue that employed residents of high-poverty neighborhoods have equivalent levels of access to social capital because of the fact of their

employment: through their jobs they are exposed to a greater number of people in a greater range of occupations. I agree that because of their jobs the employed have greater access to social capital, but their employment status does not go far enough in explaining their access to social capital because (1) they appear to have slightly greater access than the employed in low-poverty neighborhoods, and (2) the unemployed in low-poverty neighborhoods also have access to social capital that is equivalent to that of the employed in both low- and high-poverty neighborhoods, and their access greatly exceeds that of the unemployed who live in high-poverty neighborhoods. Although they are unemployed, their residence in low-poverty neighborhoods, in which greater resources exist, provides them with opportunities to make connections that allow them to get things done. For employed residents of high-poverty neighborhoods, then, a job matters, but managing the responsibilities of work and family effectively in a low-resource community probably requires greater social capital than work alone can provide.

11.   In *All Our Kin* (1974), Carol Stack characterized interclass family relationships in a similar way. Protective of the status they had attained, the more advantaged distanced themselves so as not to become overwhelmed by the obligations of exchange that would deplete them of their growing resources and make even more tenuous their shaky grasp on upward mobility. To the extent that my employed respondents from high-poverty neighborhoods also knew more unemployed residents, such that a greater share of their relations were not working, they probably experienced greater demands for assistance from people whose needs were great but whose ability to offer much in return was slight.

12.   Moss and Tilly (2001) analyzed the Multi-City Study of Urban Inequality, In-Depth Employer Survey. Fifty-six percent of employers listed interaction skills, while 51 percent mentioned workers' motivation.

13.   It was unclear how pervasive this sentiment was among Royster's blue-collar black workers. Nor does Royster make it clear what experiences led job-holders to hold this view.

14.   I obtained monthly unemployment figures from Economagic.com, "Economic Time Series Page," accessed at http://www.economagic.com/em-cgi/data.exe/blsla/lasst26000003, and calculated yearly averages based on these figures.

15.   Ronald Burt (2001) argues that although social closure may indicate when it is safe to trust, it does not necessarily produce conditions that make trust advantageous. This is because closure does not place individuals in the optimal space for taking advantage of new opportunities in the way that embeddedness in a network rich with structural holes might. Granovetter (1985) acknowledges the value of both. He highlights the importance of tightly knit networks for activating social resources, but argues that weak ties have value too. In his study, Granovetter found that job changers matched by weak ties were more likely to land high-prestige jobs because weak ties were bridges to new opportunities and resources. They provided information that individuals could not have obtained through strong ties such as relatives and close friends. Because Granovetter's job

changers were of relatively high socioeconomic status—they occupied professional, managerial, and technical positions—some have argued for a contingency to the value of weak ties: the socioeconomic status of the job-seeker. For instance, Granovetter maintains that while high-status job-seekers may benefit from weak ties, disadvantaged job-seekers probably do not. Citing past studies, Granovetter (1981) contends that individuals of low socioeconomic status are less likely to benefit from weak ties because their weak ties are more likely to be acquaintances of friends and family members occupying similar positions in the social structure, not bridges to new opportunities and resources for labor market mobility and advancement.

16. After they had interviewed the staff of the human resources department, Fernandez and Fernandez-Mateo (2006, 59) state, "none of these people responded affirmatively when asked directly whether they showed any preference for referrals as a matter of policy. The most common phrasing of these responses was that 'referrals are treated like everyone else.'"

Chapter 4

1. I use the term "job-seekers" to refer to all respondents, currently searching or not, because this chapter is based on data gathered from respondents when they were asked to think about their current or prior experiences looking for work from their perspective as job-seekers. To distinguish all "job-seekers" from those who were actually currently looking for work, I refer to the latter as "unemployed job-seekers." Half of the sample in this study were unemployed, and 37 percent were "unemployed job-seekers." Roughly 13 percent were not labor force participants—they were neither employed nor looking for work.

2. A few respondents reported submitting hundreds of résumés each day. One explanation for job-seekers' use of this relatively ineffective method of job search is the sense of efficacy or control that it provided. By submitting résumés via the Internet, job-seekers could feel as if they had crossed the digital divide while actively engaging in the job-finding process. And there is at least one additional psychological "benefit" of searching for work via the Internet—job-seekers can avoid putting themselves on the line in the way that they would if they were searching, and being rejected, face to face. By submitting résumés over the Internet, they could feel engaged in their search for a job in a way that suggested technical sophistication and connection to the larger world but also protected them from taking part fully in a process that can be emotionally and psychologically discouraging. My respondents were not atypical in submitting numerous applications that employers rarely acknowledged. In *Falling from Grace* (1988), Katherine Newman explains that members of the Forty Plus Club of New York City—"the oldest executive self-help organization in the country," the club provided both structure and social support to unemployed executives searching for work—typically submitted over one hundred résumés and letters of inquiry to employers monthly, but that these

generally yielded few callbacks or interviews. Just as with my respondents, few employers acknowledged receipt of these former executives' applications. Newman's former executives, however, were applying to employers whose lack of response appeared to be due to the downsizings of the 1980s; with few vacancies, they just stopped responding. Although the employers my respondents contacted via the Internet may also have had no positions to offer (after all, Michigan's economy was among the worst in a nation entering recession during the period of this study), it is also true that this mode of contacting employers—a mode encouraged by the job center—is not the best way to gain employment in low-level service-sector jobs, the types of jobs my respondents sought.

3. Many will interpret this as evidence that my findings about reluctance are largely a result of having drawn my sample from a job center visited by job-seekers because they lack access to social resources or are less likely to deploy the social resources they do have for job finding. However, this is not the case. First, center respondents differed little from noncenter respondents in their access to social capital. Second, a lower percentage of center respondents expressed reluctance to use personal contacts to find work than noncenter respondents. Whereas one-third of noncenter respondents claimed reluctance to use personal contacts, just one-fifth of center contacts did. Furthermore, among only residents of high- to extreme-poverty neighborhoods, a slightly higher percentage of noncenter recruits described themselves as reluctant to use personal contacts to find work than those who were recruited at the center (25 percent versus 21 percent). There are a number of reasons why recruitment from the center did not lead to a sample particularly disinclined toward personal contact use. For instance, some clients of the job center were often mandated to visit, sometimes by Work First requirements. Others had been strongly encouraged by the state to visit the center to find work in order to pay down rising child support arrears. Also, the recently unemployed were required by the state to register at the job center in order to receive unemployment compensation. Thus, center respondents were no more likely to express disfavor toward engaging a job referral network than their counterparts recruited by other strategies, and so it appears that visiting the center was less about interpersonal dynamics than it was about being mandated to do so.

4. Compared to the unemployed job-seekers in my sample, 40 percent of whom were searching through formal institutions (mostly temporary employment agencies and state employment agencies, such as the job center), Gary Green, Leann Tigges, and Irene Browne (1995) found that 6 percent of the poor in their sample searched through labor unions, 29 percent searched through state employment agencies, 22 percent searched through temporary employment agencies, and 19 percent searched through private employment agencies. Roughly 60 percent of unemployed job-seekers in my sample checked want ads and other media sources to search for work. This finding is consistent with Green, Tigges, and Browne's finding that 61 percent of the poor in their study used newspaper ads. Greater than two-thirds of unemployed job-seekers in my sample just walked in

and applied. Green, Tigges, and Browne found that 53 percent of the poor in their study searched for work in this way.

5. This is somewhat less than what others have found. For instance, Harry Holzer (1987) found that while employed job-seekers use 2.7 strategies on average to find work, unemployed job-seekers used 3.3 job search strategies. Similarly, Green, Tigges, and Browne (1995) found that poor job-seekers used 3.8 search methods on average. The difference between these studies and my own is that respondents in the other datasets—the National Longitudinal Survey of Youth (NLSY) and the Atlanta Social Survey—were given a list of job search strategies and asked if they had used any. In my study, unemployed job-seekers were asked an open-ended question about the strategies they employed to find work, reducing the likelihood, because of recall issues, that they would mention all that they had used.

6. Although often employed as synonymous with terms like prestige, status, respect, and honor, "face" is a distinct concept denoting the positive image that individuals present of themselves to the public on the basis of both performance accomplishments and ascription (Ho 1976). It is a very public declaration in which individuals communicate to the world an image of self-worth and efficacy, often in the face of internalized self-doubt and feelings of inadequacy.

Face can be both gained and lost, but it is the loss of face that garners the most attention. In Erving Goffman's (1967) words, face is a "sacred thing." The cost of losing it is far greater than what is reaped with its gain. According to David Ho (1976), there are two types of situations in which face can be lost. Individuals can expect to lose face if they are unable to fulfill their obligations or if others fail to treat them as they expect to be treated given their social status. Both types of situations deal with incongruities in social expectations—the images that individuals present of themselves are inconsistent with available evidence. Inconsistencies that are brought to light challenge individuals' claims to competence, integrity, and adequacy and threaten their status and honor in the community, often resulting in feelings of embarrassment and shame. I argue that fears of losing face prompted a significant minority of job-seekers to become disinclined toward personal contact use in the hope that such avoidance would reduce the likelihood of making themselves vulnerable to threats to face.

7. She stated, "That's the kind of thing on a good job opportunity they gonna take it before they give it to you, so. [Laughter.] That'd be my experience. If you looking for a good job, if they have a good job, then they might tell you, but other than that they going after that same offer. At least that's how I see things. Maybe if they feel like it's a big enough opportunity for everybody they would do it for you." Given the findings reported in the previous chapter, this rationale for disinclination is not unfounded. Job-holders' decisions to assist were correlated with local labor market conditions. Although job-holders' distrust was pervasive, feeding a disinclination to assist, as Michigan's economy soured a greater percentage of job-holders expressed distrust and disinclination. And while increased distrust and noncooperation could be explained by pointing to the in-

creased tenuousness of job-holders' own positions, this heightened state of being might have been at least partly a function of job-holders' sense of increased labor market competition.

8. Two of these job-seekers pointed out how much more quickly work could be found using other methods. As one explained, "I would go myself. I'd go to Labor-Ready or Manpower or something like that. I would find you get work faster." The other two pointed out that personal contacts often could not be trusted to provide accurate information. One explained, "You have to have a network for you to be successful in anything you do. [But] we gotta be concerned who the person's telling you. I got a lot of acquaintances that you don't trust. They can tell you all day and you just blow them off. They always say you can get a job at Fords and all that. Yeah. Yeah. But it depends on who was telling you. That's very important to me."

   Although searching for work through temporary employment agencies probably does lead to finding work faster, previous research finds that personal contact use is probably the most effective way of getting a job, all things considered, since the likelihood of being hired is higher for networked applicants than for non-networked applicants (Fernandez and Weinberg 1997; Newman 1999; Petersen, Saporta, and Seidel 2000; but see Fernandez and Fernandez-Mateo 2006). Networked candidates are advantaged at least in part because they tend to apply during less competitive cycles and their applications tend to be of higher quality. Presumably their contacts are screening out more high-quality applicants and advising them about how to best present themselves to employers (Fernandez and Weinberg 1997). Presumably, too, having an employee put in a good word makes a huge difference (Neckerman and Fernandez 2003).

9. Preferring restricted exchanges, this respondent stated, "I'll treat you to a dinner, girl, you hook me up with a little job. We're going to have to do lunch, get a play at the [local theater], something like that. Then we're through. Our ties are over. It's settled. [But job-holders] are expecting for some regular borrowing, exchanging some money, etc." Because she wanted to avoid more generalized exchange arrangements and the never-ending obligations that she felt job-holders sought, this respondent was disinclined to seek or accept aid from personal contacts.

   To be clear, restricted exchanges are exchanges in which the terms are clearly outlined, including who the exchange partners are, what will be exchanged, and the period within which obligations will be met. In contrast, generalized exchanges are those in which the terms are relatively unclear. There is much greater flexibility in terms of what will be exchanged, when the obligation will be fulfilled, and who exactly will benefit. Thus, within restricted exchanges, there is far less trust, greater emotional tension, and less social solidarity between exchange partners (Uehara 1990).

10. When grounded in the symbolic interactionist approach, cognitive theories of self-efficacy address individuals' beliefs that they have the ability to generate and mold the circumstances that affect their lives (for a brief review of motivational theories of self-efficacy, see Gecas 1989). Other terms

of similar meaning include locus of control (Rotter 1967, 1976), personal control (Gurin, Gurin, and Morrison 1978), self-confidence (Rosenberg 1979), and self-esteem, with its inner (self-mastery) and outer (self-worth) components (Franks and Marolla 1976). With minor variations, each of these terms attempts to capture individuals' perceptions of their own effi-cacy—that is, the extent to which they believe that their actions can have an impact on their environment in ways that they intend it to.

According to Albert Bandura (1977), individuals develop self-efficacy in early childhood as they interact with their environment. To the extent that their environments are responsive, allowing them the freedom to engage in activities that are at once challenging and rewarding, they grow with a healthy sense of themselves as powerful agents. After infancy, self-efficacy develops primarily through personal mastery. Individuals' perceptions of their own efficaciousness develop as they take on challenging tasks and complete them successfully. With such a history, individuals grow to see themselves as having personal mastery and control.

Not everyone, however, is born into an environment that is responsive to their actions and provides opportunities for personal mastery. Instead, as Viktor Gecas and Michael Schwalbe (1983) explain, personal mastery largely depends on the context of the action emerging from the social structures within which individuals are embedded. In other words, self-efficacy development is contingent on the extent to which individuals' so-cial contexts constrain their autonomy, the extent to which they have con-trol, and the extent to which resources are available to facilitate their desired actions.

Problems with unemployment and persistent joblessness help to shape individuals' perceptions of self-efficacy. Leonard Pearlin and his colleagues (1981) found that involuntary job disruptions—layoffs, ter-minations, downgradings, and leaves due to illness—negatively af-fected how individuals perceived themselves, in terms of their assess-ments of both self-worth (self-esteem) and mastery (self-efficacy). This effect of job disruption was found to be both direct and indirect. While losing their place made individuals feel less control over the circum-stances that shaped their lives, the larger effect of disruption on their sense of efficacy came through economic strain. Increased economic strain resulting from involuntary job disruptions decreased individu-als' sense that they were in control. Prolonged economic strain only magnified individuals' feelings of inadequacy, providing evidence time and again of their ineffectiveness. As Pearlin and his colleagues (1981, 345) explain:

Hardships that are an enduring testimony to one's lack of success or to the inadequacy of one's efforts to avoid problems would seem to pose the most sustained affront to one's conceptions of self-worth and of being in control over personal destiny. . . . It is the abiding problems to which people can see no end, those that seem to be-come fixtures of their existence, that are intrinsically uncongenial with positive self-concept. Although self-esteem and mastery represent quite distinct views of the self, each is particularly vulnerable to loss from the assaults of persistent hardships.

These represent the objective aspects of social context that impinge on the development of self-efficacy.

The consequences of perceived self-efficacy cannot be understated, since it affects various aspects of individuals' mental and physical well-being. For instance, Pearlin and his colleagues show that chronic life strains, such as job disruptions, often lead to depression because they diminish individuals' belief that they have control over the circumstances that affect their own lives (Seligman 1975). Self-efficacy has also been found as a mediating factor that affects whether or not one develops drug or alcohol addictions and eating disorders (Newcomb and Harlow 1986; Pearlin and Radabaugh 1976; Schneider and Agras 1985; Seeman and Anderson 1983), the extent to which addictions, phobias, and anxieties can be overcome (Bandura et al. 1980; DiClemente 1985; Seeman and Seeman 1983), and the speed with which individuals recover from illness and disease (Schwalbe and Gecas 1988). In this chapter, I contend in part that ambivalence about the use of personal contacts among the black poor develops as persistent joblessness diminishes individuals' sense of self-efficacy and that they cope through face-work.

11. This was not altogether true, however. Anthony did not like working at the lowest-level service-sector jobs, such as car washes and fast-food restaurants, because these were poorly paid and offered few if any opportunities for advancement. Consequently, Anthony felt that these jobs were best left for teenagers, not for grown men trying to raise families. Anthony had also sworn off employment through temporary employment agencies, calling one such service Fast Pimps (a play on the agency's real name, Fast Temps) to indicate the exploitative nature of these businesses for vulnerable workers like himself. He complained that although they advertised good wages, they charged their temporary workers exorbitant fees for every little service they provided such that by the time workers received their paychecks, their effective hourly rate was significantly less than the minimum wage. The problem for Anthony and others like him with felony records is that temporary employment agencies are one of the few sources of access to the labor market. Few employers are willing to hire them otherwise. Without these agencies, ex-felons' meager chances of finding work fall even further.

12. Devah Pager (2002) found that the likelihood of receiving a callback from an employer depended heavily on whether one had a criminal record, but race mattered a great deal as well. She found that whereas 34 percent of white men with no criminal record were called back and 17 percent of white ex-cons were called back, just 14 percent of black men with no criminal record were, and a mere 5 percent of black ex-cons made it to the next stage of the hiring process. Furthermore, Pager and Quillian (2005) found that even when employers said that they would be willing to hire ex-

felons, in actuality they were no more likely to hire them than were employers who were categorically against doing so.

13. Some might argue that Anthony was not reluctant to use personal contacts at all because he would allow relations to get him applications and return them for him, but this form of assistance is neither information nor influence and is no more beneficial than other forms of in-kind assistance, such as getting a ride. In other words, I categorized Anthony as a reluctant personal contact user because he avoided the type of assistance associated with personal contact use that would have best facilitated his hire.

14. Infrequent and unreliable public bus service was of little aid to Abigail. Abigail recounted how in one instance poor transportation options led, in part, to the loss of her job at the hospital. After one in a series of car breakdowns, Abigail began to take the bus to and from work. However, this was far from an easy process. The bus stopped in her neighborhood only once an hour, on the half-hour. Furthermore, it took Abigail half an hour to walk to this bus stop from her home. So she would leave her home at roughly 7:00 A.M. to catch the 7:30 bus, which got her to work at 8:15. Unfortunately, Abigail's shift began at 8:00. If she wanted to arrive at work on time via the pubic bus service, she would have to leave home at 6:00, which would get her to work forty-five minutes early. Faced with this predicament, she asked her supervisor for permission to work from 8:30 A.M. until 4:30 P.M., instead of 8:00 A.M. to 4:00 P.M., until she was able to get her transportation issues resolved. Her supervisor refused, and Abigail was later fired for excessive tardiness.

15. According to Kirschenman and Neckerman's (1991) study, employers with low-skilled blue-collar and service-sector jobs prefer applicants with long spells of unemployment to applicants who jumped from one job to the next as long as the former had good reason for being out of the labor market.

16. See Browne and Kennelly (1999), whose study not only indicates that employers perceive black women to be more beleaguered by the familial obligations associated with single-motherhood but provides countervailing evidence indicating that black women are no more likely than white women to report issues of absenteeism, tardiness, and other work-related concerns related to familial obligations. In fact, black women are less likely to report such issues, suggesting that employers are basing their perceptions less on experience than on stereotypical views of the differences between black and white women.

17. Abigail explained to me with a great deal of satisfaction that her wish for retribution had been granted. Some time later her sister stopped by to request a financial loan. The irony was not lost on Abigail. Needless to say, she did not grant her sister's request.

18. Although the plant no longer plays this role to the extent that it once did, it still represents in the minds of many a promise of something much better than they could achieve otherwise (Young 2004).

19. Chauncey explained that his current unemployment was due, in large part, to this injury. With his mobility constrained, he explained, he could only effectively perform desk jobs, a restriction that severely limited his employment options.

20. The isolation embraced by a minority of my black poor job-seekers is not specific to this class. Indeed, in *Falling from Grace* (1988), Katherine Newman reports that among the downwardly mobile managers she interviewed, a small minority also chose not to tell their family members and friends of their job loss. For instance, "Jack Rigley, a refugee from the world of big oil, was so worried about the disappointment and upset the news would cause his family that he hid the fact that he had been terminated for nearly six months. He continued to dress in a suit and tie every morning, leave the house, and stay out all day, returning home at the normal hour as if nothing had gone awry.... Rigley's experience is extreme, though he was not alone in his efforts to keep his fate a secret" (Newman 1988, 51). Just as I suggest here that my job-seekers responded in this way to better manage others' image of them, obscuring any evidence contradicting their presentation of self, Newman (1988, 270) draws from prior work (Cole 1979; Kaufman 1982) that also locates isolation in attempts to protect "[one's] self image by diminishing the importance of other people's evaluations of one's conduct or situation."

21. According to Erving Goffman (1967), individuals partake in face-work to avoid losing face. There are two types of face-work—avoidance and corrective. In the avoidance process, every attempt is made to circumvent interactions and activities that may pose a threat to face. These can be both protective and defensive. The most obvious means of protection is to steer clear of interactions and activities that may leave one's face vulnerable to challenge. When protective or defensive avoidance is unachievable or unsuccessful, face-work becomes corrective in nature, as it did in John's situation. Goffman asserts that the corrective process involves a four-stage ritual. In the first stage, a challenge is made and acknowledged. As such, the social environment is in disequilibrium, making public the incongruities between one's presentation of self and conflicting evidence. But by acknowledging the offense, the stage is set for some resolution, or equilibrium. The second stage, the offering, presents the offender with the opportunity to withdraw the challenge. This is accomplished by redefining the offense as unintended, or by redefining the face that the offender has presented as inconsistent with what she intended. The third and fourth stages involve the object's acceptance of the offering, if this is deemed adequate, and the offender's expression of appreciation at having been forgiven, saving face and bringing the social environment back into equilibrium. Of course, corrective face-work does not always unfold in this way. Conflict over face claims can go through many iterations before an offering is made, deemed sincere, and accepted. Furthermore, attempts at saving face are not always successful.

22. According to Goffman (1967), when simple avoidance is not possible and individuals find themselves in potentially threatening situations, they avoid losing face by redirecting the activity or changing the topic of conversation in the hope of circumventing those topics or activities that may bring to light information that could disprove their positive self-valuations or provide evidence to support their fears of inadequacy and self-doubt. Alternatively, they can take a defensive stance by showing all due

respect to exchange partners and being appropriately discreet, courteous, ambiguous, and even deceptive if such behavior will put their exchange partners at ease so that they will not be provoked to challenge face. If challenges arise, individuals can avoid losing face by acting as if the offending act did not take place or by acknowledging the act but in such a way that downplays its significance or redefining its intent.

23. If we examine differences categorically, we get a similar result. No open personal contact users and 3.8 percent of reluctants reported no access to any positions listed. Similar percentages of each group also reported access to one to five positions (26.9 versus 24.3 percent), six to nine positions (30.8 versus 35.1 percent), and ten or more positions (38.5 versus 40.5 percent).

24. Reluctants differed little from open personal contact users in terms of their access to workers of different skill levels, including those who were personal relations with whom they were in frequent contact with. The only exception was in access to unskilled workers who were personal contacts and frequently contacted: open personal contact users reported more such access on average than did reluctants (2.5 versus 2.1 percent).

25. Furthermore, 43 percent of open personal contact users reported having one to two discussion partners compared to 35 percent of reluctants. And while 44 percent of open personal contact users reported three or more discussion partners, just 31 percent of reluctants did. In recent studies, Peter Marsden (1987) and Miller McPherson, Lynn Smith-Lovin, and Matthew Brashears (2006) find that 24.6 percent of Americans report no discussion partners (up from 10 percent two decades before), 38 percent report one to two discussion partners (up from 31.2 percent two decades ago), and 37.1 percent list three or more discussion partners (down from 48.7 percent two decades ago).

26. I calculated yearly averages based on the monthly unemployment figures I obtained from Economagic.com, "Economic Time Series Page," accessed at http://www.economagic.com/em-cgi/data.exe/blsla/lasst26000003.

27. For a number of reasons, personal contact use also benefits employers. First, it costs less to recruit from employees than to advertise in newspapers and other sources. Second, because employees know from experience what is expected of workers on the job, they are well equipped to identify potential workers who have what it takes to be successful in that environment, and so they do a great job of recruiting and screening qualified applicants for employers (Fernandez and Weinberg 1997). Third, networked applicants who are hired receive more training assistance from their on-the-job contacts and thus learn job tasks faster than those without this social resource. Fourth, because employees recruited this way stay on the job longer, employee turnover costs are lower (Petersen, Saporta, and Seidel 2000). Finally, because networks tend to be rather homogeneous (Marsden 1987; McPherson, Smith-Lovin, and Brashears 2006; McPherson, Smith-Lovin, and Cook 2001) and because people tend to assist and be assisted during job search by people like themselves (Falcon and Melendez 2001; Smith 2000), to the extent that employers rely on word-of-mouth recruitment strategies as a primary means of worker recruitment they tend to reproduce the workforce at hand. For employers interested in excluding cer-

tain types of workers, like the black poor, word-of-mouth recruitment strategies are a relatively cheap and effective means of doing so (Kirschenman and Neckerman 1991).

Chapter 5

1. In *Flat Broke with Children* (2003), Sharon Hays also makes note of these prints in her ethnographic study of two welfare offices.
2. The extent to which clients actually saw and internalized these messages is unclear. My conversations with clients indicated that the posters were little noticed. Clients seemed aware that something occupied space on the walls, but they were hard-pressed to say what. Observations by center staff were consistent with this general impression. One resource room attendant, who had been employed at the center for two months, could remember seeing only one client taking any interest in the posters. Another hypothesized that Work First clients were the most likely to notice the posters because they spent more time in the center than any other class of visitor as a condition of their participation in the Work First program. After more than four years on the job, however, she could recall observing only one client examining the posters on the wall.

   It is possible that clients had taken in more than anyone realized. After all, the best advertisement is the one we do not realize we have seen and internalized, so much so that the thoughts it engenders occur to us as our own. What is most important here, however, is that the center attempted to communicate and instill certain values and ideals about what it takes to find and keep work and related these values to having a successful and fulfilling life generally.

   What makes it not only possible but likely that these values and ideals were successfully transmitted by the posters is that center staff valued the messages they conveyed and saw them as a panacea for many social problems, including those in their own lives. Donavon Stinson was a twenty-four-year-old black man who had worked for the center as a resource room attendant for just shy of two months. He shared that job-seekers who visited the center would be well served by paying close attention to the messages conveyed in the posters.

   Donavon was the sixth child of parents who divorced when he was five. After his parents' divorce, his mother moved him and three of his siblings to Detroit, where he was primarily raised; the two oldest siblings remained with his father to complete high school. For a time immediately after the divorce, they lived in public housing in one of Detroit's toughest neighborhoods, a move that could have significantly and negatively affected Donavon and his siblings' life chances. However, in an attempt to buffer her children from the negative influences associated with living in their new neighborhood of concentrated disadvantage, Donavon's mother adopted several "protective strategies." Foremost, she tried to provide greater structure, purpose, and supervision to their leisure time by insisting that they participate in extracurricular activities. She also put posters such as those displayed in the center on the walls in their home in the hopes that her children would internalize their messages. As a boy, Donavon largely dismissed the posters and the values they proclaimed. As a young adult, however, he found them to be of great value.

Like Donavon's mother, Joann Crawford, a thirty-four-year-old, black, single mother of two, also used miniature versions of the posters on the walls in her own home in the hopes of inspiring her sons, ages twelve and three, to challenge themselves and to become self-sufficient. This is not to say that all center staff had inspirational posters on the walls of their homes. They did not. However, every staff member defined job-seekers' difficulties in the market by at least referring to one of the values displayed on the wall, and none of these values received more attention among staff than attitude. Center staff had so embraced the values conveyed by these messages in their own lives that they informed their interactions with center clients. As a result, not only were these values and ideals highlighted on the center's walls, but they were also communicated in the materials that staff prepared for clients and in the verbal feedback staff gave to clients in face-to-face interactions.

3. A lower percentage of nonrecipients have such problems. Just 7 percent had medical problems (compared to 17 percent of recipients), just 11 percent had children with chronic medical conditions (compared to 21 percent), just 11 percent had mental health problems (compared to 24 percent), 30 percent were substance abusers (compared to 37 percent), and 22 percent had low basic skills (compared to 64 percent). In all, whereas 56 percent of nonrecipients had a moderate or severe barrier, including very low basic skills, 89 percent of recipients had such a barrier (Olson and Pavetti 1996).

4. Among nonrecipients, having these potential barriers also reduces the likelihood of employment.

5. Among parents receiving TANF in 1997, Sheila Zedlewski (1999) of the Urban Institute finds that 23 percent reported no barriers to employment, 34 percent reported one barrier, 27 percent reported two, and 17 percent reported three or more.

6. For instance, among TANF parents, Zedlewski (1999) finds that 41 percent have dropped out of high school, 43 percent lack work experience, 15 percent have a child under the age of one, 25 percent have poor general health, and 35 percent have poor mental health.

7. Similarly, Zedlewski (1999) finds that with no major obstacles to employment, 86 percent of TANF parents were either working, enrolled in school, or looking for work. Among those with one barrier to employment, 60 percent worked, attended classes, or were looking for work. An additional barrier reduced levels of "productive" activity to 43 percent, and among those with three or more barriers, productive activity declined to 27 percent. These figures obscure very high rates of unemployment, however, suggesting that the effect of major barriers is actually greater. Among those with no obstacles to employment, 52 percent were working, but 18 percent were looking for work. Among those with one barrier, just 22 percent were actually working, while 30 percent were looking for work.

Among those with two obstacles to employment, just 6 percent worked. Twenty-seven percent were looking, and 57 percent took part in no "productive" activity. For parents with three or more barriers, just 3 percent worked, only 6 percent were in school, and 18 percent were looking for work. Fully 73 percent were not engaged in any of these "productive" activities.

8. MWAs are themselves governed by the Michigan Works! Association. Established in 1987, the association touts itself as the largest, most progressive workforce development association in the country because of the "unique" partnership it has forged between the public and private sectors. Through the association, businesspeople, local elected officials, and service delivery area administrators "speak with a single voice on critical issues that affect workforce development in an effort to foster high-quality employment and training programs that serve both employers and workers by providing support activities as well as a forum for information exchange for Michigan's workforce development system" (see http://www.michiganworks.org/page.cfm/188/). MWAs are products of this collaboration.

9. I learned just how confusing this information blitz could be after observing one man's experience. It was not Rodney's first visit to the job center. He had been a couple of times before, but he had always gone away feeling dissatisfied with the assistance he received. That day's experience was no different. Yet again he left the center without receiving the information he sought. Even when his questions were as clear and pointed as they were that day, the center had never been able to assist him. His face reflected the frustration, both past and present, that arose in him from the center's inability or unwillingness to address his employment-related concerns. His anger, even hostility, seemed just barely contained, a mere seconds away from release.

A black man in his early thirties, Rodney had a felony conviction that had created an almost insurmountable obstacle to employment. To overcome this obstacle, he sought to become bonded by the state. Through the bonding process, employers received business insurance that indemnified them for losses suffered as a result of whatever dishonest acts their high-risk employees committed, including fraud, theft, burglary, and the like. Indeed, through this process, Rodney had secured employment in the past. Before moving to Michigan some eighteen months earlier, he resided in Florida, where he had been a hotel cleaning engineer for ten years, a job he was only able to acquire after becoming bonded by that state. The purpose of his visit to the center the day I observed him was to learn how he might begin the process so as to increase his chances of getting a job.

After he arrived and explained his purpose to the receptionist at the front desk, she informed him that he would have to sit through a three-minute informational session about the center's offerings and then become registered with the center by uploading a current résumé on the Michigan Talent Bank, a web-based job-matching service through which employers also posted information about job vacancies and searched for job candidates throughout the state. Until he did, she explained, he would not be served. In other words, there was no way for Rodney to obtain the information he sought without undertaking this somewhat elaborate process that clearly served some important function for the job center but often left visitors feeling impatient and frustrated. The seeds of Rodney's impatience and frustration were planted in this moment at the front desk.

The receptionist then directed Rodney to Donavon, a resource room attendant whose task for the next couple of hours was to conduct informational sessions for new visitors. At six-foot-four and at least 250 pounds, and with strikingly broad shoulders, Donavon seemed better suited to working as an NFL linebacker. But his imposing figure belied a calm, soft-spoken, gentle manner. As he began introductions, he invited Rodney to sit with him at a small table. I occupied a third seat at the table and took part as if I too were a first-time visitor to the center; at this point, Donavon had no reason to suspect otherwise. He handed us both packets of information, and then the information blitz began. Donavon detailed the packet's contents:

1. Michigan Talent Bank worksheet allowing access to the center's computers
2. Reemployment Services Initiative Targeted Industries and Occupations form
3. Southeast County Service Center registration form
4. Information verification and release form
5. Information on claiming unemployment benefits in Michigan
6. Tips for filing unemployment claims during the peak January period . . .

With the discussion of each document, I became increasingly overwhelmed and somewhat confused. Even though I was actively engaged in trying to determine what the center claimed it offered as well as how it chose to present this information, it was difficult to stay present in the situation. As I struggled, I noticed that Rodney also seemed unable, or possibly unwilling, to follow. More than that, as he slowly shuffled through the documents before him, he seemed agitated. Donavon had yet to provide Rodney with an opportunity to explain why he had come to the center. It was at this point that Rodney interrupted. In a respectful manner, he clarified that his visit had nothing to do with filing for unemployment compensation, and he began to describe the circumstances that had brought him in. Politely, Donavon cut Rodney short and proposed that if Rodney would allow him to continue, he might gain the information he sought. At that, Donavon took up where he had left off:

7. . . . An announcement about filing unemployment claims online
8. Unemployment benefit information, which provided information on how to file a claim
9. A sheet informing visitors of all of the resources provided by the center
10. A sheet providing step-by-step instructions on how to use Michigan's Talent Bank

11. Information on the Southeast County Employment Training and Community Services Group, which discussed the WIA program
12. An extensive list of Internet search sites, which included the web addresses of 107 job search sites
13. A sheet listing the weekly schedule of center workshops offered to the public
14. A separate packet of information that included the following (much of it redundant):
    a. Copies of newspaper articles referring to new programs and services at the center
    b. Information on emergency financial assistance resources
    c. Information on tax preparation assistance, especially for those qualifying for the Earned Income Tax Credit (EITC)
    d. Information on consumer services: visual, physical, psychological, and vocational assessment; physical and mental restoration; low-vision services; Braille training; orientation and mobility training
    e. Information on Michigan Rehabilitation Services
    f. Another sheet about the self-service resource room
    g. A document about a veterans' employment specialist, because veterans were given top priority
    h. More information on job leads and reference materials, face-to-face job fairs, educational and financial aid resources
    i. Information on their community scholarship
    j. Information on SOS community services

Donavon ended the session by reminding Rodney and me that we would be able to take advantage of the programs and services he had just described only by registering with the center and uploading a résumé on the Michigan Talent Bank website.

No mention was made of the bonding process. The topic had not been broached at all. This was bad enough, but after inquiring further, Rodney's agitation only grew when he learned that Donavon could offer no more information than what was found in the packet. Not only was he unaware of how to begin the bonding process, but Donavon seemed not to even know that such a process existed. Rodney stormed out of the center, which, it seemed, had once again wasted quite a bit of his time. Weeks later I asked Donavon if he had been able to assist Rodney. He had not. The day of their meeting was the last time he had seen Rodney. Presumably frustrated by having to listen to an information session that was, at best, superfluous, aggravated by Donavon's apparent ignorance about the bonding process, and irritated by the center's failures to assist him in the past, Rodney departed from the center that day not only convinced that it was unable to help a man like him but, more importantly, highly suspicious of the center's willingness to do so.

When I asked Donavon whether he was surprised by Rodney's response, he said that he was not. In the few weeks that he had worked at the center, he had found that visitors often became frustrated by having to take part in the informational session. But Donavon was convinced that the session was a valuable enterprise, if visitors would only give it a chance. Interestingly, however, Donavon explained that it was not the difficult-to-employ who were most hostile to the informational session; it was those with much higher levels of education and training who felt belittled by having to sit through the three-minute session.

10. Between July 2003 and June of the following year, over 79,000 job-seekers and 3,900 employers registered to use the center's Core Employment Services.

11. In addition to serving adults and dislocated workers, WIA's Title 1 programs also support youth employment programs and fund Job Corps, Native American programs, the Migrant and Seasonal Farmworker Program, the Veterans Workforce Investment Programs, and Youth Opportunity Grants.

12. Between July 2003 and June 2004, 90 adults and 101 dislocated workers participated in the program at Southeast County's job center. Of these, 41 adults and 28 dislocated workers entered employment. Thus, for that fiscal year the "success" rates were 46 and 28 percent, respectively.

13. Preceding MDTA, the Works Progress Administration (WPA) was enacted to reduce incredibly high rates of unemployment during the Depression by providing publicly funded employment and training for adults.

14. Under CETA, the federal government defined objectives of the program and coordinated, supervised, reviewed, monitored, and assigned performance goals and sanctions for nonperformance. States and local governments implemented programs. Local governments received grants for areas with populations of 100,000 or more, and states had responsibility for non-urbanized areas in the state (Guttman 1983). Under JTPA, this arrangement changed. The federal government became responsible for defining the objectives of the program, state governments became responsible for coordinating, supervising, reviewing, monitoring, and defining performance goals and sanctions, and local governments became responsible for the design and implementation of jobs programs. Under WIA, the federal government relinquished more power and decisionmaking authority to states and local areas (O'Shea and King 2004). In Michigan, increased responsibility on the local level has been embraced. A consequence of devolution is that jobs programs vary considerably between and within states and even within particular localities, as Dan O'Shea and Christopher King point out (2004).

15. Under MDTA and CETA, the business community had virtually no role in designing and implementing jobs programs, and to the extent that it did, it was under the authority of local government officials. According to Robert Guttman (1983), the 1978 Title VII amendment to CETA allowed for the creation of private industry councils. However, appropriations for these councils were small, and they had no independent authority; local government officials even determined membership. Because of this, the business community considered the councils too weak to make much of a difference. However, under JTPA private industry in the form of councils (called private industry councils) was given statutory authority to design and execute job-training programs *in equal partnership with local governmental officials*. Thus, JTPA also signaled a significant shift toward a business-centered, economic development approach to jobs programs.

WIA has cemented this shift (O'Shea and King 2004). Not only does WIA try to develop a strong regional economy and regional industries by assisting businesses, old and new, in realizing more effective training and retraining services, but it has shifted to serving individuals *and businesses* by assessing the needs of local businesses and promoting WIA-related services from which businesses might benefit, including tax credits, on-the-job training contracts, regularly scheduled job fairs, and other events designed to help business meet its needs. WIA's shift to a more business-centered approach marks a major turn in the federal government's approach to workforce development.

16. In 1980 alone, 750,000 low-income individuals participated in CETA programs, which served two types of economically disadvantaged individuals—those with low labor market attachment and those with chronically low wages. The various programs had the most success with the former. Individuals with the least work experience benefited the most in terms of employment and earnings. All three programs were associated with improved employment outcomes, including increases in labor force participation, the ability to find jobs, the number of hours worked, and overall earnings. However, most of the earnings increases (roughly 80 percent) were attributed to increases in labor force participation, a finding that suggests that skills upgrades had little impact on employment gains. The implications of these findings paved the way for the current form of employment programs. As concluded in U.S. Congressional Budget Office (1982, 38):

> Since most of the earnings gain from CETA training programs was due to an increase in the amount of time worked, more emphasis on job placement services and less on formal training might achieve the same results as current training programs at a lower cost per participant. In particular, job placement services could be offered through job referral assistance or through job search assistance. Job referral assistance involves locating and developing job openings and matching job seekers with openings. Job search assistance involves teaching people how to look for jobs and supervising their search. Although job referral assistance generally costs less than job search assistance, intensive group search seems to produce higher placement rates.

However, none of the CETA programs did anything to improve the earnings of workers with chronically low wages. Because individuals need to obtain greater skills to earn higher wages, researchers have suggested that more extensive training is needed than is already provided, training that would be far more expensive than the average $2,400 per participant expense.

Finally, because women were overrepresented among participants with low labor force attachment, they benefited from CETA programs a great deal more than men. Indeed, according to U.S. Congressional Budget Office (1982, 35), "The group that benefited most from this program, in terms of later earnings, was women who had been receiving welfare for roughly three or more years and who had previously worked relatively little." Because men were overrepresented among workers with chronically low wages, they benefited little from CETA programs. Furthermore, in the end it appears that the increased earnings associated with participation in CETA were equivalent to the federal government's investment in participants' training.

17. Similar to CETA, JTPA programs provided training for specific occupations, offered remedial education, and provided job search assistance. In 1995 nearly one million individuals participated in JTPA for three to four months (about four to eight weeks less than CETA) and for a cost of $2,400 per participant. However, JTPA was found to achieve modest results, at best. According to the General Accounting Office (GAO 1996), over a five-year period the earnings of JTPA participants were not significantly greater than the earnings of the control group; nor were employment rates. This report has not gone without dispute, however. In its comment on the evaluation, the Department of Labor critiqued the GAO report for not highlighting the positive outcomes associated with JTPA, including male participants' significantly higher annual earnings (by $300 to $500) for the first three years after participation compared to the control group; female participants' significantly higher annual earnings (by $300 to $600) for the first four years after participation compared to the control group; one year of higher employment among male participants compared to the control group; and three years of higher employment (by two to three percentage points) among female participants compared to the control group.

18. The reader should keep in mind, however, that the Work First program has far more participants than does WIA, and so far more money is spent on each WIA participant than on a Work First participant.

19. As Sharon Hays (2003) points out in *Flat Broke with Children*, PRWORA was intended not only to encourage work and discourage nonwork but also to promote "family values."

20. In a recent study, Joe Soss and his colleagues (2001) examined variation in the stringency of the TANF-related policies that states adopted, testing hypotheses that variation might be due to differences in policy innovation, ideology, electoral politics, desire for increased social control, racial resentment, and moralistic problem-solving. Of these factors, they find that racial resentment provides the best explanation for state variation in TANF policies. Specifically, the greater the percentage of black and Latino single mothers on a state's rolls, the more punitive the welfare policies adopted by that state. They conclude that welfare reforms have been strongly informed by racialized discourses on poverty, joblessness, and welfare dependence, to the socioeconomic detriment and moral denigration of poor people of color.

21. Work First program models vary. Researchers at the University of Michigan observed various sites throughout the state of Michigan and identified four models: job-seeking support, job search preparation, labor market sorter, and client responsibility (Anderson and Seefeldt 2000). The job-seeking support model provides job-seekers with the skills and tools they need to look for work. Its hallmark is its proactive attempt to match job-seekers with employers by developing job leads and organizing job fairs. The job search preparation model is similar to the job-seeking sup-

port model, except that it emphasizes job-seekers' more self-directed action. Although it provides access to the same tools and workshops that help clients develop the skills they need to search for and get work in a self-directed manner, no attempt is made to create job leads and organize job fairs. The opposite is true of the labor market sorter model, which focuses on matching job-seekers to jobs by creating job leads, organizing job fairs, and inviting employers to conduct on-site interviews with clients. This model highlights Work First's responsibility; the client responsibility model highlights the job-seeker's role. Here the primary objective is to have job-seekers take primary responsibility for looking for and finding work, but they are able to do so by taking advantage of the center's job postings, Internet access, phone banks, and newspapers and by getting assistance from staff in résumé writing and other skills.

22. Eligible recipients include those receiving cash assistance and noncash assistance, such as child day care, Medicaid, and food stamps. Eligible recipients also include noncustodial parents referred by the court because they are in danger of falling behind on their child support payments owing to unemployment or underemployment.

23. In *Flat Broke with Children* (2003, 41), Sharon Hays writes that "not liking your work, having problems with childcare, experiencing other family problems, having a sick child, your own illness, arguments with supervisors, having your apartment building burn down—none of these counts as good cause." Technically speaking, however, reasons for "good cause" vary considerably by state, and in some states the reasons Hays cites are taken into consideration. According to the State Policy Documentation Project (2001), transportation unavailability represented good cause in thirty-six states, unavailability of other support services represented good cause in nineteen states, and pregnancy was good cause in fifteen states, family emergency in thirty-seven states, death in the family in twenty-six states, and risky work activity in thirty-one states. In Michigan, participants can be excused for noncompliance if transportation is unavailable, if there is a family emergency, or if work presents a risk to one's health and safety.

24. Federal law requires that states sanction participants for noncompliance, but states have great leeway in shaping the form and content of their sanction policies. According to the GAO's (2000) report on state sanction policies, most states are far more stringent than is required by TANF. Nationally, and in Michigan, the overwhelming majority of sanctions meted out each month (70 percent) are for failure to meet work requirements. In Michigan in 1998, 69 percent of sanctions were meted out for failure to meet work requirements and 29 percent were for failure to meet child support enforcement efforts.

25. According to the GAO report *Welfare Reform: State Sanction Policies and Number of Families Affected* (2000), there are three types of sanction policies: partial, graduated, and full-family. Partial sanction policies are those that penalize families by reducing their benefits every time they are cited for noncompliance. For instance, Minnesota adopted a partial sanction policy (along with thirteen other states). When sanctioned for the first time for

noncompliance, Minnesota recipients' cash benefits are reduced by 10 percent, a sanction that lasts for one month. If they fail to meet requirements again, their cash benefit is reduced by 30 percent and their rent and utility allowances are reduced for six months. Graduated sanction policies are those in which families receive a partial sanction for the first infraction and a full-family sanction for every infraction thereafter. Michigan is one of twenty-two states to adopt a graduated sanction policy stance. The first time Michigan recipients fail to comply with requirements, they lose 25 percent of their cash benefit for one month. If they fail to comply a second time, they lose all of their benefits for one month. Fifteen states have adopted full-family sanction policies, in which, with every instance of noncompliance, families lose 100 percent of their benefits for one month. Florida is one such state.

26. There has been much debate about the factors that have led to the impressive increase in single mothers' employment over the 1990s. While some studies show that increases can largely be attributed to welfare reforms—welfare waivers and TANF (McKernan et al. 2000; O'Neill and Hill 2001)—others highlight the role of the expanding economy (Schoeni and Blank 2000), and still others contend that changes in the EITC account for most of the increase in employment during the 1990s (Meyer and Rosenbaum 2000, 2001).

27. This is not unlike what Hays (2003, 96) finds: "At a practical level, both caseworkers and clients regarded the massive number of new rules and regulations that came with reform as a 'hassle' and a 'pain in the neck.' Some even imagined those relentless and unforgiving rules as a series of landmines purposively installed as a test of their courage and fortitude. In any case, everyone in the welfare office struggled mightily to negotiate a way through (and around) those rules and regulations."

28. The U.S. General Accounting Office (2001), drawing from previous research, estimates that between 44 and 64 percent of TANF recipients experience multiple barriers to employment, including health problems or disabilities, human capital deficiencies, domestic violence, and substance abuse. To address these issues, the report recommends (1) that "HHS promote research and provide guidance that would enable states to estimate the number of hard-to-employ TANF recipients who will reach their 60-month limit on benefits; and (2) that HHS expand its efforts to help states better understand how to use the flexibility the law gives them to create appropriate programs for hard-to-employ recipients" (6). In commenting on the draft report, however, the Department of Health and Human Services disagreed with both of these recommendations.

29. Work First participants represent a cheap and captive workforce because they are obligated to accept any job offer they receive from an employer and they cannot quit their job or have their employment terminated for almost any reason. Indeed, some observers, including the participants themselves, have likened this system to slavery because its rules and regulations enforce work requirements without full consideration of workers' needs (Hays 2003).

References

Aguilar, John L. 1984. "Trust and Exchange: Expressive and Instrumental Dimensions of Reciprocity in a Peasant Community." *Ethos* 12(1): 3–29.

Amato, Paul. 1993. "Urban-Rural Differences in Helping Friends and Family Members." *Social Psychology Quarterly* 56(4): 240–62.

Anderson, Elijah. 1990. *Streetwise: Race, Class, and Change in an Urban Community.* Chicago, Ill.: University of Chicago Press.

———. 1999. *Code of the Street: Decency, Violence, and the Moral Life of the Inner City.* New York: W. W. Norton & Co.

Anderson, Nathaniel, and Kristin S. Seefeldt. 2000. *Inside Michigan Work First Programs.* Ann Arbor, Mich.: University of Michigan, Michigan Program on Poverty and Social Welfare Policy.

Ardener, Shirley. 1964. "The Comparative Study of Rotating Credit Associations." *Journal of the Royal Anthropological Institute* 94: 201–29.

Aschenbrenner, Joyce. 1975. *Lifelines: Black Families in Chicago.* New York: Holt, Rinehart and Winston.

Bandura, Albert. 1977. "Toward a Unifying Theory of Behavioral Change." *Psychological Review* 84: 191–215.

———. 1997. *Self-Efficacy: The Exercise of Control.* New York: W. H. Freeman.

Bandura, Albert, Nancy E. Adams, Arthur B. Hardy, and Gary N. Howell. 1980. "Tests of the Generality of Self-Efficacy Theory." *Cognitive Therapy and Research* 4(1): 39–66.

Bassuk, E. L., L. F. Weinreb, J. C. Buckner, A. Browne, A. Saloman, and S. S. Bassuk. 1996. "The Characteristics and Needs of Sheltered Homeless and Low-Income Housed Mothers." *Journal of the American Medical Association* 276: 640–6.

Belle, D. 1990. "Poverty and Women's Mental Health." *American Psychologist* 45: 385–9.

Benin, Mary, and Verna M. Keith. 1995. "The Social Support of Employed African American and Anglo Mothers." *Journal of Family Issues* 16(3): 275–97.

Bertrand, Marianne, and Sendhil Mullainathan. 2004. "Are Emily and Brendan More Employable Than Lakisha and Jamal? A Field Experiment on Labor Market Discrimination." Working paper 9873. Cambridge, Mass.: National Bureau of Economic Research (June 20).

Billingsley, Andrew. 1968. *Black Families in White America.* Englewood Cliffs, N.J.: Prentice-Hall.

Blau, Peter. 1964. *Exchange and Power in Social Life.* New York: John Wiley & Sons.

Blumer, Herbert. 1969. *Symbolic Interactionism: Perspective and Method.* Berkeley, Calif.: University of California Press.

Bonnett, Aubrey W. 1981. "Structured Adaptation of Black Migrants from the Caribbean: An Examination of an Indigenous Banking System in Brooklyn." *Phylon* 42: 346–55.

Bound, John, and Harry J. Holzer. 1993. "Industrial Shifts, Skills Levels, and the Labor Market for White and Black Males." *Review of Economics and Statistics* 75(3): 387–96.

Bourdieu, Pierre. 1985. "Forms of Capital." In *Handbook of Theory and Research for the Sociology of Education*, edited by John G. Richardson. Westport, Conn.: Greenwood Press.

Boxman, E. A. W., P. M. De Graaf, and Henk D. Flap. 1991. "The Impact of Social and Human Capital on the Income Attainment of Dutch Managers." *Social Networks* 13: 51–73.

Brehm, John, and Wendy Rahn. 1997. "Individual-Level Evidence for the Causes and Consequences of Social Capital." *American Journal of Political Science* 41: 999–1023.

Brewster, Karin L., and Irene Padavic. 2002. "No More Kin Care? Change in Black Mothers' Reliance on Relatives for Child Care, 1977–1994." *Gender and Society* 16(4): 546–63.

Briggs, Xavier de Souza. 1998. "Brown Kids in White Suburbs: Housing Mobility and the Many Faces of Social Capital." *Housing Policy Debate* 9(1): 177–221.

Browne, Angela. 1993. "Family Violence and Homelessness: The Relevance of Trauma Histories in the Lives of Homeless Women." *American Journal of Orthopsychiatry* 63(3): 370–84.

Browne, Irene, and Ivy Kennelly. 1999. "Stereotypes and Realities: Images of Black Women in the Labor Market." In *Latinas and African American Women at Work: Race, Gender, and Economic Inequality*, edited by Irene Browne. New York: Russell Sage Foundation.

Burt, Ronald S. 1992. *Structural Holes: The Social Structure of Competition.* Cambridge, Mass.: Harvard University Press.

———. 1997. "The Contingent Value of Social Capital." *Administrative Science Quarterly* 42: 339–65.

———. 2001. "Bandwidth and Echo: Trust, Information, and Gossip in Social Networks." In *Networks and Markets*, edited by James E. Rauch and Alessandra Casella. New York: Russell Sage Foundation.

Campbell, Karen, Peter V. Marsden, and Jeanne S. Hurlbert. 1986. "Social Resources and Socioeconomic Status." *Social Networks* 8(1): 97–116.

Cappelli, Peter. 1995. "Is the 'Skills Gap' Really About Attitudes?" *California Management Review* 37(4): 108–24.

Cole, Robert. 1979. *Work, Mobility, and Participation: A Comparative Study of American and Japanese Industry.* Berkeley: University of California Press.

Coleman, James. 1988. "Social Capital in the Creation of Human Capital." *American Journal of Sociology* 94: S95–121.

———. 1990. *Foundations of Social Theory.* Cambridge, Mass.: Belknap Press of Harvard University Press.

Colten, M. E., C. Cosenza, and M. A. Allard. 1996. *Domestic Violence Among*

Massachusetts AFDC Recipients: Preliminary Results. Boston, Mass.: University of Massachusetts, Center for Survey Research.

Cook, Karen S., and Russell Hardin. 2001. "Norms of Cooperativeness and Networks of Trust." In *Social Norms*, edited by Michael Hechter and Karl-Dieter Opp. New York: Russell Sage Foundation.

Cook, Karen S., Russell Hardin, and Margaret Levi. 2005. *Cooperation Without Trust?* New York: Russell Sage Foundation.

Corcoran, Mary. 1999. "The Economic Progress of African American Women." In *Latinas and African American Women at Work: Race, Gender, and Economic Inequality*, edited by Irene Browne. New York: Russell Sage Foundation.

Corcoran, Mary, Linda Datcher, and Greg J. Duncan. 1980. "Information and Influence Networks in Labor Markets." In *Five Thousand American Families: Patterns of Economic Progress*, vol. 8, edited by Greg J. Duncan and James N. Morgan. Ann Arbor, Mich.: Institute for Social Research.

Curcio, William. 1996. *The Passaic County Study of AFDC Recipients in a Welfare-to-Work Program: A Preliminary Analysis.* Passaic Co., N.J.: Passaic County Family Development Program.

Danziger, Sandra K., Mary Corcoran, Sheldon Danziger, Colleen Heflin, Ariel Kalil, Judith Levine, Daniel Rosen, Kristin S. Seefeldt, Kristine Siefert, and Richard Tolman. 2000. "Barriers to Employment of Welfare Recipients." In *Prosperity for All?* edited by Robert Cherry and William M. Rodgers III. New York: Russell Sage Foundation.

Danziger, Sandra K., and Kristin S. Seefeldt. 2002. "Barriers to Employment and the 'Hard to Serve': Implications for Services, Sanctions, and Time Limits." *Social Policy and Society* 2(2): 151–60.

De Graaf, Nan Dirk, and Hendrik Derk Flap. 1988. "With a Little Help from My Friends." *Social Forces* 67(2): 452–72.

DiClemente, Carlo C. 1985. "Perceived Efficacy in Smoking Cessation." Presented at the Annual Meeting of the American Association of Advanced Science, Los Angeles, Calif.

DiTomaso, Nancy. 2006. "Social Capital: Nobody Makes It on Their Own." Paper presented to the annual meeting of the American Sociological Association. Montreal, August, 2006.

Dohan, Daniel. 2003. *The Price of Poverty: Money, Work, and Culture in the Mexican American Barrio.* Berkeley, Calif.: University of California Press.

Drake, St. Clair, and Horace R. Cayton. 1945/1993. *Black Metropolis: A Study of Negro Life in a Northern City.* Chicago, Ill.: University of Chicago Press.

Drentea, Patricia. 1998. "Consequences of Women's Formal and Informal Job Search Methods for Employment in Female-Dominated Jobs." *Gender and Society* 12: 321–38.

Du Bois, W. E. B. 1996. *The Philadelphia Negro: A Social Study.* Philadelphia, Pa.: University of Pennsylvania Press. (Orig. pub. in 1899.)

Edin, Kathryn, and Laura Lein. 1997. *Making Ends Meet: How Single Mothers Survive Welfare and Low-Wage Work.* New York: Russell Sage Foundation.

Eggebeen, David J. 1992. "From Generation unto Generation: Parent-Child Support in Aging American Families." *Generations* 16(3): 45–49.

Eggebeen, David J., and Dennis P. Hogan. 1990. "Giving Between Generations in American Families." *Human Nature* 1(2): 211–32.

Elliot, James R., and Mario Sims. 2001. "Ghettos and Barrios: The Impact of

Neighborhood Poverty and Race on Job Matching Among Blacks and Latinos." *Social Problems* 48(3): 341–61.

Ellwood, David T. 1988. *Poor Support: Poverty in the American Family.* New York: Basic Books.

———. 2000. "The Impact of the Earned Income Tax Credit and Social Policy Reforms on Work, Marriage, and Living Arrangements." *National Tax Journal* 53 (4, pt. 2): 1027–62.

Falcon, Luis M. 1995. "Social Networks and Employment for Latinos, Blacks, and Whites." *New England Journal of Public Policy* 11(1): 17–28.

Falcon, Luis M., and Edwin Melendez. 2001. "Racial and Ethnic Differences in Job Searching in Urban Centers." In *Urban Inequality: Evidence from Four Cities,* edited by Alice O'Connor, Chris Tilly, and Lawrence Bobo. New York: Russell Sage Foundation.

Fernandez, Roberto, and Isabel Fernandez-Mateo. 2006. "Networks, Race, and Hiring." *American Sociological Review* 71(1): 42–71.

Fernandez, Roberto, and David Harris. 1992. "Social Isolation and the Underclass." In *Drugs, Crime, and Social Isolation: Barriers to Urban Opportunity,* edited by Adele V. Harrell and George E. Peterson. Washington: Urban Institute Press.

Fernandez, Roberto, and Nancy Weinberg. 1997. "Sifting and Sorting: Personal Contacts and Hiring in a Retail Bank." *American Sociological Review* 62: 883–902.

Fevre, Ralph. 1989. "Informal Practices, Flexible Firms, and Private Labor Markets." *Sociology* 23(1): 91–109.

Foley, Michael W., John D. McCarthy, and Mark Chaves. 2001. "Social Capital, Religious Institutions, and Poor Communities." In *Social Capital and Poor Communities,* edited by Susan Saegert, J. Phillip Thompson, and Mark R. Warren. New York: Russell Sage Foundation.

Franks, David D., and Joseph Marolla. 1976. "Efficacious Action and Social Approval as Interacting Dimensions of Self-esteem: A Tentative Formulation Through Construct Validation." *Sociometry* 39(4): 324–41.

Freeman, Richard, and William Rodgers. 2000. "Area Economic Conditions and the Labor Market Outcomes of Young Men in the 1990s." In *Prosperity for All? Tight Labor Markets and African-American Employment,* edited by Robert Cherry and William M. Rodgers III. New York: Russell Sage Foundation.

Furstenberg, Frank F., Jr., Thomas D. Cook, Jacquelynne Eccles, Glen H. Elder Jr., and Arnold Sameroff. 1999. *Managing to Make It: Urban Families and Adolescent Success.* Chicago, Ill.: University of Chicago Press.

Gallagher, Jerome, Megan Gallagher, Kevin Perese, Susan Schreiber, and Keith Watson. 1998. "One Year After Federal Welfare Reform: A Description of State Temporary Assistance for Needy Families (TANF) Decisions as of October 1997." Assessing the New Federalism Series. Occasional paper 6. Washington: Urban Institute.

Gallup, George, Jr., and D. Michael Lindsay. 1999. *Surveying the Religious Landscape: Trends in U.S. Beliefs.* Harrisburg, Penn.: Morehouse.

Garfinkel, Irwin, and Sara S. McLanahan. 1986. *Single Mothers and Their Children.* Washington: Urban Institute Press.

Gecas, Viktor. 1989. "The Social Psychology of Self-Efficacy." *Annual Review of Sociology* 15: 291–316.

Gecas, Viktor, and Michael L. Schwalbe. 1983. "Beyond the Looking-Glass Self: Social Structures and Efficacy-Based Self-esteem." *Social Psychology Quarterly* 46(2): 77–88.

Geertz, Clifford. 1962. "The Rotating Credit Association: A 'Middle Rung' in Development." *Economic Development and Cultural Change* 1(3): 241–63.

Glynn, Timothy P. 1998. "The Limited Viability of Negligent Supervision, Retention, Hiring, and Infliction of Emotional Distress Claims in Employment Discrimination Cases in Minnesota." *William Mitchell Law Review* 24: 581–633.

Goffman, Erving. 1967. *Interaction Ritual: Essays on Face-to-Face Behavior.* New York: Pantheon Books.

Gould, Roger. 2002. "The Origins of Status Hierarchies: A Formal Theory and Empirical Test." *American Journal of Sociology* 107(5): 1143-78.

Granovetter, Mark. 1981. "Toward a Sociological Theory of Income Differences." In *Sociological Perspectives on Labor Markets*, edited by Ivar Berg. New York: Academic Press.

———. 1974/1995. *Getting a Job: A Study of Contacts and Careers*, 2nd ed. Chicago, Ill.: University of Chicago Press.

———. 1985. "Economic Action and Social Structure: The Problem of Embeddedness." *American Journal of Sociology* 91: 481–510.

Green, Gary P., Leann M. Tigges, and Irene Browne. 1995. "Social Resources, Job Search, and Poverty in Atlanta." *Research in Community Sociology* 5: 161–82.

Green, Gary P., Leann M. Tigges, and Daniel Diaz. 1999. "Racial and Ethnic Differences in Job-Search Strategies in Atlanta, Boston, and Los Angeles." *Social Science Quarterly* 80(2): 263–78.

Gurin, Patricia, Gerald Gurin, and Betty M. Morrison. 1978. "Personal and Ideological Aspects of Internal and External Control." *Social Psychology* 41(4): 275–96.

Guttman, Robert. 1983. "Job Training Partnership Act: New Help for the Unemployed." *Monthly Labor Review* (March): 3–10.

Hahn, Jeffrey M. 1991. "Pre-employment Information Services: Employers Beware?" *Employee Relations Law Journal* 17(1): 45–69.

Hanson, Susan, and Geraldine Pratt. 1991. "Job Search and the Occupational Segregation of Women." *Annals of the Association of American Geographers* 81(2): 229–53.

Hardin, Russell. 1993. "The Street-Level Epistemology of Trust." *Politics and Society* 21(4): 505–29.

———. 2002. *Trust and Trustworthiness.* New York: Russell Sage Foundation.

———. 2004. "Distrust: Manifestations and Management." In *Distrust*, edited by Russell Hardin. New York: Russell Sage Foundation.

Harris, Kathleen Mullan. 1993. "Work and Welfare Among Single Mothers in Poverty." *American Journal of Sociology* 99: 317–52.

Harris, Louis, and Associates. 1989. *The Unfinished Agenda on Race in America*, vol. 1. Report for NAACP Legal Defense and Educational Fund (June-September).

Hays, Sharon. 2003. *Flat Broke with Children: Women in the Age of Welfare Reform.* New York: Oxford University Press.

Hays, William C., and Charles H. Mindel. 1973. "Extended Kinship Relations in Black and White Families." *Journal of Marriage and the Family* 35: 51–57.

Heiss, Jerold. 1975. *The Case of the Black Family: A Social Inquiry.* New York: Columbia University Press.

Heymann, S. Jody, Alison Earle, and Brian Egleston. 1995. *Parental Availability for the Care of Sick Children.* Boston: Harvard Medical School, Department of Health Care Policy.

Ho, David Yau-fai. 1976. "On the Concept of Face." *American Journal of Sociology* 81(4): 867–84.

Hochschild, Jennifer L. 1995. *Facing Up to the American Dream: Race, Class, and the Soul of the Nation.* Princeton, N.J.: Princeton University Press.

Hofferth, Sandra L. 1984. "Kin Networks, Race, and Family Structure." *Journal of Marriage and the Family* 46: 791–806.

Hogan, Dennis P., David J. Eggebeen, and Clifford C. Clogg. 1993. "The Structure of Intergenerational Exchanges in American Families." *American Journal of Sociology* 98(6): 1428–58.

Hogan, Dennis P., Ling-xin Hao, and William Parish. 1990. "Race, Kin Networks, and Assistance to Mother-Headed Families." *Social Forces* 68(3): 797–812.

Holzer, Harry J. 1986. "Reservation Wages and Their Labor Market Effects for White and Black Male Youth." *Journal of Human Resources* 21(Spring): 157–77.

———. 1987. "Informal Job Search and Black Youth Unemployment." *American Economic Review* 77(3): 446–52.

———. 1996. *What Employers Want: Job Prospects for Less-Educated Workers.* New York: Russell Sage Foundation.

———. 1997. "Why Do Small Establishments Hire Fewer Blacks Than Large Ones?" Discussion paper 1119-97. Madison, Wisc.: University of Wisconsin, Institute for Research on Poverty.

Holzer, Harry J., and Keith R. Ihlanfeldt. 1998. "Customer Discrimination and Employment Outcomes for Minority Workers." *Quarterly Journal of Economics* (August): 835–67.

Holzer, Harry J., and Paul Offner. 2002. "Trends in Employment Outcomes of Young Black Men, 1979–2000." Discussion paper 1247-02. Madison, Wisc.: University of Wisconsin, Institute for Research on Poverty.

———. 2004. "The Puzzle of Black Male Unemployment." *The Public Interest* (Winter): 74–84.

Holzer, Harry J., Paul Offner, and Elaine Sorensen. 2004. "Declining Employment Among Young Black Less-Educated Men: The Role of Incarceration and Child Support." Urban Institute Research Paper, no. 411035.

———. 2005. "What Explains the Continuing Decline in Labor Force Activity Among Young Black Men?" *Labor History* 46(1): 37–55.

Holzer, Harry J., Steven Raphael, and Michael A. Stoll. 2002a. "Will Employers Hire Ex-offenders? Employer Preferences, Background Checks, and Their Determinants." Discussion paper 1243-02. Madison, Wisc.: University of Wisconsin, Institute for Research on Poverty.

———. 2002b. "Perceived Criminality, Criminal Background Checks, and the

Racial Hiring Practices of Employers." Discussion paper 1254-02. Madison: University of Wisconsin, Institute for Research on Poverty.

Isaacs, Kenneth S., James M. Alexander, and Ernest A. Haggard. 1963. "Faith, Trust, and Gullibility." *The International Journal of Psycho-Analysis* 44: 461–69

Iversen, Roberta, and Naomi Farber. 1996. "Transmission of Family Values, Work, and Welfare Among Poor Urban Black Women." *Work and Occupations* 23(4): 437–60.

Jargowsky, Paul A. 1997. *Poverty and Place: Ghetto, Barrios, and the American City.* New York: Russell Sage Foundation.

Jayakody, Rukmalie, Linda M. Chatters, and Robert Joseph Taylor. 1993. "Family Support to Single and Married African American Mothers: The Provision of Financial, Emotional, and Child Care Assistance." *Journal of Marriage and the Family* 55(May): 261–76.

Jenkins, Richard, Alan Bryman, Janet Ford, Teresa Keil, and Alan Beardsworth. 1983. "Information in the Labor Market: The Impact of Recession." *Sociology* 17(2): 260–7.

Jones, Rachel, and Ye Luo. 1999. "The Culture of Poverty and African-American Culture: An Empirical Assessment." *Sociological Perspective* 42(3): 439–58.

Kalil, Ariel, Mary E. Corcoran, Sandra K. Danziger, Richard Tolman, Kristin S. Seefeldt, Daniel Rosen, and Yunju Nam. 1998. "Getting Jobs, Keeping Jobs, and Earning a Living Wage: Can Welfare Reform Work?" Discussion Paper 1170-98. Madison, Wisc.: University of Wisconsin, Institute for Research on Poverty.

Kalil, Ariel, Kristin S. Seefeldt, and Hui-chen Wang. 2002. "Sanctions and Material Hardship Under TANF." *Social Service Review* (December): 642–62.

Kaplan, Elaine Bell. 1997. *Not Our Kind of Girl: Unraveling the Myths of Black Teenage Motherhood.* Berkeley, Calif.: University of California Press.

Kasarda, John. 1995. "Industrial Restructuring and the Changing Location of Jobs." In *State of the Union: America in the 1990s,* vol. 1, *Economic Trends,* edited by Reynolds Farley. New York: Russell Sage Foundation.

Kasinitz, Philip, and Jan Rosenberg. 1996. "Missing the Connection: Social Isolation and Employment on the Brooklyn Waterfront." *Social Problems* 43(2): 180–96.

Kasschau, Patricia. 1977. "Age and Race Discrimination Reported by Middle-Aged and Older Persons." *Social Forces* 55(3): 728–42.

Kaufman, Harold G. 1982. *Professionals in Search of Work: Coping with the Stress of Job Loss and Underemployment.* New York: John Wiley and Sons.

Kessler, R. C., A. Sonnega, E. Bromet, M. Hughes, and C. B. Nelson. 1995. "Post-Traumatic Stress Disorder in the National Comorbidy Survey." *Archives of General Psychiatry* 52: 1048–60.

King, Valerie. 2002. "Parental Divorce and Interpersonal Trust in Adult Offspring." *Journal of Marriage and Family* 64(3): 642–56.

Kirschenman, Joleen, and Kathryn Neckerman. 1991. "'We'd Love to Hire Them, but . . .': The Meaning of Race for Employers." In *The Urban Underclass,* edited by Christopher Jencks and Paul E. Peterson. Washington: Brookings Institution Press.

Kollock, Peter. 1994. "The Emergence of Exchange Structures: An Experimental

232   References

Study of Uncertainty, Commitment, and Trust." *American Journal of Sociology* 100(2): 313–34.

Kramer, Frederica D. 1998. "The Hard-to-Place: Understanding the Population and Strategies to Serve Them." *Welfare Information Network* 2(5): 1–17.

Kreps, David M. 1996. "Markets and Hierarchies and (Mathematical) Economic Theory." *Industrial and Corporate Change* 5(2): 561–96.

Ladner, Joyce. 1972. *Tomorrow's Tomorrow: The Black Woman.* Garden City, N.Y.: Doubleday.

Lawler, Edward, and Jeongkoo Yoon. 1996. "Commitment in Exchange Relations: Test of a Theory of Relational Cohesion." *American Sociological Review* 61(1): 89–108.

———. 1998. "Network Structure and Emotion in Exchange Relations." *American Sociological Review* 63(6): 871–94.

Lee, Yean-Ju, and Isik A. Aytac. 1998. "Intergenerational Financial Support Among Whites, African Americans, and Latinos." *Journal of Marriage and the Family* 60(May): 426–41.

Levitan, Mark. 2004. *Annual Report: A Crisis of Black Male Employment.* New York: Community Service Society.

Lewis, Oscar. 1968. "The Culture of Poverty." In *On Understanding Poverty: Perspectives from the Social Sciences,* edited by Daniel P. Moynihan. New York: Basic Books.

Licht, Walter. 1992. *Getting Work: Philadelphia, 1840-1950.* Cambridge, Mass.: Harvard University Press.

Liebow, Elliot. 1967. *Tally's Corner: A Study of Streetcorner Men.* Boston, Mass.: Little, Brown and Co.

Light, Ivan. 1972. *Ethnic Enterprise in America.* Berkeley, Calif.: University of California Press.

Lin, Nan. 1999. "Social Networks and Status Attainment." *Annual Review of Sociology* 25: 467–487.

———. 2001. *Social Capital: A Theory of Social Structure and Action.* Cambridge: Cambridge University Press.

Lin, Nan and Mary Dumin. 1986. "Access to Occupations Through Social Ties." *Social Networks* 8: 365-85.

Lin, Nan, Walter M. Ensel, and John C. Vaughn. 1981. "Social Resources and Strength of Ties: Structural Factors in Occupational Status Attainment." *American Sociological Review* 46(4): 393–405.

Lin, Nan, Yang-chih Fu, and Ray-May Hsung. 2001. "Position Generator: Measurement Techniques for Investigations of Social Capital." In *Social Capital: Theory and Research,* edited by Nan Lin, Karen Cook, and Ronald S. Burt. New York: Aldine de Gruyter.

Lincoln, C. Eric, and Lawrence H. Mamiya. 1990. *The Black Church in the African American Experience.* Durham, N.C.: Duke University Press.

Lloyd, Susan. 1996. *The Effects of Violence on Women's Employment.* Working paper 97-4. Evanston, Ill.: Northwestern University, Institute for Policy Research.

Loprest, Pamela J., and Gregory Acs. 1996. *Profile of Disability Among Families on AFDC.* Report to the Henry J. Kaiser Family Foundation. Washington: Urban Institute.

Loprest, Pamela J., and Sheila R. Zedlewski. 1999. *Current and Former Welfare Recipients: How Do They Differ?* Assessing the New Federalism Series. Washington: Urban Institute.

Loury, Glenn C. 1977. "A Dynamic Theory of Racial Income Differences." In *Women, Minorities, and Employment Discrimination*, edited by Phyllis A. Wallace and Annette M. LaMond. Lexington, Mass.: D. C. Heath.

MacLeod, Jay. 1995. *Ain't No Makin' It: Aspirations and Attainment in a Low-Income Neighborhood*. Boulder, Colo.: Westview Press.

Marsden, Peter V. 1987. "Core Discussion Networks of Americans." *American Sociological Review* 52: 122–31.

Marsden, Peter V., and Jeanne S. Hurlbert. 1988. "Social Resources and Mobility Outcomes: A Replication and Extension." *Social Forces* 66(4): 1038–59.

Massey, Douglas, and Nancy Denton. 1993. *American Apartheid: Segregation and the Making of the Underclass*. Cambridge, Mass.: Harvard University Press.

McKernan, Signe-Mary, Robert I. Lerman, Nancy Pindus, and Jesse Valente. 2000. "The Relationship Between Metropolitan and Nonmetropolitan Locations, Changing Welfare Policies, and the Employment of Single Mothers." Working paper 192. Chicago, Ill.: Northwestern University/University of Chicago, Joint Center for Poverty Research.

McPherson, Miller, Lynn Smith-Lovin, and Matthew E. Brashears. 2006. "Social Isolation in America: Changes in Core Discussion Networks over Two Decades." *American Sociological Review* 71: 353–75.

McPherson, Miller, Lynn Smith-Lovin, and James Cook. 2001. "Birds of a Feather: Homophily in Social Networks." *Annual Review of Sociology* 27(1): 415–44.

McRoberts, Omar M. 2003. *Streets of Glory: Church and Community in a Black Urban Neighborhood*. Chicago, Ill.: University of Chicago Press.

Mead, Lawrence M. 1985. *Beyond Entitlement: The Social Obligations of Citizenship*. New York: Free Press.

———. 1992. *The New Politics of Poverty: The Nonworking Poor in America*. New York: Basic Books.

Menjívar, Cecilia. 2000. *Fragmented Ties: Salvadoran Immigrant Networks in America*. Berkeley, Calif.: University of California Press.

Meyer, Bruce D., and Dan T. Rosenbaum. 2000. "Making Single Mothers Work: Recent Tax and Welfare Policy and Its Effects." *National Tax Journal* 53(4, pt. 2): 1027–62.

———. 2001. "Welfare, the Earned Income Tax Credit, and the Labor Supply of Single Mothers." *Quarterly Journal of Economics* 116(3): 1063–1114.

Meyers, Marcia K., Anna Lukemeyer, and Timothy Smeeding. 1996. "Work, Welfare, and the Burden of Disability: Caring for Special Needs Children in Poor Families." Income Security Policy Series, paper 12. Syracuse, N.Y.: Syracuse University, Maxwell School of Citizenship and Public Affairs, Center for Policy Research.

Moffitt, Robert. 1983. "An Economic Model of Welfare Stigma." *American Economic Review* 73(5): 1023–35.

Molm, Linda D., Nobuyuki Takahashi, and Gretchen Peterson. 2000. "Risk and Trust in Social Exchange: An Experimental Test of a Classical Proposition." *American Journal of Sociology* 105(5): 1396–1427.

Moore, Kristin A., Martha J. Zaslow, Mary Jo Coiro, Suzanne M. Miller, and Ellen B. Magenheim. 1995. *The JOBS Evaluation: How Well Are They Faring? AFDC Families with Preschool-Aged Children in Atlanta at the Outset of the JOBS Evaluation.* Washington: U.S. Department of Health and Human Services, Office of the Assistant Secretary for Planning and Evaluation.

Morenoff, Jeffrey, Robert J. Sampson, and Stephen W. Raudenbush. 2001. "Neighborhood Inequality, Collective Efficacy, and the Spatial Dynamics of Urban Violence." *Criminology* 39(3): 517–59.

Moss, Philip, and Chris Tilly. 2001. *Stories Employers Tell: Race, Skill, and Hiring in America.* New York: Russell Sage Foundation.

Moynihan, Daniel Patrick. 1967. "The Negro Family: The Case for National Action." In *The Moynihan Report and the Politics of Controversy* by Lee Rainwater and William L. Yancey. Cambridge, Mass.: MIT Press.

Neckerman, Kathryn M., and Roberto M. Fernandez. 2003. "Keeping a Job: Network Hiring and Turnover in a Retail Bank." *Research in the Sociology of Organizations* 20: 299–318.

Neckerman, Kathryn M., and Joleen Kirschenman. 1991. "Hiring Strategies, Racial Bias, and Inner-City Workers." *Social Problems* 38(4): 433–47.

Newcomb, Michael D., and L. L. Harlow. 1986. "Life Events and Substance Use Among Adolescents: Mediating Effects of Perceived Loss of Control and Meaninglessness in Life." *Journal of Personality and Social Psychology* 51: 564–77.

Newman, Katherine S. 1988. *Falling from Grace: Downward Mobility in the Age of Affluence.* Berkeley, Calif.: University of California Press.

———. 1999. *No Shame in My Game: The Working Poor in the Inner City.* New York: Knopf and Russell Sage Foundation.

Newman, Katherine S., and Chauncy Lennon. 1995. "Finding Work in the Inner City: How Hard Is It Now? How Hard Will It Be for AFDC Recipients?" Working paper 76. New York: Russell Sage Foundation.

Nichols-Casebolt, Ann M. 1986. "The Psychological Effects of Income-Testing Income Support Benefits." *Social Service Review* 60(June): 287–303.

Nightingale, Demetra S., Regina Yudd, Stacey Anderson, and Burt Barnow. 1991. *The Learning Disabled in Employment and Training Programs.* Washington: U.S. Department of Labor.

Noonan, Mary C., Sandra S. Smith, and Mary E. Corcoran. 2007. "Examining the Impact of Welfare Reform, Labor Market Conditions, and the Earned Income Tax Credit on the Employment of Black and White Single Mothers." *Social Science Research* 36: 95–130.

Olson, Krista K., and LaDonna Pavetti. 1996. *Personal and Family Challenges to the Successful Transition from Welfare to Work.* Prepared for the Office of the Assistant Secretary for Planning and Evaluation and the Administration for Children and Families, contract 100-95-0021. Washington: Urban Institute.

O'Neill, June E., and M. Anne Hill. 2001. "Gaining Ground? Measuring the Impact of Welfare Reform on Welfare and Work." Civic report 17. New York: Manhattan Institute, Center for Civic Innovation.

O'Shea, Dan, and Christopher King. 2004. "Michigan Case Study." *The Workforce Investment Act in Eight States: State Cases from a Field Evaluation*, vol. 1.

Pager, Devah. 2002. "The Mark of a Criminal Record." *American Journal of Sociology* 108(5): 937–75.

Pager, Devah, and Lincoln Quillian. 2005. "Walking the Talk? What Employers Say Versus What They Do." *American Sociological Review* 70(3): 355–80.

Parent, T. Wayne. 1985. "A Liberal Legacy: Blacks Blaming Themselves for Economic Failures." *Journal of Black Studies* 16(1): 3–20.

Parish, William, Lingxin Hao, and Dennis P. Hogan. 1991. "Family Support Networks, Welfare, and Work Among Young Mothers." *Journal of Marriage and the Family* 53: 203–15.

Patterson, Orlando. 1998. *The Ordeal of Integration: Progress and Resentment in America's "Racial" Crisis.* New York: Basic Civitas.

Pavetti, LaDonna Ann. 1993. "The Dynamics of Welfare and Work: Exploring the Process by Which Women Work Their Way Off Welfare." PhD dissertation, Harvard University.

———. 1995. ". . . And Employment for All? Lessons from Utah's Single Parent Employment Demonstration Project." Paper presented to the seventeenth annual research conference of the Association for Public Policy Analysis and Management. Washington, November 2–4, 2005.

Pearlin, Leonard I., Elizabeth G. Menaghan, Morton A. Lieberman, and Joseph T. Mullan. 1981. "The Stress Process." *Journal of Health and Social Behavior* 22(4): 337–56.

Pearlin, Leonard I., and Clarice W. Radabaugh 1976. "Economic Strains and the Coping Function of Alcohol." *American Journal of Sociology* 82(3): 652–63.

Pescosolido, Bernice A. 1992. "Beyond Rational Choice: The Social Dynamics of How People Seek Help." *American Journal of Sociology* 97(4): 1096–1138.

Petersen, Trond, Ishak Saporta, and Marc-David L. Seidel. 2000. "Offering a Job: Meritocracy and Social Networks." *American Journal of Sociology* 106(3): 763–816.

Peterson, Debra F. 1996. "The Effect of Race on Kinship Support: A Meta-analysis." PhD dissertation, Department of Sociology, University of Nebraska.

Petterson, Stephen. 1997. "Are Young Black Men Really Less Willing to Work?" *American Sociological Review* 62(August): 605–13.

Pettit, Becky, and Bruce Western. 2004. "Mass Incarceration and the Life Course: Race and Class Inequality in U.S. Incarceration." *American Sociological Review* 69: 151–69.

Podolny, Joel M. 1993. "Status-Based Model of Market Competition." *American Journal of Sociology* 98(4): 829–72.

Portes, Alejandro. 1998. "Social Capital: Its Origins and Applications in Modern Sociology." *Annual Review of Sociology* 24: 1–24.

Portes, Alejandro, and Julia Sensenbrenner. 1993. "Embeddedness and Immigration: Notes on the Social Determinants of Economic Action." *American Journal of Sociology* 98: 1320–50.

Quint, Janet C., Barbara L. Fink, and Sharon L. Rowser. 1991. *New Chance: Implementing a Comprehensive Program for Disadvantaged Young Mothers and Their Children.* New York: Manpower Demonstration Research Corporation.

Rankin, Bruce, and James Quane. 2000. "Neighborhood Poverty and the Social Isolation of Inner-City African American Families." *Social Forces* 79(1): 139–64.

Raphael, Jody. 1995. *Domestic Violence: Telling the Untold Welfare-to-Work Story.* Chicago, Ill.: Taylor Institute.

Roschelle, Anne R. 1997. *No More Kin: Exploring Race, Class, and Gender in Family Networks.* Thousand Oaks, Calif.: Sage Publications.

Rosenberg, Morris. 1979. *Conceiving the Self.* New York: Basic Books.

Rotenburg, Ken J. 1995. "The Socialization of Trust: Parents' and Children's Interpersonal Trust." *International Journal of Behavioral Development* 18(4): 713–26.

Rotter, Julian. 1967. "A New Scale for the Measurement of Interpersonal Trust." *Journal of Personality* 35(4): 651–65.

———. 1971. "Generalized Expectancies for Interpersonal Trust." *American Psychologist* 26(5): 443–50.

———. 1976. "Generalized Expectancies for Internal Versus External Control of Reinforcement." *Psychological Monographs* 80: 1–28.

———. 1980. "Interpersonal Trust, Trustworthiness, and Gullibility." *American Psychologist* 35(1): 1–7.

Royster, Deirdre. 2003. *Race and the Invisible Hand: How White Networks Exclude Black Men from Blue-Collar Jobs.* Berkeley, Calif.: University of California Press.

Sampson, Robert J., and W. Byron Groves. 1989. "Community Structure and Crime: Testing Social-Disorganization Theory." *American Journal of Sociology* 94(4): 774–802.

Sampson, Robert J., Jeffrey Morenoff, and Felton Earls. 1999. "Beyond Social Capital: Spatial Dynamics of Collective Efficacy for Children." *American Sociological Review* 64(5): 633–60.

Sampson, Robert J., and William Julius Wilson. 1995. "Toward a Theory of Race, Crime, and Urban Inequality." In *Crime and Inequality*, edited by John Hagan and Ruth Petersen. Stanford, Calif.: Stanford University Press.

Sanchez Jankowski, Martin. 1991. *Islands in the Street: Gangs and American Urban Society.* Berkeley, Calif.: University of California Press.

Sandfort, Jodi R., Ariel Kalil, and Julie A. Gottschalk. 1999. "The Mirror Has Two Faces: Welfare Clients and Front-Line Workers View Policy Reforms." *Journal of Poverty* 3(3): 71–91.

Sarkisian, Natalia, and Naomi Gerstel. 2004. "Kin Support Among Blacks and Whites: Race and Family Organization." *American Sociological Review* 69(December): 812–37.

Schlozman, Kay Lehman, and Sidney Verba. 1979. *Injury to Insult: Unemployment, Class, and Political Response.* Cambridge, Mass.: Harvard University Press.

Schneider, J. A., and W. S. Agras. 1985. "A Cognitive Behavioral Group Treatment of Bulimia." *British Journal of Psychiatry* 146: 66–69.

Schoeni, Robert F., and Rebecca M. Blank. 2000. "What Has Welfare Reform Accomplished? Impacts on Welfare Participation, Employment, Income, Poverty, and Family Structure." Working paper 7627. New York: National Bureau of Economic Research.

Schwalbe, Michael L., and Viktor Gecas. 1988. "Social Psychological Consequences of Job-Related Disabilities." In *Work Experience and Psychological Development Through the Life Span*, edited by Jeylan T. Mortimer and Kathryn M. Borman. Boulder, Colo.: Westview.

Seefeldt, Kristin, Sheldon Danziger, and Sandra K. Danziger. 2003. "Michigan's Welfare System," chapter in *Michigan at the Millennium: A Benchmark and Analysis of its Fiscal and Economic Structure*, C. Ballard, P.N. Comant, D.C. Drake, R.C. Fisher, and E.R. Gerber, eds. East Lansing, Mich.: Michigan University Press.

Seeman, Melvin, and Carolyn. S. Anderson. 1983. "Alienation and Alcohol: The Role of Work, Mastery, and Community Drinking Behavior." *American Sociological Review* 48(February): 60–77.

Seeman, Melvin, and Teresa E. Seeman. 1983. "Health Behavior and Personal Autonomy: A Longitudinal Study of the Sense of Control in Illness." *Journal of Health and Social Behavior* 24(June): 144–60.

Seligman, Martin E. P. 1975. *Helplessness: On Depression, Development, and Death.* San Francisco, Calif.: W. H. Freeman & Co.

Sennett, Richard, and Jonathan Cobb. 1972. *The Hidden Injuries of Class.* New York: Alfred A. Knopf.

Shapiro, Carl. 1982. "Consumer Information, Product Quality, and Seller Reputation." *Bell Journal of Economics* 13(1): 20–35.

Shaw, Clifford R., and Henry D. McKay. 1942/1969. *Juvenile Delinquency and Urban Areas: A Study of Rates of Delinquency in Relation to Differential Characteristics of Local Communities in American Cities.* Chicago, Ill.: University of Chicago Press.

Shih, Johanna. 2002. "'. . . Yeah, I Could Hire This One, but I Know It's Gonna Be a Problem': How Race, Nativity, and Gender Affect Employers' Perceptions of the Manageability of Job Seekers." *Ethnic and Racial Studies* 25(1): 99–119.

Shook, Kristen. 1999. *Does the Loss of Welfare Income Increase the Risk of Involvement with the Child Welfare System?* Ann Arbor, Mich.: University of Michigan, Poverty Research and Training Center.

Sigelman, Lee, and Steven A. Tuch. 1997. "Metastereotypes: Blacks' Perceptions of Whites' Stereotypes of Blacks." *Public Opinion Quarterly* 61(1): 87–101.

Sigelman, Lee, and Susan Welch. 1991. *Black Americans' Views of Racial Inequality: The Dream Deferred.* Cambridge, Mass.: Harvard University Press.

Small, Mario Luis. 2004. *Villa Victoria: The Transformation of Social Capital in a Boston Barrio.* Chicago, Ill.: University of Chicago Press.

———. 2006. "Neighborhood Institutions as Resource Brokers: Child Care Centers, Interorganizational Ties, and Resource Access Among the Poor." *Social Problems* 53(2): 274–92.

Small, Mario, and Monica McDermott. 2006. "The Presence of Organizational Resources in Poor Urban Neighborhoods: An Analysis of Average and Contextual Effects." *Social Forces* 84(3): 1697–1724.

Small, Mario L., and Laura Stark. 2005. "Are Poor Neighborhoods Resource-Deprived? A Case Study of Child Care Centers in New York." *Social Science Quarterly* 86(S1): 1013–36.

Smith, R. Drew. 2001. "Churches and the Urban Poor: Interaction and Social Distance." *Sociology of Religion: A Quarterly Review* 62(3): 301–13.

Smith, Sandra S. 2000. "Mobilizing Social Resources: Race, Ethnic, and Gender

Differences in Social Capital and Persisting Wage Inequalities." *Sociological Quarterly* 41(4): 509–37.

———. 2005. "'Don't Put My Name on It': Social Capital Activation and Job-Finding Assistance Among the Black Urban Poor." *American Journal of Sociology* 111(1): 1–57.

———. 2007. "What Who-You-Know Will Do For You: Racial and Ethnic Differences in Job Contacts' Method of Assistance." Paper presented at the Annual Meetings of the International Sunbelt Social Network Conference, Corfu, Greece, May, 2007.

Smith, Tom W. 1997. "Factors Relating to Misanthropy in Contemporary American Society." *Social Science Research* 26: 170–96.

Sosin, Michael. 1991. "Concentration of Poverty and Social Isolation of the Inner-City Poor." Paper presented to the Chicago Urban Poverty and Family Life Conference. Chicago, Ill. October 10–12, 1991.

Soss, Joe, Sanford Schram, Thomas Vartanian, and Erin O'Brien. 2001. "Setting the Terms of Relief: Explaining State Policy Choices in the Devolution Revolution." *American Journal of Political Science* 24: 69–86.

Spence, A. Michael. 1974. *Market Signaling: Informational Transfer in Hiring and Related Processes*. Cambridge, Mass.: Harvard University Press.

Stack, Carol. 1974. *All Our Kin: Strategies for Survival in a Black Community*. New York: Harper & Row.

State Policy Documentation Project. 2001. "State Policies Regarding TANF Work Activities and Requirements." http://www.spdp.org, a joint project of the Center for Law and Social Policy and the Center for Budget and Policy Priorities.

Steel, J.L. 1991. "International Correlates of Trust and Self-Disclosure." *Psychological Reports* 68: 1319–20.

Steele, Claude, and Joshua Aronson. 1995. "Stereotype Threat and the Intellectual Test Performance of African Americans." *Journal of Personality and Social Psychology* 69: 797–811.

———. 1998. "Stereotype Threat and the Test Performance of Academically Successful African Americans." In *Black-White Test Score Gap*, edited by Christopher Jencks and Meredith Phillips. New York: Brookings Institution Press.

Sugrue, Thomas J. 1996. *The Origins of the Urban Crisis: Race and Inequality in Postwar Detroit*. Princeton, N.J.: Princeton University Press.

Suttles, Gerald. 1968. *The Social Order of the Slum: Ethnicity and Territory in the Inner City*. Chicago, Ill.: University of Chicago Press.

Thernstrom, Stephan, and Abigail Thernstrom. 1998. *America in Black and White: One Nation, Indivisible*. New York: Simon & Schuster.

Turner, Margery Austin, Michael Fix, and Raymond J. Struyk. 1991. *Opportunities Denied, Opportunities Diminished: Racial Discrimination in Hiring*. Washington and Lanham, Md.: Urban Institute Press.

Uehara, Edwina. 1990. "Dual Exchange Theory, Social Networks, and Informal Social Support." *American Journal of Sociology* 96(3): 521–57.

U.S. Congressional Budget Office (CBO) and National Commission for Employment Policy (NCEP). 1982. *CETA Training Programs—Do They Work for Adults?* Washington: CBO-NCEP (July).

U.S. Department of Health and Human Services, Office of the Assistant Secretary for Planning and Evaluation, and National Institute on Drug Abuse. 1994. *Patterns of Substance Use Among Women and Parents*. Washington: DHHS/ASPE.

U.S. General Accounting Office (GAO). 1996. *Job Training Partnership Act: Long Term Earnings and Employment Outcomes*. Report to Congressional Requesters. GAO/HEHS-96-40. Washington: GAO (March).

———. 2000. *Welfare Reform: State Sanction Policies and Number of Families Affected*. Report to Congressional Requesters. GAO/HEHS-00-44. Washington: GAO (March).

———. 2001. *Welfare Reform: Moving Hard-to-Employ Recipients into the Workforce*. Report to the Chairman, Subcommittee on Human Resources, Committee on Ways and Means, House of Representatives. GAO-01-368. Washington: GAO (March).

Wacquant, Loic. 1998. "Negative Social Capital: State Breakdown and Social Destitution in America's Urban Core." *Journal of Housing and the Built Environment* 13(1): 25–40.

Wacquant, Loic J. D., and William J. Wilson. 1989. "The Cost of Racial and Class Exclusion in the Inner City." *Annals of the American Academy of Political and Social Science* 501: 8–25.

Waldinger, Roger. 1996. *Still the Promised City?: African-American and New Immigrants in Postindustrial New York*. Cambridge, Mass.: Harvard University Press.

———. 1997. "Black/Immigrant Competition Reassessed: New Evidence from Los Angeles." *Sociological Perspectives* 40(3): 365–86.

Waters, Mary C. 1999. *Black Identities: West Indian Immigrant Dreams and American Realities*. New York and Cambridge, Mass.: Russell Sage Foundation and Harvard University Press.

Weissman, Marsha, and Candace Mayer LaRue. 1998. "Earning Trust from Youths with None to Spare." *Child Welfare League of America* 77: 579–94.

West, Candace, and Don H. Zimmerman. 1987. "Doing Gender." *Gender and Society* 1(2): 125–51.

Wial, Howard. 1991. "Getting a Good Job: Mobility in a Segmented Labor Market." *Industrial Relations* 30(3): 396–415.

Wilson, Robert. 1985. "Reputations in Games and Markets." In *Game-Theoretic Models of Bargaining*, edited by Alvin E. Roth. Cambridge: Cambridge University Press.

Wilson, William Julius. 1987. *The Truly Disadvantaged: The Inner City, the Underclass, and Public Policy*. Chicago, Ill.: University of Chicago Press.

———. 1996. *When Work Disappears: The World of the New Urban Poor*. New York: Alfred A. Knopf.

Wood, Stephen. 1985. "Recruitment Systems in the Recession." *British Journal of Industrial Relations* 23(3): 103–20.

Wrightsman, Lawrence S. 1991. "Interpersonal Trust and Attitudes Toward Human Nature." In *Measures of Personality and Social Psychological Attitudes*, edited by John Paul Robinson, Phillip R. Shaver, and Lawrence S. Wrightsman. San Diego, Calif.: Academic Press.

Yamagishi, Toshio. 2001. "Trust as a Form of Social Intelligence." In *Trust in Society*, edited by Karen S. Cook. New York: Russell Sage Foundation.

Yamagishi, Toshio, and Karen S. Cook. 1993. "Generalized Exchange and Social Dilemmas." *Social Psychology Quarterly* 56(4): 235–48.

Yamagishi, Toshio, Masako Kikuchi, and Motoko Kosugi. 1999. "Trust, Gullibility, and Social Intelligence." *Asian Journal of Social Psychology* 2(1): 145–61.

Young, Alford, Jr. 2004. *The Minds of Marginalized Black Men: Making Sense of Mobility, Opportunity, and Future Life Chances.* Princeton, N.J.: Princeton University Press.

Zedlewski, Sheila R. 1999. "Work-Related Activities and Limitations of Current Welfare Recipients." Assessing the New Federalism Series. Discussion paper 99-06. Washington: Urban Institute.

Zill, Nicholas, Kristin A. Moore, Christine Winquist Nord, and Thomas Stief. 1991. *Welfare Mothers as Potential Employees: A Statistical Profile Based on National Survey Data.* Washington: Child Trends.

Index